MILLION DOLLAR LES PAUL

In Search Of The Most Valuable Guitar In The World

MILLION DOLLAR LES PAUL

In Search Of The Most Valuable Guitar in The World

TONY BACON

MILLION DOLLAR LES PAUL

In Search Of The Most Valuable Guitar In The World

Tony Bacon

A GENUINE JAWBONE BOOK
First edition 2008
Published in the UK and the USA by Jawbone Press,
2A Union Court,
20-22 Union Road,
London SW4 6JP,
England
www.jawbonepress.com

ISBN: 978-1-906002-14-5

Editor: Siobhan Pascoe
Design: Adam Yeldham

Origination and print by Colorprint (Hong Kong)

08 09 10 11 12 5 4 3 2 1

CONTENTS

Keith Richards (above), early 1965, with the first Les Paul Burst owned by a famous player; guitar pictured today (right). Eric Clapton with his first Burst: at the Pontiac Club, London, summer 65 (three snaps) and at Decca studio (top right) in May 66 to cut Mayall 'Beano' album.

Gibson
Bigsby
PATENT

Marshall

Eric Clapton with borrowed Burst (above) at early Cream gig, in Windsor, July 1966, and (opposite) with his second Burst, bought from Andy Summers, in early 67 in Denmark (top) and England (below).

Billy Gibbons with 'Pearly Gates' Burst on stage in Texas, 1975. Michael Bloomfield with Burst: at Fillmore East in late 68 (centre) and in the studio (right) for Super Session (jacket pictured) in May 68.

MIKE BLOOMFIELD
AL KOOPER
STEVE STILLS
SUPER SESSION

Mick Taylor (above) with ex-Keith Richards Burst, in John Mayall's band, 1969. Peter Green with his famous 'reversed-pickup' Burst (guitar pictured today, right) at De Lane Lea studio, London, May 69 (centre) and backstage a month later (right).

Gibson

Jimmy Page and his favoured Burst (with rear pickup in various states) on stage with Led Zeppelin: California 1975 (left); Denmark 70 (centre); and England 73 (above). The guitar today is pictured here.

Gibson

Duane Allman (opposite, below) with his 'Hot 'Lanta' Burst, and the guitar today (far left). Ben Wells of Black Stone Cherry (opposite, top) in 07 with his Les Paul Classic. Paul Kossoff (above) with Burst in late 70 (guitar today, opposite, top).

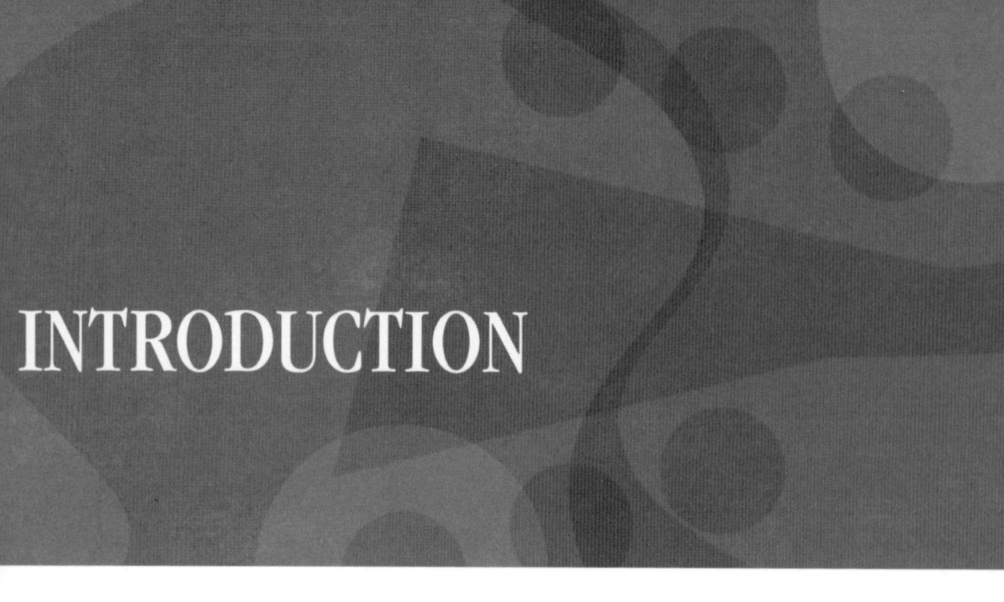

INTRODUCTION

"OK, I need to get started. Shall I wear gloves?" Edwin Wilson is talking to Jimmy Page. He is about to delve into the innards of Page's famous old 'Number 1' Les Paul, which has served the guitarist so well since the early days of Led Zeppelin.

Wilson is Gibson's Historic Program Manager and is used to doing this sort of thing. Gibson now recognises the importance and value of the greatest players of its original Les Paul sunburst model, the 'Burst' as it's known, and occasionally produces no-detail-too-small copies of these iconic guitars in limited runs. Wilson is often the man charged with going to the instrument and making the measurements.

"No, that's OK," replies Page. So, asks Wilson, I can pull the pickups out? "Oh yeah," says Page. "Take it apart. Do whatever you want to do."

Wilson is surprised but pleased. He's had owners of far less noteworthy instruments insist that he wear gloves before he even gets in the same room as their guitar. An amenable man, he was happy to oblige them.

"But when Jimmy Page said that," Wilson tells me later, "I realised that one of the things that makes his guitar the coolest Les Paul ever is that he knows very well what that guitar is. He knows that it's a tool for him. It's not something he hangs up on the wall. And that made it very easy to go through the guitar and do my thing."[1]

This is what we have come to with the sunburst Gibson Les Paul. Fifty years ago, almost to the day as I write this, the Gibson guitar company made a small and apparently insignificant change to one its models. Today, examples of that model, made from mid 1958 and in production for less than three years, have become among the most revered and the most valuable electric guitars of all time.

Page is one of a handful of key players who helped to create the legend of this instrument. But Page and other players of his generation, like many musicians, usually consider their guitars as tools, and not much more. They care for them and keep them close to hand but, as Wilson says, they know very well what they are. Many collectors and admirers of the Burst see the instrument rather differently.

In a world where music exists mostly as an invisible stream of ones and zeroes on computers and iPods, and in which it is possible to become a pop star without touching an instrument, it's comforting to possess an object as tangible and real as a solidbody electric guitar. It must be more comforting still to own a genuine 1959 Gibson Les Paul Burst.

Instruments built in that year are seen by most players and expert collectors as the peak of perfection in a Les Paul guitar. Everything came together. As we shall see, ever since that time, guitarists, guitar makers, and guitar nuts have wondered how Gibson achieved such an extraordinary mix of mahogany, plastic, maple, rosewood, metal, and even, some say, magic.

The appeal for many collectors is a reminder of their youth, when guitars had a magical power, particularly those they saw in the hands of their heroes. Some pay big sums in an effort to recapture that youth. The sunburst Les Paul has gradually increased in value over the years since it was introduced to become an instrument that now sells regularly for well into six figures. In this book, my quest has been to see whether there is such a thing as a million-dollar Les Paul. It has been an extraordinary journey.

Quite a few years back I talked to Les Paul himself – the man for whom Gibson named the original guitar when it first appeared in the early 50s – and I asked what he was playing at his regular weekly gig in New York City.

He said: "I play a guitar that I just love, it's called a Les Paul Heritage 80. It's a great, beautiful guitar." That's a newer version of the old sunburst Les Paul model, I clarified. "Yes," he said, "which is what Jimmy Page played. That's what they all play."[2]

1. BIRTH

Les Paul, Gibson, and the origins of the Les Paul Guitar

The Les Paul guitar was born more than 50 years ago, in 1952, when the Gibson company of Kalamazoo, Michigan, put on sale its first solidbody electric 'Spanish' guitar.

Today, we don't think twice about such an instrument. To most people, that's what 'electric guitar' means: a six-string with a solid wooden body, a long fretted neck, pickups and controls. It's the kind of guitar on which almost every kind of music is made now: pop music, rock music, country music, any flavour you like. But back in the early 50s it was a shocking new idea.

Les Paul was an important character in that early story. At the time of writing, remarkably, he's still out there, playing every week at a club in New York City, an apparently irrepressible 93-year-old guitarist.

"I can't wait to get up and out of bed and I can't wait to get to my guitar and play it," he tells me, as enthusiastic now as he's ever been for his adored instrument. "I love it so much. It's so personal. And yet it defies explanation. It's an awesome instrument."[1]

He was born Lester William Polfus in Waukesha, Wisconsin, in 1916, and started professional life early, as a talented teenage guitarist. At 17 he was broadcasting on local radio stations, playing country as Rhubarb Red and jazz too. The kid had a natural technical facility, which he used not only to make music but also to make his own odds and ends of instrumental and electrical gadgetry.

Like some other performers in the 30s, the young Lester became interested in amplifying his guitar. He says that in his early teens he made a pickup out of a telephone mouthpiece and concocted an amplifier from his parents' radio, all because he wanted to bring his guitar to the attention of the audience at a local roadhouse gig.

It was around this time that a handful of instrument makers – Rickenbacker and National among them – began selling the first commercial electric guitars. These were regular hollowbody archtop acoustics with electric pickups and controls bolted on, sometimes literally. By the middle of the 30s, Gibson was in this avant-garde market too with an 'electric Spanish' guitar and amplifier, and so was their biggest competitor, Epiphone of New York City.

Meanwhile, Lester Polfus had permanently adopted a suitably shortened version of his name – Les Paul – and for three years from 1938 led a jazz-based trio broadcasting out of New York on the Fred Waring show. He shifted from an acoustic archtop model to various Gibson electrics, including an ES-150 and an experimental L-7 and L-5. But he wanted something more – something that none of the guitar companies of the day seemed to want to produce.

I've interviewed Les several times since the first time I called him at his New Jersey home back in 1989. He's never less than entertaining. He's a fine story-teller, a man who loves to place himself close to almost any musical development you care to name. He comes across as a natural extemporiser.

He interviews like he plays: humorous, engaging, and unquestionably the centre of attention.

What was it he wanted that the other guitar companies weren't making? "I had in mind a guitar that sustained and reproduced the sound of the string with nothing added: no distortion, no change in the response," says Les. Those early hollowbody electrics of the 30s suffered from feedback as players turned up their amplifiers too loud, and the crude pickups and amplifiers of the time did not reproduce string tone accurately.

"I wanted the string to do its thing," he continues, getting into the groove. "No top vibrating, no added enhancement – either advantageous or disadvantageous. I wanted to be sure that you just plucked the string and that's what you heard. That was my whole idea."[2] He started by stuffing rags into the open f-holes of his hollowbody guitars. When that posed its own problems, he took a different route.

He looked at Rickenbacker's 'Frying Pan', an early and crude electric semi-solid guitar. "I said that's not the way to go. You couldn't hold it in your lap. The pickup was in the wrong place. And it was made of steel, so if you got under hot lights, well … everything was wrong with it. So I just went on my way"[3]

Toward the end of the 30s, Les made some friends at the Epiphone guitar factory and arranged to visit at quiet times when he could experiment with instrument ideas. The result was what he called the 'log' and a couple of 'clunkers'. The log nickname came from a four-by-four solid block of pine that he fitted between two sawn halves of a dismembered Epiphone body, adding a Gibson neck, a Larson Bros fingerboard, a Kauffman vibrato, and his own pickups. Les didn't use his log much, but he played the clunkers regularly on stage and in the recording studio throughout the early 50s.

Other pioneers were exploring the idea of solidbody electric guitars in America, not least Rickenbacker, National, Bigsby, and Fender, all in

California. They liked the idea of a solidbody electric because it was easier to construct than an acoustic guitar, using a body or body-section made of solid wood to support the strings and pickups. For the player, it could cut down the irritating feedback that amplified acoustic guitars often suffered. A solidbody guitar reduced the effect that the body had on the instrument's overall tone – something that players of electric hollowbody guitars criticised – but the solidity had the benefit of more accurately reproducing and sustaining the sound of the strings.

The guys at Epiphone were mystified by Les's semi-solid testbed guitars. They'd ask him what that the hell he was up to with this odd-looking thing. It's the log, he'd tell them, a solidbody guitar. And, inevitably, they came back with the obvious question: "Why?" But Les had other ideas. "I was aiming at Gibson, I wasn't aiming at Epi. Gibson was the biggest in the business and that's where I wanted to go."[4]

Gibson was certainly big and undoubtedly successful. Founded as the Gibson Mandolin-Guitar Manufacturing company in Kalamazoo, Michigan, in 1902, the firm had built an enviable reputation among musicians for fine, potent instruments, their mandolins in particular achieving wide popularity. The guitar had grown in importance during the 20s and 30s, and any company that wanted to succeed among guitarists had to be seen as inventive and forward-thinking. Gibson had obliged with many six-string innovations, including the effective L-5 archtop of the early 20s.

The Chicago Musical Instrument Company (CMI) bought a controlling interest in Gibson in 1944. CMI had been set up some 25 years earlier in Chicago, Illinois, by Maurice H. Berlin, and under the deal Berlin became the boss of Gibson's new parent company. The manufacturing base remained at the original factory, purpose-built in 1917 at Kalamazoo, an industrial and commercial centre in a farming area more or less half way between Detroit and Chicago. Lincolnwood, Illinois, a suburb of Chicago, was the location for Gibson's new sales and administration headquarters at CMI.

It was probably around 1946 that Les Paul took one of his experimental guitars to Maurice Berlin at CMI in Chicago. His idea was to convince Gibson to market such a guitar. No doubt with all the courtesy that a pressurised city businessman could summon up, Berlin showed the musician the door. "They laughed at the log," remembers Les.[5]

Meanwhile, Les was busy becoming famous. He was a member of the original Jazz At The Philharmonic touring and recording supergroup organised by Verve Records boss Norman Granz, and had been in the Armed Forces Radio Service during the war, operating out of their HQ in Hollywood, California, entertaining the troops. Among the singers he backed was Bing Crosby. After World War II was over, Les played prominent guitar on Crosby's Number One hit 'It's Been A Long Long Time' (1945), credited to Bing Crosby With The Les Paul Trio. Almost instantly, it brought Les to a wider audience. Crosby showed a keen interest in new recording developments and from 1947 was an early adopter of tape recorders for his radio show. He encouraged Les to build a studio into the garage of the guitarist's home in Hollywood.

It was in that small home studio that Les discovered some important recording techniques. At first he recorded onto aluminium discs, then tape, which he'd seen his friend Crosby use successfully. His method was to build up multiple layers of instruments by using two recording machines. He would add new material to an existing recording at each pass of the tape and could vary the tape-speed to produce impossibly high and fast guitar passages. With this homegrown technology – and later with the facilities afforded by a single, modified tape recorder – Les created on record a magical orchestra of massed guitars playing catchy instrumental tunes.

Les Paul and his 'New Sound' was signed to Capitol Records, and his first multi-guitar single, 'Lover', became a Number 21 hit in America in 1948. Jazzman Sidney Bechet had done a technically similar thing seven years earlier for his multi-instrument 'Sheik Of Araby' and singer Patti Page's hit 'Confess' later in 1948 used the same kind of recording techniques. But it was Les who made overdubbing his own, and more of the distinctive hits followed, many with his singing wife Mary Ford.

The Tennessee Waltz' went to Number Six in the US charts in 1950, but it was 'How High The Moon' that struck gold for "America's musical sweethearts", providing Les & Mary with a Number One smash in April 1951. The duo made a host of personal appearances and played a string of sell-out concerts. They were heard on NBC Radio's *Les Paul Show* every week for six months during 1949 and 1950.

By 1951, Les Paul was a big recording star and just about the most famous guitarist in America. *Time* magazine wrote: "So far this year, Paul and Ford have turned out about one bestseller a month. If they keep it up, they will sell close to six million records before the year is over – and that's tops in Tin Pan Alley's books. One secret of their success is a tape recorder on which Paul dubs multiple guitar and vocal passages, layer-cake style. The result is a reverberating volcano of polyphony."[6]

At the same time, a small California company added its own modest eruption to the quickly evolving sound-world of the electric guitarist. So far, Fender Electric Instruments had been turning out a few amplifiers and electric lap-steel guitars. But in 1950 they quietly launched the world's first commercial solidbody electric 'Spanish' guitar. The innovation was at first called the Fender Esquire or Broadcaster, and in 1951 Fender renamed the instrument as the Telecaster.

Despite the ambitions of players like Les Paul, Fender's burst of activity did not instantly convert guitarists everywhere to the new tones and the potential to play safely at higher volumes offered by these new solidbody instruments from the West Coast. For now, Fender's novel electrics were used by a handful of country players and western-swing guitarists, mostly local to Fender's workshop in Fullerton, California.

Slowly the word spread, and Fender's rise to the upper reaches of the electric guitar market began. Of course, other makers noticed. National, Supro, Kay, and Harmony brought out affordable solidbody models for budding players. Over in Kalamazoo, Gibson had their ears to the ground as well. Gibson's approach of conservative professionalism attracted most of the major jazz guitarists of the day to play the company's hollowbody archtop acoustic and electric guitars, but a development like this, even if it was contrary to Gibson's entire game-plan, could not to be overlooked.

Ted McCarty had joined Gibson in March 1948, having worked at the Wurlitzer organ company for 12 years. In summer 1950 he was made president at Gibson, replacing the outgoing Guy Hart. McCarty recalled that Maurice Berlin, head of parent company CMI, appointed him expressly to improve Gibson's business performance, which had been suffering since World War II. Gibson had suspended most musical-instrument production during the war and was finding it hard to get back into full-scale guitar production. McCarty's immediate aim when he joined was to improve systems, communication, and efficiency in the factories. "I went there on March 15 1948," he remembered. "We lost money in March; we lost money in April; we made money in May and we made it for the next 18 years that I was there."[7]

I met Ted McCarty back in 1992 during a research trip to the States. I was strapped into a tiny plane and braced myself for the hop over Lake Michigan from Chicago to Kalamazoo. "Yes, there really is a Kalamazoo," said the apologetic sign in the hut that passed for the airport lounge. And yes, the old Gibson factory was still there, used in part by the Heritage guitar company, which was run by ex-Gibson workers who didn't care to move to the company's shiny new Nashville plant in 1984.

I went to see McCarty, who was in his 80s then and almost totally blind, but still busy running the Bigsby company in Kalamazoo. Sad to say, he died in 2001, but I'm glad I spent that day with him back in 92. He seemed like a man with a hundred ideas running around his head. At lunch I foolishly offered the view that it would be great for the USA if Bill Clinton won the upcoming presidential election, and I think it would be fair to say from the soup incident that Ted was not a Democrat. Back safely at the Bigsby office, friends again, we settled down and I switched on my cassette recorder.

By 1950, Gibson's line of electric guitars consisted of seven models, from the ES-125 retailing at $97.50 to the ES-5 at $375. These were all hollowbody archtop guitars with f-holes and they conformed to the regular 'amplified acoustic' type of instrument, which Gibson had done much to popularise.

Then along came that Fender solidbody electric from California. McCarty remembered the reaction at Gibson. "We were watching what Leo Fender was doing, realising that he was gaining popularity in the west," McCarty told me. "I watched him and watched him, and said we've got to get into that business. I thought we were giving him a free run, and he was about the only one making that kind of guitar with the real shrill sound, which the country and western boys liked. It was becoming popular.

"We talked it over and decided to start out and make a solidbody for ourselves. We had a lot to learn about the solidbody guitar. It's different to the acoustic. Built differently, sounds different, responds differently."

McCarty's recollection was that Gibson started work on their own solidbody guitar project soon after the appearance of Fender's Broadcaster in late 1950 and that he and the company's top engineers were involved in the project. McCarty told me emphatically that it was Gibson, not Les Paul, who designed the new solidbody instrument that became the Les Paul Model. "We started trying to learn something about a solidbody guitar. I was working with the rest of the engineers, and we would sit down, like in a think tank, and we would talk about this guitar: let's do this; let's try that."

Exactly how many people at the company were involved in the design of the new instrument remains unclear. McCarty calculated that there were at least four, including himself: John Huis, who was his vice president in charge of production, plus "one of the fellows in charge of the wood department" and "one of the guitar players in final assembly". McCarty also mentioned Gibson employees Julius Bellson and Wilbur Marker as being "in on the thing", and it's likely that Gibson's sales people would have been consulted through Clarence Havenga, the vice president in charge of sales (and apparently known throughout the building as Mister Guitar).

"We eventually came up with a guitar that was attractive," said McCarty, "and as far as we were concerned it had the tone, it had the resonance, and it also had the sustain – but not too much. And to get to that point took us about a year."

Early in 1952 the local paper, *The Kalamazoo Gazette*, said Gibson had files bulging with instrument ideas that musicians had sent in. There were enough suggestions "to create the combined pandemonium of a four-alarm fire, dog fight, curfew chorus, and mouse-frightened female".[8] And according to McCarty "only a few" of the ideas were impractical. Presumably, somewhere in those files lurked Les Paul's idea for a semi-solid electric guitar, his 'log' that he'd brought to the company years earlier. He'd been turned away then. But market conditions were changing fast.

"We thought we had our guitar," said McCarty, "and now we needed an excuse to make it. So I got to thinking. At that time Les Paul and Mary Ford were riding very high. They were probably the number one vocal team in the United States. They were earning a million dollars a year. And knowing Les and Mary, I decided maybe I ought to show this guitar to them."[9]

Les Paul's own recollections of the events that led to Gibson producing the Les Paul Model guitar are different. He says that Gibson first contacted him early in 1951, when Fender started making its solidbody electric. He remembers that Maurice Berlin told Marc Carlucci, his second-in-command at Gibson parent company CMI, to contact Les. "They said to find that guy with the broomstick with the pickups on it," he recalls, laughing. "They came around right away, soon as they heard what Fender was doing. And I said well, you guys are a little bit behind the times. But OK, let's go."

Les says that after Gibson contacted him and declared their interest in developing a solidbody guitar, they held a meeting at the CMI HQ in Chicago. Present were Berlin, Carlucci, and CMI's attorney, Marv Henrickson, who also represented Les. "They finalised their deal," says Les, "and hammered out the specifics of the new guitar's design. Then the research and development began in earnest."[10]

Accompanied by Les's business manager, Phil Braunstein, McCarty took the prototype to Les and Mary, who were at a hunting lodge in Stroudsburg, Pennsylvania, near the Delaware Water Gap park, probably in late 1951 or early 1952. Les had turned the living room into a studio, taking advantage of the building's isolated position to make a peaceful recording retreat.

McCarty said that he visited Stroudsburg to try to interest Les in publicly playing the new guitar in return for a royalty on sales. Les too recalls that the lodge was where he saw the first prototype of what became the Gibson Les Paul Model. McCarty remembered that Les loved the prototype, saying to Mary: "I think we ought to join them, what do you think?" She said she liked it too.

An agreement was reached that night, said McCarty. He and Les and Braunstein sat down and worked out a contract. First they decided on the royalty Gibson would pay for every Les Paul guitar sold. Les says it was five per cent. The term of the contract was set at five years.

McCarty: "We each had a copy, written out long-hand. Les could take it to his attorney and I could take it to ours, and if there were any questions, then we would get together and work them out. But not a single word in that contract was changed. So anyway, I came back to the factory. Now we had a Les Paul model."[11]

Les says he had a much bigger involvement in the design of the Les Paul guitar than McCarty's story allows. He states categorically: "I designed everything on there except the arched top. I had a flat top. The arch was contributed by Maurice Berlin. He told me he liked violins and took me by his vault to show me his collection.

"Berlin said that at Gibson they had something that nobody else had, a shaper so they could make an arched belly on that guitar. It would be very expensive for Fender or whoever to make one like it. He asked if I'd have any objection to a violin top, and I said no, that was a wonderful idea. So then they introduced me to Ted McCarty, and we signed the agreement with Gibson."[12]

But McCarty was adamant when recalling his version of the story. "I have told you exactly how it got to be a Les Paul. We spent a year designing that guitar, and Les never saw it until I took it to Pennsylvania."[13]

The Les Paul was not Gibson's first guitar named for a musician, something that today would be called a signature model. Gibson's first signature instrument was the Nick Lucas acoustic flat-top, launched back in 1928. Lucas, touted as the "singing troubadour", was the first American to become a big star through popular guitar/vocal records – in a similar way to Les Paul. Lucas's big hits were 'I'm Looking Over A Four-Leafed Clover' and 'Tiptoe Through The Tulips' but he also made some nifty guitar-rich solo tracks with hip titles like 'Pickin The Guitar' and 'Teasin The Frets'. Despite the signature model, Lucas continued to play his favoured Gibson L-1 flat-top guitar.

It will never be clear exactly who designed what on the original Gibson Les Paul Model, but my guess is that Gibson was responsible for virtually all of it. What I'm certain of is that Les's respected playing and commercial success along with Gibson's weighty experience in manufacturing and marketing guitars made for a strong and impressive combination. It must have created quite a stir over at Fender.

Gibson launched the new Les Paul Model guitar in the summer of 1952, priced at $210. This was about $20 more than Fender's Telecaster. (In today's money, you'd need to spend around $1,600 to match the buying power of $210 in 1952.) Early samples of the new guitar were shipped to Gibson's case manufacturer, Geib, at the end of April, and to Les Paul himself late in May. Some stores began to receive stock in June.

Makers usually unveiled new instruments officially during the annual trade-only NAMM convention, organised by the National Association of Music Merchants. All the important instrument-business people, from store managers to manufacturers, would attend the show. The 1952 convention was held at the Hotel New Yorker in New York City at the end of July, but Gibson also hosted a special pre-NAMM musicians' clinic at the nearby Waldorf Astoria a few days before the convention.

The idea for the clinic, reported *The Music Trades*, was that professional musicians, who couldn't officially attend the NAMM show, as well as the business folk, would have the opportunity to preview and play the latest Gibson instruments. "Especially Gibson's new Les Paul model electronic guitar," noted the magazine. "Tiger Haynes, reported to be the premier colored guitarist, spent at least an hour on the Les Paul Model, and we doubt that suite 4-V will ever be the same again."[14] Other guitarists who visited and tried the new Les Paul included session players and jazz guitarists such as George Barnes, Mundell Lowe, Tony Mottola, and Billy Mure.

Les Paul himself began using the new Gibson solidbody immediately, in line with his endorsement contract. He says he used one for the first time in June 1952, on stage at the Paramount Theater in New York City. He and Mary toured

Europe that September, and a British musicians' newspaper spotted the unusual new instruments played by the "guitar boffin" and his singing partner. "He'd brought his own special amplifiers, four specially-made and surprisingly small guitars with cutaway shoulders to help with the high-speed treble, and plenty of spare tubes."[15]

Today, the gold-finish Les Paul Model is known as a Goldtop, for obvious reasons, and that's what we'll call it too. The new Goldtop's solid body cleverly combined a carved maple top bonded to a mahogany base, a sandwich that united the darker tonality of mahogany with the brighter sonic edge of maple.

Les says that the gold colour was his idea. "Gold means rich," he explains, "it means expensive, the best, superb."[16] Gibson had made a one-off all-gold hollowbody guitar in 1951 for Les to present to a terminally ill patient he'd met during a special appearance at a hospital in Milwaukee. That presentation guitar probably prompted Gibson's all-gold electric archtop ES-295 model of 1952 and must have been the inspiration for the colour of the Les Paul Model too.

During 1953, Gibson dropped the original 'trapeze' bridge–tailpiece unit of the original Goldtop and fitted a new bar-shaped bridge-and-tailpiece that mounted to the body. It was a more stable unit, and the strings now wrapped over the top of the bridge, giving improved sustain and intonation. Also, the guitar's neck 'pitch', or angle, was made steeper. The result was a much happier and more playable instrument.

The Goldtop sold well in relation to Gibson's other models during these early years. Gibson's shipping records reveal an annual total of 1,716 Goldtops in 1952, rising to a record 2,245 the following year, and 1,504 in 1954. Most of the hollowbody electrics were nowhere near that, although the ES-175 peaked at 1,278 in 1953.

Gibson's historian at the time, Julius Bellson, was intrigued by the new sales hike and consulted the records to chart the progress of the company's electric instruments, both solidbody and hollowbody. He estimated that back in 1938, electric guitars made up no more than ten per cent of Gibson guitar sales, but that the proportion of electrics to the rest had risen to 15 per cent by 1940, to 50 per cent by 1951, and that by 1953 electric guitars provided no less than 65 per cent of the company's total guitar sales. The buoyant new Les Paul Model helped that figure considerably.

Gibson, confident now that solidbody electrics could provide a profitable new line, introduced two new Les Paul models in 1954 alongside the Goldtop: the Custom and the Junior. The two-pickup Les Paul Custom looked classy with its all-black finish, multiple binding, block-shape position markers in an ebony fingerboard, and gold-plated hardware, and was indeed more expensive than the Goldtop.

Les said that he chose black for the Custom because "when you're on stage with a black tuxedo and a black guitar, the people can see your hands flying with a spotlight on them".[17]

The Custom had an all-mahogany body, as favoured by Les himself, rather than the maple–mahogany mix of the Goldtop, giving the new guitar what some players felt was a rather more mellow tone. Les insists that Gibson got the arrangements the wrong way around, and that as far as he was concerned the cheaper Goldtop should have been all-mahogany while the costlier Custom should have sported the more elaborate maple-and-mahogany combination.

The Les Paul Custom was promoted in Gibson catalogues as "the fretless wonder" because of its very low, flat fretwire, different to the frets used on other Les Pauls at the time. Some players thought it helped them play more speedily but many missed the fret contact that helped them 'dig in'.

The budget-price Junior was designed for and aimed at beginners and did not pretend to be anything other than a cheaper guitar. Later, that no-

nonsense simplicity would help it become a rock'n'roll workhorse. The outline shape of its body was the same as the Goldtop and Custom, but the most obvious difference to its partners was a flat-top solid mahogany body, a single P-90 pickup governed by single volume and tone controls, and an unbound rosewood fingerboard with simple dot-shape position markers. It was finished in Gibson's traditional two-colour brown-to-yellow sunburst.

The Custom was the first Les Paul to use Gibson's new Tune-o-matic bridge, in conjunction with a separate bar tailpiece. Patented by McCarty, the Tune-o-matic meant that for the first time on Gibson guitars it was possible to individually adjust the length of each string, which improved tuning accuracy. From 1955 it also became a feature of the Goldtop model, the same year that the Les Paul Special debuted, effectively a two-pickup version of the Junior.

Meanwhile, in the Gibson electronics department, run by Walt Fuller, Seth Lover started work on a new pickup. Lover was a radio and electronics expert who had worked on and off for Gibson in the 40s and early 50s while he also taught and did installation jobs for the US Navy. After several comings and goings, Lover had rejoined Gibson's electronics department permanently in 1952.

He had already designed the Alnico neck pickup of the 1954 Custom, but his new pickup would turn out to have a far greater and lasting impact than that shortlived design. Lover was charged with finding a way to cut down the hum and electrical interference that plagued standard single-coil pickups, Gibson's P-90 included. It was one of the main problems that players complained about on their electric guitars of the time.

Gibson began to use Lover's new humbucking pickups in the early months of 1957 and started to replace the old P-90 single-coils on the Les Paul Goldtop and Custom with the new humbuckers during that year. The Custom was promoted to a three-pickup instrument in its new humbucker get-up. Players gradually came to appreciate that humbuckers and a Les Paul guitar made for a congenial mixture, and today many guitarists and collectors covet early Gibson humbucking pickups.

By July 1957, Gibson was able to present an impressive Les Paul line of models in the pricelist, as follows: Les Paul Junior (brown/yellow sunburst) $120; Les Paul Junior three-quarter (brown/yellow sunburst) $120; Les Paul TV (effectively a beige-finish Junior) $132.50; Les Paul Special (beige) $179.50; Les Paul Model (Goldtop) $247.50; and Les Paul Custom (black) $375.

Sales of these original Les Paul guitars reached an overall peak in 1956 and 1957, with the cheaper Junior hitting a record-so-far 3,129 units in '56. But famous musicians were still generally cautious of the relatively new-fangled solidbody electric guitar, although there were clearly a number of more adventurous players who recognised the musical benefits – as well as the fact that a guitar as flashy as a Goldtop was a visual bonus too.

In 1958, Gibson made a radical design change to three of the Les Paul models and a cosmetic alteration to another. Remarkably, that small visual alteration provides the basis for the most desired and collectable Les Paul guitar ever made, and the basis for the story in this book.

"Guitarists the world over are familiar with Gibson's famous series of Les Paul Guitars," the company proclaimed in *The Gibson Gazette* at the end of 1958. "They include some of the finest solidbody instruments manufactured today – and lead the field in popularity. It is with great pride that Gibson announces exciting improvements."

The Junior, Junior three-quarter, and TV were revamped with a completely new double-cutaway body shape. The Junior's fresh look was enhanced with a new cherry red finish. The TV adopted the new double-cutaway design as well, with a more yellow shade of TV finish. The new double-cutaway Special was offered in cherry or the new TV-style yellow.

The Goldtop was the model that fell victim to the small cosmetic alteration. Back to the *Gazette*, under the headline Les Paul Guitar In Cherry Red. "A beautiful red cherry sunburst finish is the news here! This guitar now has a rich, rubbed appearance that cannot be equaled at any price, and the 'new look' that is tops with today's guitarists. If the illustration above were in color, you would see exactly what we mean – this instrument is a true beauty. In the future, all Les Paul guitars will be shipped in cherry sunburst finish – there will be no increase in price.

"All other features of this wonderful guitar will remain exactly the same. Two powerful humbucking pickups give the instrument increased sustain and a clear sparkling tone. Any guitarist will appreciate the wide range of tonal colorings produced by the Les Paul. Tune-o-matic bridge permits adjusting string action and individual string lengths for perfect intonation. Graceful cutaway design with attractive inlaid rosewood fingerboard. Separate tone and volume controls for each pickup that can be preset – three-way toggle switch to activate either or both pickups."[18]

This report brings us to an important matter in the story of this new sunburst Les Paul: exactly what is the model name? Up to now, in Goldtop style, it's officially been the Les Paul Model. This seems logical: that's what it says on the headstock, which has a scripty 'Les Paul' in signature style with 'MODEL' underneath in block capitals. Gibson's regular pricelists continued to name the sunburst version as the Les Paul Model, and that's what the headstock continued to say too. But the May 1960 catalogue lists it as the Les Paul Standard – and that's what many people still call it. Among the cognoscenti, it is a Burst. Short for sunburst. Nothing to do with burst pipes.

Gibson had made a simple marketing decision. They knew sales of the Les Paul Model, a.k.a. the Goldtop, had declined. They knew something had to be done to stimulate renewed interest in this relatively high-price model. The think-tank decided that it was the fault of the unusual gold finish, figuring that some players found it too unconventional. So they acted: they changed the look, applying the new sunburst finish to the maple top in a bid to attract new (and perhaps more conservative) customers.

It's likely Gibson had wind of Fender's new model for 1958: a sunburst-finished solidbody called the Jazzmaster. Was this those damned west-coasters trying to coax Gibson's beloved jazz players over to a solid electric? Perhaps that helped Gibson to decide the kind of finish to shift to on the revised Les Paul.

Probably the first two proper sunburst Les Pauls were shipped from the factory on May 28 1958, logged in Gibson's records simply as "LP Spec finish". Gibson had the new look ready to show off in Room 727 at the Palmer House in Chicago during the summer NAMM show in 1958, which took place from July 21 to 24. The sunburst look would not last long and would be gone by the end of 1960, as would the single-cutaway Les Paul design itself.

The *Gazette* announcement in late 1958 pitched the price of the new sunburst Les Paul at $247.50 (zone 1), with the "plush lined" case adding $42. That $247.50 would have the same buying power as about $1,775 in today's money. By the February 1959 list, the price had gone up to $265 (zone 1) and in November the zone 2 price was $280, while Gibson's October 1960 pricelist (zone 2) shows the "cherry finish" Les Paul Standard model for $318. (The two zones reflected Gibson's higher shipping costs to the furthest states: zone 2 prices were a touch higher to reflect that.)

And – this will unsettle today's buyer used to clicking just a few more times for that 50-cent saving – the list price was pretty much always what you would have to pay.

Gibson's new cherry sunburst meant that the maple body top was now clearly visible through the finish. On Goldtops, that cap had always been hidden under the opaque gold paint. But now that the maple showed through the virtually transparent sunburst finish, Gibson's woodworkers were a little more careful with its appearance. Some of the Bursts made between 1958 and 1960 feature some gloriously striking patterned maple. This pattern is known technically as figure, but most guitar people call it flame. A great Les Paul of the period must have a flame top for most collectors, who place higher values on the full-on look.

The quality of the maple used for the tops was never advertised or promoted by Gibson, because it was simply down to the wood that happened to be available, whether figured or plain. If a good-looking Burst came along every now and again, that was a bonus. Some were remarkably attractive; some were extremely plain.

At Gibson in the late 50s, these Les Pauls continued to come off the line, but no priority at all was given to them. The sole photograph that has turned up of the Gibson booth at the 58 NAMM show does not reveal a Burst, even lurking in the background, although the new Flying V is clearly on display. Les Pauls had not been selling, and the new-look sunburst models were almost an afterthought. The March 1959 catalogue still showed a Goldtop (with P-90s); nobody even bothered to change it.

To an extent, Gibson's hunch about a different look for the guitar was proved right. Consulting their shipping records, they would have seen that sales of the Goldtop declined from a high of 2,245 during 1953 to just a few hundred in 1958 before the new sunburst finish. After the look was revised, sales climbed to 643 in 1959, but they would dip again in 1960.

By late 1960, the sunburst Les Paul experiment was over. Gibson decided that the change of finish had not been enough and that the only way to attract new customers was to completely redesign the entire Les Paul line. This would result in what we now know as the Gibson SG models. Confusingly, for a short while, some of the new-design models still had the Les Paul name on them, and these are usually known now as SG/Les Paul models.

Among guitar fans, the sunburst Les Paul has since become the most highly prized solidbody electric guitar ever. Today, as we're about to find out, they regularly fetch huge sums, far in excess of almost all other collectable electric guitars. Those with especially beautiful figure visible through an unfaded finish are rated the highest.

The Burst turned into one of Gibson's sleeping giants. As far as Gibson was concerned, the story ended badly for this Les Paul model. New sunburst Les Pauls were ignored by famous players at the time, but the instrument has now become an ultra-collectable icon. Players and collectors gradually came to realise that the guitar's inherent musicality and its short production run – around 1,450 were made between 1958 and 1960 – added up to a modern classic.

As we'll discover, the Burst's re-evaluation was prompted originally in the middle and later years of the 60s when several top guitarists discovered that it had enormous potential for high-volume blues-based rock. It turned out that the Les Paul guitar's inherent tonality coupled with its humbucking pickups – and all played through a loud tube amp – made a wonderful noise. It would become apparent before too long that the model had reached its absolute zenith in the 1958–60 Burst.

2. ORIGINALITY

An interview with an early owner of a sunburst Les Paul

Randy Larson bought a used sunburst Les Paul guitar in 1962 for $185. In May 2006 he sold it at auction for $192,000. "I loved that guitar," he says, "so at first I thought to myself there was no way I was going to sell it. And then when I did auction the thing off, I was amazed how emotional an experience it was. I was depressed!"

Today, Randy is the pastor of a church on Long Island, New York. Back in 1962, he was a 16-year-old growing up on a farm in North Dakota. He'd been playing guitar for a few years and wanted a better instrument than the cheap Kay with which he'd started out and which he had now outgrown. He wanted a nicer guitar. He certainly got one.

As a teenager, Randy mostly played in his local church, accompanying hymns, and practiced at home. His father had been a farmer for most of his life but, following a mild heart attack, decided to quit and concentrate on what he loved doing most, which was playing music. Randy's dad taught piano and organ full-time and led an active local three-piece combo.

"My influences were a couple of guys who played guitar and were probably a few years older than me," says Randy. "I was buying Chet Atkins albums and trying to play like Chet. I remember getting one of his books and trying to play fingerstyle – and I got a couple of the tunes down pretty good."

But those were not for church, presumably? "No," he laughs, "not for church. That was outside of church. The churches I was in back then always had organs and pianos, so we kind of fit in with that."

The clarinet player in his dad's group happened to own Anderson's, the music store in town. That's where Randy went at the end of December 1962. He particularly liked the look of that Gibson Les Paul hanging on the wall. It was a couple of years old, a 1960 model, and used.

"It was a beautiful guitar to look at – I loved the sunburst finish on it – and it was real easy to play compared to my Kay. It was like cutting a knife through some soft butter, that's how I always described it. I could finally play that F chord, you know? The one you struggle to get the barre on."

Much less easy was finding the necessary $185. "I just had some odd jobs, putting together some things," Randy recalls. "I definitely had to save up for my Les Paul. That was a decent little amount of money to save up for in 1962 as a 16-year-old."

Shortly afterward, he graduated from senior high school and went to Bible College in Minneapolis. Naturally, his Les Paul went with him. "That's where I really started playing it. I picked up a Fender Deluxe Reverb amp for $150. So, unknowingly, I scored a couple of fantastic items. But at the time, who knew?"

At Bible College, Randy continued to play in local churches and also in the various chapels at the school. "I never actually played in a rock band or anything like that," he explains. "Which is kind of unusual. Usually young guys get a guitar and they get some kind of a band going. But it never came across my path, it never seemed to be the thing to do for me."

Next up for Randy and his sunburst Les Paul, after he graduated from Bible College, was a job with Teen Challenge, an anti-drug programme in New York City. It's still going strong today, describing itself as "the faith-based solution to the drug epidemic". Randy ended up at Teen Challenge for 18 happy years.

"I played my guitar all the time there in the services we had. The organisation did a lot of stuff out in the street, through all the boroughs in New York City. We'd go into the drug areas and play music. We had a little trio, me and an English couple who'd come out to work with us. We'd sing some gospel music, some spirituals, and I would accompany on the Les Paul."

There's a pleasant irony if you care to look. Here was Randy in the 60s and through the 70s spreading the word and doing his bit for the anti-drug message, all the while with a Les Paul in his hands. At the same time, other musicians – among them the rock gods who appeared to advocate and often indulged in drugs – were using the same guitar in very different circumstances. In the same city, in the same country, but almost as if in some kind of parallel universe.

"Yes," smiles Randy, "my guitar career has primarily been church related. I've never made money with it, you know? I've never played out where I've made any money. After Teen Challenge, I did what I'm doing now, pastoring this church here on Long Island. I used my Les Paul in a worship band for the last 20 years or so, playing at least twice a month in church. I used it right up until I sold it."

There's another matter to consider. Had Randy been in a rock band and been like many other guitarists in that other world, he might well have chopped and changed instruments as fashions came and went. He might well have sold his Les Paul sooner rather than later, keen to keep up with his bandmates and his fellow guitarists in the search for The Latest Thing. Instead, he stuck with the one guitar he loved.

Remarkably, during the 40 years and more that Randy owned the instrument, no one ever said that the sunburst Gibson Les Paul he played regularly in public might be worth anything. Not, that is, until 2005 and his good friend Don – who also plays guitar and is also in the church – started to speak his mind. Don had gone off to do some work in Ohio, where he got chatting to a local music-store owner. Just talking around guitar stuff, as you do.

Don mentioned over coffee and strings that his friend had a nice guitar, but he couldn't bring to mind any details beyond the fact that it was old and had a Gibson logo on the head. "But it was enough," laughs Randy, "it was enough to pique the interest of the owner of that store. He said to Don, now when you go back to New York, you get your friend to take some pictures and send them over to me."

Snap, snap. Pictures duly taken and emailed off. It didn't take long for Excited Of Ohio to get back to them. "Don said to me, right, now this guy's really interested in your guitar. He thinks it might be worth something.

"I didn't believe him. I'm like: you're kidding me. Nobody wants this guitar. It's old. But this guy went crazy. He said he had buyers that would give me $100,000 right now. I still didn't believe it. I thought it must be some kind of scam."

Don is one of those guys who likes to do research, so he began to read up on the guitar and scout around for info. After a short interlude, he got back to Randy with some news. "He said to me that he really did think this guitar might be worth something. It really might be. And he said, you know what? Maybe you shouldn't be playing it."

Randy was not impressed. He loved his guitar. It had been a friend all these years, and he wasn't about to go selling it. Meanwhile, Don would yell at him: "Hey, someone could walk on by and knock the thing over! And then what would you have?"

Well yes, Randy thought to himself, that's probably true. That could happen. "So I was a little more careful. But I didn't have another guitar, so what am I going to do? I just figured I'd carry on playing it."

At last — and more to keep Don quiet than anything else – Randy emailed the Gibson company. They said, as they habitually do in such situations, that they are not in a position to value old guitars. Instead, they suggested he go look in the *Blue Book* of guitar prices. This didn't prove easy, but eventually Randy located a copy at the public library in a town a few miles away. Running his finger down the list of Les Pauls, he stopped at his model, a 1960 sunburst, and looked across to the value range. He checked back and did it again, to be sure. There it was in black and white. $50,000 to $60,000.

"When I saw that," says Randy, "I thought wow! Maybe there is something to this story." Don was pleased. At last his friend was seeing some sense. He suggested they take the old Gibson along to the local branch of one of the big guitar-store chains.

Which is what they did. The manager looked at the guitar. Soon all his workmates crowded around it. They ooh-ed and aah-ed over the Les Paul. The manager called his boss, saying he hadn't seen a guitar like this in I don't know how many years. People took pictures with their phones. Somebody started to take it apart a little. They started to criticise a few things.

"So now he's trying to tear it down," says Randy. "He's looked at it and now he's trying to minimise it. So they put everything back together and I left them. There was no way I was going to let these guys touch it. But the excitement that they showed made me believe that this thing is probably worth more money than I ever thought."

Don meanwhile gets in touch with Christie's auction house. "We went into New York City with the guitar. It was pouring rain. We drove in. It cost me $50 to park in the garage underneath Christie's. I was like oh, man, 50 bucks: this thing better be worth some money."

They met Kerry Keane, the auctioneer's instrument specialist. "Kerry was great," says Randy. "He looked it over. He didn't take it apart. He didn't trash it. He knew what he was looking at: he said yes, this guitar is worth a lot of money. He showed me an earlier one they'd auctioned, I think it was a 59 model that had gone for $250,000.

"So right on the spot, right then and there, I signed the thing over to him. I guess I'd gone through all this process. And Kerry wasn't trying to beat me out of it. He really understood guitars, and I trusted him."

The guitar came up for auction at Christie's instrument sale in May 2006. Randy and Don and their wives attended. "There it is, sitting on a stand next to this Stradivarius violin, which ultimately went for over three million dollars, the highest instrument price ever in their history, I think. So I'm saying to myself OK, that's good: my guitar is up there next to a Stradivarius. That's where it really should be, you know?

"I'm feeling a little sad at this point. The reality is here and now. They are going to sell this guitar. When I left it there at Christie's that day, it still hadn't hit me that it was going to be gone. I still owned it, so to speak. But I knew that day at the auction that this was it."

Randy's 1960 sunburst Gibson Les Paul went under the hammer for $192,000. "When it was over, my friends said right, do you want to go talk to the guy that bought it? He was right there. But I said no – and that's when I knew, emotionally, that this was really hard for me. So we left."

Two or three weeks go by, and Randy's wife asks him if he's going to go and get a new guitar, like he said he would. Randy is still not keen, still troubled by the sale. But he goes along anyway. They look in maybe six big-name stores. "I was like a spoiled brat," he smiles. "These were all probably great guitars, old ones, new ones, and I'm like … nothing really connected."

On the way back home, without a new guitar to show for his trouble, Randy suddenly remembers a friend telling him about a store in the town he's driving through right now. He turns off the main drag, finds the street, locates the store, a nondescript brick building with a window and a sign in it.

He leaves his wife in the car to go take a look. No signs of life in the store. He goes around the back. There's somebody inside, working on a guitar at a bench. He knocks. "This guy opens up. I says, you guys sell guitars? He says yes, come on in."

Randy goes and gets his wife. The tewo of them go into the store, past the workbench, and down a small hallway. He hears some guys talking in a room off the hallway.

"I look into the room, and there hanging on the wall is my guitar. My Les Paul. The one that I sold. This can't be! So I walk into the room, and when I turn around, the guy that's talking is the guy that bought the guitar, the guy that bid on it at Christie's. My mouth is open. This is unreal. Unreal."

But it is most certainly real, and another strange twist in the story of one particular sunburst Les Paul.

The store owners are freaked out too at first, but they gather themselves together and remember to take some pictures of ex-owner with ex-guitar. "Two great guys," says Randy. "It was just hilarious. But I guess that was the moment that I knew for sure that yes, really, it's over now. That was it. Those guys love guitars, they know guitars, and somebody's going to buy it and will be really glad to have it."

He went out the next week, conscience clear, and bought himself a PRS McCarty Model. He didn't know until it was explained to him that this was named for Ted McCarty, who had been president of Gibson at the time the original Les Paul guitar was designed.

"When I heard that, I thought OK, this is the guitar for me. And I love playing it."

How about the large sum of money? "I gave a huge chunk to Teen

Challenge, the drug and alcohol ministry that I had been in," says Randy. "I gave another large sum to the church. And then I put most of it into my retirement fund, which was sorely lacking at that point.

"When I think about it now," he sighs, "I was just this farm kid from a little town in a sort of unknown state. To look back to when I purchased that guitar is just amazing to me. How do things like that happen?"[1]

3. BLUESBREAKER

How Eric Clapton, Keith Richards, Michael Bloomfield, and others rediscovered a classic

Not one well-known guitarist played the 1958–60 sunburst Les Paul during the model's own short lifetime. By contrast, the Goldtop, the earlier incarnation of the instrument, had turned up in the hands of quite a few familiar players. But then a lot more Goldtops were made during that model's five-year life.

Rhythm & blues masters Hubert Sumlin and Jody Williams each played a Goldtop with Howlin' Wolf, and rockabilly rebel Carl Perkins put the same model to good use, but it was bluesmen who seemed to take the biggest shine to Goldtops. Muddy Waters, Guitar Slim, Freddie King, Buddy Guy, B.B. King, and John Lee Hooker all strapped one on at some time or another in the 50s.

Most of those became famous for using other electrics – Buddy Guy with his Strat, B.B. with his Gibson thinlines – but Freddie King cut nearly all his wonderfully bustling bluesy instrumentals with his Goldtop, not least the classic 'Hide Away', which he recorded in summer 1960. It was a big American hit the following year, grazing the pop Top 30, and it reached the ears of just about any blues player you care to name – including one particular Englishman whom we'll meet a little later.

Frannie Beecher of proto-rock'n'rollers Bill Haley & His Comets played a Les Paul Custom, given to him by Gibson in an early endorsement deal. "Bill Haley recommends that you see the magnificent Gibson line at your local dealer," ran a 50s Gibson ad, with Beecher and his black Custom clearly visible at Haley's side. It was the model for the way that electric guitars would be promoted for decades to come.

As for the sunburst Les Paul ... well, it seemed as if Gibson was justified in its decision to drop the model in 1960. No one wanted a Burst back then. A Goldtop had a kitsch kind of bluesy charm, enough to add a sparkle to the frontline of any electric band. But a conservative sunburst, with a finish similar to those big boxes the jazz guys used? No thanks. That seemed to sum up the general response from the growing ranks of budding rock'n'rollers.

As the 60s dawned, Fender's Stratocasters and Telecasters were just the job for the pros in that world. Gibson's replacement for the single-cutaway Les Paul was the new SG solidbody, with what Gibson described as an "ultra thin, hand contoured, double cutaway body". The SG style was a radical departure for Gibson. The body edges looked almost as if a sculptor had been at work rather than a guitar-maker, chiselling away at a modernistic amalgam of bevels and points and angles.

Gibson could hardly have failed to notice Fender's growing success with the sleek, stylish Stratocaster; after all, the earliest Fender solidbody guitar had prompted the launch of the Les Paul in the first place, back at the start of the 50s and the start of the solidbody electric guitar.

While Fender and Gibson fought for the high-end market, big-volume Chicago makers like Harmony and Kay and the mail-order merchants, Danelectro among them, were happy to serve the would-be stars. The single-cutaway old-style Les Paul, in Goldtop, black Custom, or sunburst style, already seemed old-fashioned.

That was in the United States. However, the story of the revival of those old Les Pauls, and especially the Bursts, starts in the UK. A number of young English boys who wanted to play the electric guitar would turn out to have the most profound effect upon this instrument and the way it would be perceived by many of its fans over the coming decades. What those boys wanted most was an American instrument. That is what their heroes played. So clearly that is what they needed. But lack of funds and a government decree determined otherwise. For the time being.

Thanks to a post-war, cash-strapped British government, the importing of musical instruments and gramophone records "from the dollar areas" was banned in 1951, along with some other luxury goods. This government embargo on US instrument imports was presumably designed to boost the home industry. Remarkably, it was not lifted until the summer of 1959. During the decade, budding British guitar players had to make do with European-made instruments. Brands such as Hofner and Futurama became better known than Gibson and Fender.

Around the end of 59, stores began advertising the arrival of the Yankee produce – and some with less than total enthusiasm. "Most American models have now reached us: Gibson, Guild, Harmony etc," ran an ad by the Stanley Lewis store in London. "The comparison between the [European] instruments and the American is interesting, and some customers may now decide that after comparing the two, it will be worth having a Hofner or Framus after all, especially as the prices are so very much lower, but we leave this for you to decide."[1] Maybe Lewis's had large stocks of Euro guitars that they thought might now be difficult to shift. Anyway, most British guitarists decided they still wanted those American guitars, as a dream or a now-closer reality.

And so as the 60s got underway, with the post-war restrictions on American trade finally lifted, British guitarists could at last buy new American guitars – assuming, that is, they had the cash, or had parents willing to sign the forms and act as guarantor for their wild offspring to acquire a guitar on hire purchase (the name of the scheme then for buying on credit). These were the primary routes to the magical state known as Actually Owning A Real American Guitar.

Albert Lee was one of those who wanted to join this select club. Later, of course, he would rise to fame – playing with Emmylou Harris, Eric Clapton, The Crickets, and others – and make some great records of his own. Back in 1961, however, the unknown 17-year-old was on a mission. "I had it in mind to go out and buy a Gibson," he recalls, speaking at his home now in California. "I don't know why. I guess I was a big Scotty Moore fan and liked the idea of a Gibson."

In the same way as many young guitar nuts back then, he was drawn to the guitar shops of London's West End, the central part of town around the main shopping areas of Oxford Street and Regent Street. The guitar shops were mainly to be found along Charing Cross Road and Shaftesbury Avenue. Mecca came in the form of the Selmer store on Charing Cross Road.

"I was in Selmer's one day looking at guitars and wondering which one I could afford," smiles Lee. "I was there every Saturday. Selmer had more guitars than anybody else. Lew Davis was just up the street, and further down Charing Cross Road was Jennings. It was there that I bought my Czechoslovakian-made Grazioso, later called a Futurama. That was expensive: I paid £85 [about $240] secondhand for it. It was kind of like an American guitar and looked a *bit* like Buddy Holly's guitar – three pickups and a tremolo. What did I know? We hadn't seen a Stratocaster. I had a Hofner President with a pickup in it before that."

The teenager drooled over the wares on display in Selmer, along with all the other youngsters up west for a nice day out in 1961. "This guy heard me playing. He said oh, are you in a band? His name was Bob Xavier. He said do you want to join a band? I went over to his house, and he opened up this guitar case, and there's this brand new Les Paul Custom, with a Bigsby. Sure, OK, I'll join your band!"

Lee took over the payments on the luscious black Les Paul. "At the time, it was a guitar I didn't think was in my budget. I was looking for something around £120 or so, and this Custom was well over £200. But I just loved this guitar." Lee played the Les Paul for five years or so, with Bob Xavier and then in British rhythm & blues singer Chris Farlowe's band, The Thunderbirds.

He was mates with another young budding guitarist, Jimmy Page. The two had met while Lee was playing in the house band at the 2-Is coffee bar in central London. Page, who'd started playing with Neil Christian's Crusaders, would drop by the music dive, and soon the two guitar nuts struck up a friendship.

"We'd go to each other's houses," says Lee, "just young kids. He was a month or so younger than me. At that time I had a Supro amp with a 15-inch Jensen speaker. He really liked the sound of my Les Paul Custom and my Supro, to the extent that he went out and bought the same set-up. This would have been 1962, maybe 63. He went to Selmer's, and they still had a couple of these Les Pauls. Not on the wall, but they had a couple in their warehouse. They weren't that popular at the time. He bought that and a smaller Supro."[2]

Like Lee, Page's first electric guitar was one of the basic Stratocaster-ish Grazioso/Futurama guitars made in Czechoslovakia (now the Czech Republic). Soon, he moved on to some much better guitars, including a Gretsch Chet Atkins 6120 and a Gibson thinline stereo model, which he may have traded for the Les Paul Custom.

Page moved on from The Crusaders to become a session player on London's busy studio scene of the mid 60s, appearing on many a now-collectable vinyl single and album, working for music-industry figures as diverse as Mickie Most and Burt Bacharach. Page's Custom was his main electric guitar for these sessions.

"I chose that Les Paul Custom purely because it had three pickups and such a good range of sounds. It seemed to be the best all-rounder at the time," Page said in 1972. "Even though I [was] one of the first to have a Les Paul, I didn't often get the chance to get going on it. On the odd occasion, I was able to put a bit of feedback on some record or other, but it was only after all the other musicians had gone home, because when I played like that they just used to put their fingers in their ears. The limitations were often really frustrating – a factor which eventually led to my leaving session work – because I rarely had a chance to roar into something. The sax players and violinists used to look at me as though I were some kind of joke."[3]

As the 60s progressed and his career developed, Page moved away from the Custom. As we'll see, he would rediscover the Les Paul in two-humbucker sunburst form and become one of the Burst's most important players. But for now he put the Custom aside. "I didn't feel that particular model was good for blues," he explained. "It's called the 'Fretless Wonder' and the frets are filed real fine, but it just doesn't happen for the blues."[4]

Despite their later fame, neither Albert Lee nor Jimmy Page caused much excitement at the time by playing their Les Paul Customs. Apart from their small circle of like-minded friends, not too many people yet appreciated their taste in solidbody guitars. And then, along came Keith Richards.

Here was an unquestionably famous guitarist. By the start of 1964, the Stones had notched up two Top 20 British 45s and in the summer scored their first Number One, 'It's All Over Now'. Richards wanted American electric guitars just like everybody else, but he was in a much better position to indulge himself. By early 64 he had two: a Harmony Meteor and an Epiphone Casino. It was probably on the group's first US tour, in June, that he bought a sunburst Les Paul. The tour included dates in Texas, as well as recording sessions at the Chess studio in Chicago.

Richards' guitar marked the start of the Burst legend. It was the first time anywhere in the world that a significant and publicly visible player had chosen the model. The guitar would, it turned out, have a long and varied career itself.

For now, Richards was one very proud guitarist. His new baby – or rather his new old baby – was a 1959 Les Paul Model in sunburst finish. It had been fitted with a Bigsby vibrato at some point after it left the Gibson factory. Maybe when Richards had bought it on that US tour he found it needed some work, because as far as photographic evidence suggests, he didn't appear with it in public until September – notably during a Pathe News film shot at a Stones show in Hull in northern England on the 21st.

At the end of the following month, the Stones went to the States for a second tour, this time for three weeks. Right at the start, within days of arriving, they played CBS TV's *Ed Sullivan Show*. This was the programme that had done so much to bring The Beatles to an American audience earlier in the year. Just as they had for The Beatles, almost every budding guitarist in America was ready and waiting in front of their TV set – and here came Richards playing his Les Paul on 'Around And Around' and 'Time Is On My Side'. Cue several million guitar fans saying to themselves: "But what the hell is that guitar?"

Remember, this was a model that Gibson had dropped from production in 1960. Even if the *Ed Sullivan* viewers had flipped through the current Gibson catalogue, all they would have seen in the solidbody electric section was a bunch of SGs, Melody Makers, and Firebird models – and nobody was going to muddle any of those with a 50s Les Paul.

Back in Britain, too, Richards was widely seen on TV with his sunburst Les Paul – presenting 'The Last Time' on *Ready Steady Go!* and *Top Of The Pops* around the end of February 1965, for example. Again, guitar fans were intrigued by the rare Burst on their screens. Later that year, in August, Jimmy Page's Custom too caused a stir when it appeared prominently in a photograph in the musicians' magazine *Beat Instrumental*. But by now another key player had discovered the sunburst Les Paul for himself.

Maybe Richards showed his new guitar to his friend Eric Clapton? Whatever the circumstances, Clapton acquired a sunburst Les Paul of his own, probably toward the end of May 1965. In the mythology of the Burst, this guitar would become the most revered of all instruments – not only because Clapton played his finest-ever recorded work with it, but also because he did not have the guitar for very long.

But we're getting ahead of ourselves. Eric Clapton was in John Mayall's Bluesbreakers at this time. He'd joined the band in April 1965 after leaving The Yardbirds a few months earlier, so he'd only been with Mayall a very short time when he got the Les Paul. For the first weeks with Mayall he was playing a Telecaster. The attraction of the Mayall band to Clapton was that they played pure blues, which was exactly what the 21-year-old guitarist wanted to do. "He loves the blues so much," said Yardbirds singer Keith Relf, "I suppose he did not like it being played badly by a white shower like us."[5]

Now that he was in a real blues band, Clapton wanted a real blues guitar. Just about his favourite blues guitarists was Freddie King, and there on the front of King's 1962 album *Let's Hide Away And Dance Away* was the guitarist playing an old-style Les Paul Goldtop. Or was it? The record company, King Records (no relation), did not appear to have spent money on the finest printing methods. The colour picture of Freddie showed a guitar that didn't exactly look gold, more a sort of brown-ish colour. More like a sunburst finish than a gold one, perhaps.

With that image in his mind, Clapton went shopping. Of course, he went to the London West End shops, just like Albert Lee, Jimmy Page, and all the rest. That's where the best guitars were. That's where the American guitars were. One and the same thing.

Clapton probably already had a suspicion that older guitars were somehow better, too. A little later, he told a journalist angling for advice for young guitarists: "When you're starting, always buy a secondhand guitar, because it will be 'broken in' and easier to play, apart from the fact that the older the guitar the better it seems to have been made."[6] This is in essence what would become the vintage guitar argument, in one sentence.

Anyway, to Clapton's shopping trip. Selmer was the shop to head for first. As Albert Lee says, that was the one with more guitars than anywhere else. Selmer London had been set up back in 1929 by brothers Ben and Lew Davis when they secured an agency deal to sell Selmer's made-in-France saxophones. They distributed and manufactured a range of different instruments and opened two stores in the West End: Selmer was at 114-116 Charing Cross Road, on the corner of Flitcroft Street, and a short distance north on the same side of the road was Lew Davis, at number 134, almost at the corner of Denmark Place.

Denmark Street, which ran off to the east on the stretch of Charing Cross Road between the two shops, was London's own Tin Pan Alley, with management offices, demo studios, and other music-biz spots.

Clapton remembered buying his first sunburst Les Paul "at Lew Davis's shop in Charing Cross Road; it's Selmer's now. He had a couple imported from the States, and I managed to get hold of one. ... I was very pleased with my sound while I was with John [Mayall]. Those Gibsons have the perfect blues sound."[7] In a later interview he said: "It had humbuckers and was almost brand new." He mentioned the original case with its "lovely" puple lining and summed up the whole package as "just magnificent".[8]

Clapton's recollection seems confused. We already know that most guitarists regarded Selmer as the place to go for guitars, and I think that is where Clapton got his Les Paul. Even if he did go into the Lew Davis shop – when he says "it's Selmer's now" in this 1968 interview, he means that the Davis store at number 134 had closed by then – he may have been asked to wait a few minutes while the axe in question was walked the short distance up the road from Selmer.

Both shops advertised regularly in *Melody Maker*, the music paper that was read by musicians and that carried most ads for gear. The Lew Davis store did not advertise any Gibson Les Pauls during this period. Selmer's ads boasted quite a few, although not, infuriatingly, the one that appears to be Clapton's. This was the hip guitar of the moment, and stock would move quickly. But at least the ads tell us more or less what Clapton would have paid for his.

Selmer advertised three Les Pauls for sale during May and June 1965, one with a Bigsby, another "with trem arm" (which could also describe the SG-style model), and one simply described "with case". They ranged in price from 120 guineas to 130 guineas. Some luxury goods were priced then in guineas; one guinea equalled one pound and one shilling. Averaging out the prices, that means Clapton must have paid about £130 for his.

Christopher Hjort researched and wrote about this period of Clapton's career for his 2007 book *Strange Brew*. Hjort has pinpointed the time of Clapton's acquisition during 1965 of this most famous of guitars down to a ten-day window between May 26 and June 4. On May 25, a budding young guitarist named Peter Green saw Clapton play with the Mayall band at a club in north London. It made a great impression on Green, who vividly remembered later that Clapton was still playing his Telecaster that night. Ten days later, on June 4, a local-paper photographer snapped Clapton playing his newly-acquired Les Paul in Guildford. It seems Clapton must have gone shopping in the West End during his days off leading up to that gig on the 4th.

How many 21st century pounds or dollars would we need to spend to match the roughly £130 that Clapton paid for his Burst? The British retail price index tells us that £130 in 1965 would be about £1,800 in today's money. As for dollars, the exchange rate in 1965 was $2.80 to £1, making that £130 about $365. And $365 in 1965 would be about $2,400 in today's money. Consider too that a brand new Gibson SG Standard was $305 in 1965, a new Fender Stratocaster $281. However you look at it, Clapton was prepared to make a sizeable investment.

No definitive evidence has emerged to determine the year in which Clapton's Burst had been made by Gibson, although some say an aside or two from Clapton later about it having a "slim neck" indicates that it was a 1960 model. Clapton didn't do very much to his new-old guitar apart from play it and love it, but the small changes he made to the instrument are now deemed significant.

It may have been Clapton who changed the original Kluson tuners to more robust Grover units; someone did, either a previous owner or Clapton himself. Probably late in 1965, Clapton took off the metal covers of the guitar's pickups, at first the neck pickup, revealing the twin 'bobbins' below. Perhaps he was just curious; perhaps he thought it would make the pickup sound better. That's what he'd decided by the time of an interview in the first months of 1966. "You've probably heard about me taking the covers off my pickups," he said. "This is something I would definitely recommend for any guitarist. The improvement soundwise is unbelievable."[9]

The sonic difference is debatable, but anything that Eric Clapton did, everyone wanted to try. If I do that to my guitar, I will sound like Clapton. Well, no. But what the cover-removal did reveal was the colour of the twin pickup bobbins, on Bursts sometimes black and sometimes white, or even a combination of the two. This is another small difference that has since taken on almost mystical significance for some Burst fans.

Another general change that players were beginning to adopt and that Clapton helped bring to wider attention was the use of lighter strings. String-bending was an established technique – some styles, including blues, would hardly exist without the expressive pitch-bending it allowed – and guitarists would mess around with their string sets to assist the trick.

Clapton and others at first did this by discarding the regular low-E string, moving each string down a notch – the A in place of the E, D in place of the A, and so on – and then replacing the now-missing high-E with a thinner banjo string. Soon, custom-made string sets by brands such as Fender (Rock & Roll strings) provided the right balance. The lightness not only made it easier to achieve big bends but also to use vibrato in the left hand. Clapton used both techniques to full effect, and his vibrato in particular became the envy of many onlookers.

"I would hit a note, hold it, and give it some vibrato with my fingers, until it sustained, and then the distortion would turn into feedback," Clapton wrote later in his autobiography. "It was all of these things, plus the distortion, that created what I suppose you could call my sound."[10]

One of the first opportunities Clapton had to put his new pairing of a Les Paul and a Marshall amp on to tape came in August 1965, when Jimmy Page produced a session featuring Clapton with John Mayall's Bluesbreakers for Immediate Records. It would provide Mayall's next single, 'I'm Your Witch Doctor'.

"He had all that sound down," Page recalled later, "and the engineer, who was co-operating up to that point, but was used to doing orchestras and big-bands, suddenly turned off the machine and said, 'This guitarist is unrecordable!' I told him to just record it and I'd take full responsibility. The guy just couldn't believe that someone was getting that kind of sound from a guitar on purpose. Feedback, tremolo – he'd never heard anything like it."[11] This would not be the last time that recording personnel were affronted by Clapton's sonic assault on their gear.

In the world of the sunburst Les Paul guitar, all roads lead to Eric Clapton. More specifically, to the album he recorded called *Blues Breakers John Mayall With Eric Clapton*. More specifically still – and as we are discovering, you can never have too many specifics in Les Paul-land – it concerns what happened at the Decca recording studio at 165 Broadhurst Gardens, West Hampstead, north London, early in May 1966.

No surviving documents have ever revealed the exact date. But it was probably on a Monday morning, May 2, just around the corner from West Hampstead tube station, that you could have wandered through the front door at Decca and into number 2 studio to see engineer Gus Dudgeon draining the last of his tea-cup and completing his set-up. Or so he thought.

Dudgeon recalled later that Clapton absolutely insisted that he wasn't going to play with a 'tame' sound and wanted to play loud in order to get the Ericaceous sound. Very loud. Nobody had done that at Decca, as far as Dudgeon could remember. This was a recording studio. Why would you want to play at a gig volume level? Dudgeon waited for producer Mike Vernon to arrive and sort it out. Vernon asked if it was essential, and Clapton said it was. Clapton said the sound changed and the sustain disappeared if you turned it down. So Dudgeon went over to the microphone he'd carefully set up and moved it away to a safer distance from Clapton's guitar amplifier, a 45-watt Marshall model 1962 combo with two 12-inch speakers. And the band began to play. Loudly.

"Clapton made a handful of recordings with that first Les Paul, about half of which are collected on the *Blues Breakers* album," says Hjort. "Clapton and Mayall distilled their own British brand of Chicago blues on that record, and the guitar playing is phenomenal." Clapton is self-assured, with an unparalleled melodic sense; he employs a graceful phrasing but a dirty guitar tone that, reckons Hjort, was the equal of the power demonstrated by original blues guitar stars like Freddie King and Otis Rush. It is a remarkable record that still sounds phenomenal today.

It's not just the stuff in the grooves that tickles the Les Paul fancier. The record's jacket was important too. First, it provides the album's nickname. On the front, Clapton sits with his bandmates and reads a copy of the *Beano* comic. This is an easy one: the record is now widely known as the *Beano* album. Certainly more succinct than *Blues Breakers John Mayall With Eric Clapton.* And on the rear is a small black-and-white photo of Clapton tuning his Les Paul, carefully avoiding the ciggie stuck on the end. That would have been photoshop'd out today, for a start.

Even though the photograph only showed part of the back of the guitar, keen-eyed Clapton fans could work out what it was. It's arguable that this one image began the entire 'vintage guitar' fashion, a trend based on the debatable notion that old guitars are inherently better than new ones. Whatever the arguments, it was certainly Clapton more than any other musician who turned the ears and hearts of his fellow players toward the new sound of the old Les Paul guitars.

Beyond the essential *Beano* album, Clapton and his first Les Paul are heard to brilliant effect on about a dozen other tracks from that time. Hjort reports: "There's a two-song session with American bluesman Champion Jack Dupree, a couple of singles with John Mayall, and several home recordings with Jimmy Page, later cleaned up and repackaged on countless compilations over the years. The Dupree track 'Third Degree' is a delightful highlight with a wild, distorted solo that is reminiscent of Buddy Guy, and another good one is 'Bernard Jenkins', a sprightly piano–guitar duet with Mayall, with Clapton equally expert as fiery soloist or understated accompanist."[12]

Hjort accurately assesses that Clapton's talent in those years transcends time and that the recordings on the *Beano* LP in particular sound as fresh today as they did when they were cut more than 40 years ago. Few fans of the best guitar playing will disagree: the Mayall album is one of the great white blues albums, not least for Clapton's inspired combination of controlled distortion and feedback, and his fine vibrato style and keen melodic ideas, all wrapped up in that beautiful tone and natural sustain. High spots are many, including 'Have You Heard', 'Key To Love', and 'Stepping Out', and it all came together for the blistering cover of Freddie King's 'Hideaway' – a great moment for Clapton's new guitar, inspired by the King album that includes this very track.

By the time the *Beano* album was released in late July 1966, the restless Clapton was already rehearsing his next band, with bassist Jack Bruce and drummer Ginger Baker. Mayall's LP made a respectable Number Six on the UK charts but soon died away, its reputation only growing in later years. Cream, on the other hand, became superstars very quickly. In a sense, this was to be the band's undoing. There was no doubt about their talent – they did not call themselves Cream on a whim – but their enormous success exerted pressures on the trio that they could hardly have foreseen when they began rehearsals in a scout hut in north London that July.

It quickly became apparent to Clapton, Bruce, and Baker that they had something special, but Clapton was distraught when his beloved Les Paul was stolen during one of those rehearsals, before he'd had a chance to play it with the new group in public or in the studio. The calamity was mentioned during an interview in August for *Record Mirror*. Clapton was in a restaurant with journalist Richard Green, who wrote: "Eric's culinary lesson was interrupted by a man at the table opposite calling over and asking if he knew anyone who wanted to buy a certain make of guitar. The two had a discussion, then Eric told me about his favourite guitar."

Clapton described the robbery of his sunburst Les Paul. "Someone stole it at the rehearsal room … I wouldn't have sold it. It was worth about £400 to me. It was the only one I had and the one I always played. I'm borrowing guitars now. I'd like to get another Les Paul; there are only about six or seven in the country. I might get a Rickenbacker."

The *Mirror* printed a description of the guitar in an attempt (futile, as it turned out) to have it returned. "It's a Les Paul Standard, five or six years old, small and solid. It has one cutaway and is a red-gold colour with Grover machine heads. The back is very scratched and there are several cigarette burns on the front. The strap is a big, black leather belt with the names Buddy Guy, Big Maceo, and Otis Rush carved on the inside."

Clapton told the writer how the cheeky thief made a return visit to complete his prize. The guitar had gone missing during Cream's rehearsals, probably in the last week of July. The group played their first gigs the following week, including a date at Klooks Kleek, a club a few doors along from the Decca studio in Hampstead, north London. "Someone stole the case at Klooks Kleek," said a dejected Clapton. "That takes a lot of doing, to walk out of Klooks Kleek with my guitar case. Whoever took the guitar must have come back for the case."[13]

Since then, many, many Les Pauls have been hopefully offered as this famous ex-Clapton guitar, known to Les Paul fans as the Beanoburst, but no proof has ever accompanied such instruments. As Peter Green put it in 1999: "Eric's Les Paul would go for 50 million now. It was a special one."[14] Well, maybe not 50 million, Pete. Not yet, anyway. And besides, first you have to find it. Or fake it.

So what was Clapton playing on those first Cream dates? A fan's snap exists of him at Cream's debut gig, at the Twisted Wheel in Manchester on July 30th, and good quality pictures survive of him playing at the Windsor National Jazz & Blues Festival the following day. The sunburst Les Paul he's playing differs visually from the stolen one: most obviously it has a Bigsby vibrato, and it also has both pickup covers intact and the original Kluson tuners. In other words, much like Keith Richards' sunburst. Maybe a loaner for a friend in need? Richards was on tour with the Stones in the States and now regularly playing two other Les Pauls, a Goldtop with P-90 pickups and a black Custom. But no doubt a few select phone calls could have secured the Burst for Clapton in England. It remains a possibility, but no more than that.

(That travelled Bigsby'd Burst certainly turned up later in capable hands. The Stones guitarist sold it to yet another Mayall guitarist, the talented Mick Taylor, in September 1967. Ironically, Taylor arrived with the guitar when he joined the Stones in the summer of '69.)

Back again to summer 66, and following Cream's debut gigs, Clapton tried a Les Paul Special for a few dates, a humbler guitar without humbuckers. No doubt he did not consider that seriously for very long. By the middle of September, he would manage to persuade Andy Summers, then of Zoot Money's Big Roll Band and later of The Police, to part with another fine sunburst Les Paul.

Summers wrote in his 2006 memoir *One Train Later* that he had bought the guitar in – have a guess – London's Charing Cross Road. "When Eric sees me with it, he asks me where I bought it. I innocently tell him that they have another one for sale for 80 quid and he could go get it. … So Eric gets the other Les Paul and eventually changes the sound of rock guitar for ever."

Clapton started calling Summers soon after the robbery, asking if he would sell him the guitar. Summers had in fact moved to a Telecaster, which he considered a hipper instrument, and anyway thought his Gibson's back pickup might be faulty. But at first he declined Clapton's offers, knowing that these original Les Pauls were now sought-after instruments.

Reports had begun to appear in the musicians' press in Britain. One of the first to identify the trend was the players' magazine *Beat Instrumental*, in summer 1966. "Les Paul Customs are in great demand!" shrieked the headline. While a Custom was specified, most guitarists would have been pleased to find any kind of original Les Paul guitar. Eagle-eyed fans of Clapton would have specified a sunburst model. But information was scarce on these discontinued instruments from Kalamazoo, Michigan, and to some, 'Custom' was simply a generic term for all the various old Les Pauls – black, gold, or sunburst.

The *Beat* reporter wrote: "If you have a Les Paul Custom you want to sell, come to London and get a very good price for it from almost anyone. Rarest of the lot seems to be the three-pickup job which Jimmy Page uses. If you have one of these you're rich."[15]

Page himself said in summer 66 that he'd still got his Les Paul Custom (though he used a Telecaster with The Yardbirds) and was aware that big money was being offered for them. "Now everybody wants one. I heard a story the other day, although I don't know if it's absolutely true, that Gordon Waller [of Peter & Gordon] met a guitarist with a model like mine and offered him £500 for it. Even then the bloke wouldn't let it go."[16]

Letters pleading for help began to appear in the magazine columns. "I am having great difficulty in obtaining a Gibson Les Paul Custom guitar," wrote a reader. "Have you any idea where I can obtain one? If you think this is impossible, perhaps you could tell me which guitar is similar in tone?"

The magazine replied that the original Les Paul "is a much sought after instrument. It is impossible to obtain a new one, and even secondhand models are very scarce. If you want one, then you will have to be very patient."[17] They went on to recommend as an alternative one of the slowly growing band of Japanese-made copy guitars being imported to Europe and the USA. These oriental 'replicas' were of poor quality at the time – but at least they looked similar and were available.

Demand continued to increase. In a later news item, a reporter contemplated the sorry state of supply and demand. "So many people are interested in obtaining one of the almost legendary Les Paul guitars that we've done a bit of checking. Some guitarists insist that new Les Pauls can still be bought, but they're wrong ... so if you're offered a guitar, and told it's a Les Paul, be very wary."[18] This may well be the first appearance in print of the words "legendary Les Paul" and "be very wary" in close proximity. It is a mantra that has been repeated regularly ever since.

Meanwhile, back in summer 1966, Eric Clapton persisted in his attempts to buy Andy Summers' sunburst Les Paul, offering an attractive £200. Summers said later that his Les Paul was a 1958 model; others have speculated from photographs that it was more likely a 1960.[19] Anyway, Summers weakened, well aware that Clapton was offering more money than Summers had paid for the guitar.

"One night, I drag it out from under the bed and open the case with its plush pink lining," Summers wrote. "I play it for a few minutes. 'I dunno: £200, back pickup doesn't work.' It feels like the love affair with this one is over. I am not a Les Paul man and I reach for the phone.

"Twenty-four hours later, with the din of The Supremes in the background singing 'Baby Love', I lean across a table in a dark booth as [Cream manager] Robert Stigwood hands me a wad of notes, remarking that it's too much money for a bloody guitar. The next day, I drop off the Les Paul at [a studio] in the West End where [Eric is] in the middle of recording with Jack and Ginger."

In that 2006 memoir, Summers also took time to reflect on the true value of his sale. "The terms Les Paul and Clapton become synonymous [and] the star of the Sunburst Les Paul begins to ascend. Before Clapton, it was regarded as a weird failure, but after *Fresh Cream* the little Gibson becomes the absolute guitar. ... What if I hadn't sold my guitar to Eric? Maybe it would have turned out differently, and the Les Paul become merely another interesting historical clunker rather than a cultural icon. But possibly because of our little interchange, it ultimately becomes a 'Stradivarius' of rock guitars."[20] That overlooks the all-important first Burst that Clapton owned, of course, but otherwise the point is well made.

It was the ex-Summers Les Paul that Clapton used to record most of the group's first album, *Fresh Cream*, including gems such as 'Spoonful' on which he demonstrates an impressive command of dynamics and sets forth the full range of tones available from his guitar–amp combination. He also used that guitar for the remarkable single 'I Feel Free'. That A-side alone turned the heads of many a guitar player who had not switched on to or perhaps even heard the Mayall album. And this was something quite different.

"I am playing more smoothly now," Clapton explained. "I'm developing what I call my 'woman tone'. It's a sweet sound, something like the solo on 'I Feel Free'. It's more like the human voice than a guitar. You wouldn't think that it was a guitar for the first few passages. It calls for the correct use of distortion."[21]

Not for Clapton the rasping distortion of the new fuzz pedals, however. What he did was to turn the tone control of the Les Paul's neck pickup all the way down and the volume all the way up through his powerful Marshall 100-watt amp. Instant woman tone. At some point, Clapton removed both pickup covers from the Summers Burst, revealing double-black bobbins, and also took off the plastic: truss-rod cover, pickguard, pickup-selector switch tip, pickup-selector surround.

Meanwhile, over in the USA, Michael Bloomfield had come to the attention of guitarists on the first two Paul Butterfield Blues Band albums: the first eponymous record appeared in summer 1965 and *East-West* in August 66. Later, Bob Weir, guitarist in The Grateful Dead, summed up the impact. "I first became a fan of Michael Bloomfield when that first Butterfield record came out. We were all just awestruck. ... He was also sort of a teacher," said Weir, "because we'd all go and watch him and learn how he was doing some of the things that he was doing, making some of those wonderful sounds."[22]

After *East-West* burst out in summer 66 – with listeners dazed by the extended title-track where Bloomfield and Elvin Bishop solo in a proto raga-rock saga – the Butterfield band came to Britain, in October. Bloomfield had made that first album in 65 with a Telecaster, but later that year had shifted to a Les Paul Goldtop with P-90 pickups, inspired by his beloved Chicago blues guitarists who also played Goldtops.

I asked David Dann, whose excellent website[23] charts the guitarist's career, to nominate a couple of tracks to represent Bloomfield's Goldtop recordings. He zones in on *East-West*, the record that revealed the first Butterfield Band at a creative peak. "The title track and 'Work Song' set the benchmark for all the blues-rock guitarists who would follow," says Dann, who notes Bloomfield's use of modes and unorthodox scales and the Goldtop's clean signal and clearly-articulated notes.

On 'East-West, Live Version #1' from *East-West Live*, despite the quality of the recording at the Whisky A Go Go in early 66, Dann is in awe of Bloomfield's soloing on the guitarist's cranked-up but barely distorted Goldtop. "His tone is bell-like at times, raw and aggressive at others. The Gibson's ability to hold a note at high volume without feeding back is clearly demonstrated in some passages, and the overall effect enhances the tamboura-like drone of the piece. This is an extraordinary performance by a gifted young musician using an instrument perfectly configured to meet the demands of loud, intricate, virtuosic electric music."

Bloomfield brought his Goldtop along for the late-66 UK tour. "The Paul Butterfield Band from Chicago visited here last week with a good reputation but without ever having had a hit record in this country," reported the British music paper *Record Mirror*. "People like Jeff Beck had returned from

American visits extolling the virtues of the band who had only been heard in Britain via a couple of singles and LPs.

"Paul's lead guitarist, Mike Bloomfield, said his big ambition was to meet Eric Clapton and to get the same equipment as Eric Clapton. Two days later, the Butterfield outfit and the Cream played together at a London 'in' club. Then the Americans joined the Georgie Fame–Chris Farlowe tour, where they are reported to be doing very well."[24]

Bloomfield's big ambition came true not only at that 'in' club but also a few days later in Leeds, where Cream and the Butterfield band played separate gigs on October 22: Cream at the University Hop; Butterfield at the Odeon, on the third date of the Fame–Farlowe tour. After the Butterfield band played their second house, they legged it across to the University, in time for Bloomfield and Clapton to meet and play a little in the interval – Bloomfield with his Goldtop and Clapton with his Burst – and in time to have a look at Cream's second set. "I really appreciated seeing that," said Bloomfield afterward.[25]

After meeting and playing with Clapton, it seems Bloomfield really did have it in mind that he needed "the same equipment". Exactly the same equipment. A Les Paul with those pickups and that top. Albert Lee was playing with Chris Farlowe on the tour and had time to get to know Bloomfield. "Mike was a real nice guy," remembers Lee. "He was playing a Goldtop, but he told me he was looking for a sunburst Standard and asked me if I knew anyone who had one. I thought ah yes, my friend Kostas has one. I knew he'd bought one, but I couldn't find him, couldn't get hold of him. Obviously Mike eventually found one."[26]

Bloomfield eventually got a Burst back in the States. Dan Erlewine is now a well-known guitar repairer, but in 1966 he was a young guitarist in a Detroit blues band called The Prime Movers (which included one James Newell Osterberg Jr., later Iggy Pop). Erlewine got to know Bloomfield well when the Butterfield band played locally. He noticed that Bloomfield played a Goldtop and remembered renting a similar guitar from the shop he worked in, the Herb David Guitar Studio in Ann Arbor, Michigan.

Erlewine rushed over to the shop with his Fender Jazzmaster, ready to trade. "I said, where's that electric guitar you had? It was mainly acoustics there. Herb said oh, George Mallory bought it. I thought, oh shit!" Erlewine dashed straight to his friend Mallory's and secured the beautiful sunburst Les Paul. "Being a soul man, you can imagine why George would be more taken with the Jazzmaster. So we switched, and I had his sunburst."

Then Erlewine began to wonder about the differences between the various Les Paul models, and mostly the pickups: P-90s on Bloomfield's Goldtop; humbuckers on Erlewine's newly-acquired Burst. "His Goldtop sounded killer. I'm sure he used that on 'East-West'. We watched them practice that song many times before they recorded it – and you know how long that would take. But I was always fascinated by Bloomfield's playing on that, and the sound of the P-90s just made it killer. That was another reason I wanted a Goldtop. You can't have that sound in a sunburst. You can't do that."

Erlewine and Bloomfield's guitars were destined for a trade. Bloomfield had seen what Clapton's Burst could do, and he wanted one of those. Erlewine had seen what Bloomfield's Goldtop could do and wanted one of those. All of this was, of course, a long time ago, and no one can be quite sure now of the exact date of the switchover. Bloomfield died young in 1981, so he's not saying, and he does not seem to have specified the event in any surviving interviews.

Erlewine's best guess is spring of 1967 going into the summer, when Bloomfield was leaving Butterfield and setting up his new band, The Electric Flag. "I kept in touch with Bloomfield," says Erlewine. "He moved out west, called me, said do you want to sell your sunburst? I said, do you want it?

And he said yeah. He said he'd give me the Goldtop and a hundred bucks. OK! And I did it. He was a hero to me. And he always treated me nice."[27]

Bloomfield expert David Dann makes an educated guess of late May 1967 for the switch. As part of his research, Dann put together a photo timeline so that he could work out what Bloomfield played when. "I believe the last shots of the Goldtop come from the Butterfield performance at Town Hall, New York City, on November 26 1966. By that time it was in pretty sorry shape, with a missing lead-pickup tone knob and a taped-on jack plate.

"Those pictures are a full seven months before the sunburst made its appearance, at the Monterey Pop Festival in June 1967," continues Dann, "so that's the window of time for the trade with Erlewine. Michael probably played a Gibson Byrdland, a thinline hollowbody electric model, to record *The Trip* movie soundtrack with the Flag around April 67. The Goldtop may have been essentially unplayable at the time he gave it to Erlewine, which would explain why it wasn't seen for those months leading up to Monterey and why he was using the Byrdland. Michael was known to use whatever guitar was at hand in the studio when he was recording."[28]

Late in August 1967, The Electric Flag were supporting Cream for a six-night residency at the Fillmore Auditorium in San Francisco, and Bloomfield invited Erlewine and his band, The Prime Movers, to California to hang out for a month or so. Erlewine: "Bloomfield comes down one day and says, 'You guys are playing at the Fillmore tonight.' We go, 'What? We are not.' He says, 'Yes, you've got to, we can't go on.' Barry Goldberg, their keyboard player, was ill." A startled Prime Movers found themselves opening for Clapton's Cream.

On other nights during the Fillmore residency, Erlewine was rewarded with a close-as-you-can-get view of Bloomfield playing the Burst. "Out he comes with The Electric Flag," recalls Erlewine, "and he's playing my sunburst. And my heart broke! Because now I wanted that guitar again, because of what he played and the difference it made. I hadn't heard him play in half a year or more, and I was stunned by the way he got around. I was proud of him. Clapton played his SG with all the painting on it, and that knocked me out too. There was this big American band and this big British band, and Mike Bloomfield was holding his own or better with Eric Clapton."[29]

How did Bloomfield's Burst sound at its best? David Dann makes some more choices of key tracks. First up is 'Really' from the 1968 album *Super Session*. "This tune perhaps captures the range and tone of Michael's Burst better than any other studio recording. Done at the behest of organist and producer Al Kooper in May 1968, *Super Session* became Bloomfield's only million-seller. Michael plays straight B.B. King-inflected blues, spinning out chorus after chorus of flawlessly phrased lines while demonstrating the vocal capabilities of the guitar with string-stretches and tremolos.

"After Kooper's solo," Dann continues, "Michael returns to play a remarably languid chorus, quietly exhibiting not only his ability to greatly vary the dynamic within a single piece but also proving that the Les Paul can maintain its punch regardless of the intensity of a player's attack. This is the recording that established the Les Paul–Fender Twin Reverb combo as de rigueur for all aspiring young guitar slingers."

Dann's second choice is 'Long Hard Journey' (also known as 'One More Mile') from *Barry Goldberg And Friends*, probably recorded at a 1969 Shrine Auditorium show put together by organist Goldberg. "Despite its ad hoc creation – Bloomfield can be heard shouting out the key at the start – his Burst rides the waves of his improvisations without faltering, the tone always pure and the notes invariably clear.

"At one point during Goldberg's solo, Bloomfield drops in a four-note phrase high on the neck that literally screams," says Dann. "It's a sound that can only be made with a Les Paul, and it was a sound that Bloomfield was particularly adept at creating." The piece lasts six minutes, but Dann reckons it qualifies as a blues masterpiece in miniature.[30]

Quite what happened to Bloomfield's Burst is another of those where-are-they-now stories that seem to crowd guitar history. Bloomfield's brother, Allen, is aware of the interest but is almost as baffled as the rest of us. "Lots of rumours have been flying around regarding the whereabouts today of the sunburst Les Paul, but most are just vacant conversation," says Bloomfield. "After his death, we went to Michael's house and someone had already stolen many of his guitars. I had no inventory of what he actually owned, so there was no way of determining what was taken. That Les Paul was allegedly shipped to a gig in Canada but Michael never showed and the promoter kept the guitar as compensation. Fact or fiction? Who knows."[31]

Over in England, Eric Clapton was not having much luck hanging on to his Les Pauls. The ex-Andy Summers Burst went the same way as Clapton's first, stolen in the first months of 1967, probably March. It was around this same time that Clapton acquired a used Gibson SG Standard – ironically, the model that had replaced the sunburst Les Paul. It had the same humbucker pickups, the same control layout, but a very new and different double-cutaway sculpted body.

Clapton had his SG painted in psychedelic style by The Fool, a Dutch art group. A generous interpreter might describe part of the design as an explosive multi-coloured sunburst. That's in addition to the winged fairy figure and the stars and the clouds. Clapton liked this one – and managed to keep hold of it, too. He used the decorated machine as his main stage guitar until 1968 and recorded with it extensively as well, not least on much of *Disraeli Gears*.

Cream did go on to great success, as I hardly need remind you. Big American tours and little time to develop their repertoire meant the band was forced to improvise at length, changing the nature of their musical direction, at least on stage. Clapton did play a few other sunburst Les Pauls in his career, although in more recent years he has been most associated with the Fender Stratocaster.

Clapton's generosity meant that a good friend ended up with a humbucker'd Les Paul in summer 1968. Beatles roadie Mal Evans alerted fans to a guitar newly acquired by George Harrison during the group's recordings for *The White Album*. Evans reported in his monthly column in a Beatle fan magazine that Harrison now had Lucy, "the fantastic solid red Gibson guitar that was given to George at the beginning of August by Eric Clapton".[32]

The guitar was originally a 57 Goldtop and had been owned by Rick Derringer, guitarist in The McCoys, and before that by John Sebastian of The Lovin' Spoonful. Derringer, who would go on to success with Edgar Winter and Steely Dan, decided the guitar was so beat up it could do with a fresh new finish and, living not far from the Gibson factory, delivered it there, probably in 1966, with instructions to paint it in a shiny SG cherry finish. He got it back – and decided its quality had changed too much. He soon traded it for another guitar at the Dan Armstrong store in New York City. Which is where Clapton acquired it – and Clapton in turn gave it to his Beatle chum.

Harrison loved the humbuckers and the whole guitar, using Lucy for more *White Album* tracks and on into 1969, including his solos on the exciting three-way six-string exchange with Lennon and McCartney at the close of 'The End', the last proper track on the group's last album, *Abbey Road*. But the most famous piece recorded with Lucy was when Harrison let Clapton play it once more for the solo on 'While My Guitar Gently Weeps', cut in September 1968. Clapton was the only non-Beatle ever allowed to play a guitar solo on a Beatles record. He did very well.

Our investigation here has necessarily reduced a lively and exciting time for guitar playing to a sequence of events, a trail from this player to that one, this store to another, of so much cash and a good deal of imagination. Guitarists came upon the tools they needed. Eric Clapton found a couple of sunburst Les Paul guitars and made some great music with them. I wonder what he would have thought then if he'd known I'd be hunting for a million-dollar example 40-something years later? I doubt he would have believed it.

How did the guitar Clapton used affect what he was trying to say? Musicians need something approaching transparency in an instrument, and yet at the same time have tangible requirements: a great tone and responsive playability, to name two of the most important to an electric guitarist. Great tone is what great players seem to spend all their lives chasing.

How did Clapton feel about what he was doing? "I'm not interested in guitar, sound, technique, but in people and what you can do to them via music," he told a journalist in March 1966. "My guitar is a medium through which I can make contact to myself. It's very, very lonely. This is blues. Expression. I am contacting myself through the guitar and telling myself I have a power."[33]

That power translated through to a key trio of records he made in 1966 and 67 – the Mayall *Blues Breakers* (or *Beano*) album, the 'I Feel Free' 45, and *Fresh Cream* – and defined the tone and the expression that a great player could achieve. This great player happened to stumble on a great instrument to make his music: the original sunburst Les Paul. And for many players and guitar fans, those recordings have yet to be beaten. So it is that the model of guitar that Clapton used to make that music and those records has taken on a mythical quality.

4. PEARLY

An interview with Les Paul devotee Billy Gibbons of ZZ Top

One of the budding musicians who listened in awe to what Eric Clapton was getting up to with John Mayall and then Cream was Billy Gibbons. He also saw Keith Richards on TV with the Stones and, more importantly, a sunburst Les Paul.

At the time, Gibbons was 15, and soon began stumbling along in early bands, even if he was yet to find his feet. Which he did later – and very effectively too – in the mighty ZZ Top. With the aid of a beautiful Les Paul Burst. With all that in mind, it seemed churlish not to go and talk to the man about his most vibrant history.

We meet at a characterless motel in Texas in spring 2008. Is that a knowing look from the receptionist as I ask for the (false) name with which Gibbons has checked in? This is no doubt an essential subterfuge for someone who's been in ZZ Top since its formation in 1970. Who recorded the first of their many million-selling albums, *Tres Hombres*, just a few years later. Who began touring the world from 1976, and who fused crunching Les Pauls, slabs of pop, some sharp-dressed beards, video stardom, and a mess of synth grooves to make the fabulous *Eliminator* in 83. The band are still going strong as I write this.

Back in Texas, however, I knock at Room 203. The man with the beard answers. He is not long awake. He excuses himself for a moment to obtain a diet Coke from the machine in the hall. He returns. We sit and talk about old times in Texas. It seems to be a favourite subject.

"I stand among the many who seemed to think that the appearance of Clapton on the reverse side of the Mayall *Blues Breakers* album, that first disc, was indicative, because the sound was so fierce and so attractive," suggests Mr Gibbons. He's awake now.

"The appeal drew everyone to attempt to suss out where this sound was coming from. The photograph was a clue and has been reproduced many times. Many references drew the obvious conclusion. Ah, look in the background: there's a Marshall, but it's not very big. Ah, look at that: they don't make those any more – but it's *one of those old Les Pauls*."

These were the thoughts of a growing youth. Way back in the day, when the sunshine was just that bit warmer and the guitars oh so mysterious and unattainable, 12-year-old Billy had spied a couple of brothers who lived at the end of his block in Houston. They were 15 and 16. They had a band that would set up in the front of the house and play and practice on the weekend. Three guitars and drums. No bass. "And they had the good stuff!" proclaims Gibbons, taking a swig of Coke to wash down the memory.

They had the red SG/Les Paul with the sideways vibrola. They had the sunburst Jazzmaster with the anodised guard. They had the triple-pickup Black Beauty Les Paul with the gold-plated hardware. "I was just amazed." This is understandable. "Not only were they cool, they had a band, number one, but they had hot rod cars. Man! These cats were on it.

"My parents were a bit skittish about the whole thing, but they couldn't stop me. So I kind of had the reference there to the old and the new Les

Paul – the SG and the Custom – but I would have been happy with any of them. Any of the three! Their band was called The Van-tels. They even had a record."

It was all too much. The red SG had been 'pinstriped', a decorative doo-dah normally reserved for hot-rod cars. "I said wow man, where did you get that? I'd badgered my folks for a year straight, from the time I turned 12 to the Christmas day. I have a birthday that falls on December 16. I kept on: *I need an electric guitar. I need an electric guitar.* Sure enough, Christmas Day, just after I turned 13, there it was: a Gibson Melody Maker, single cutaway, single pickup. It was good enough," he laughs, putting the drained Coke bottle aside and settling down for some serious talking.

The next day, Gibbons found out that a noted car customiser had just come to Houston from California and that this was the gentleman who had painstakingly pinstriped brother two's guitar. "The day after Christmas, my dad drove me over to the custom shop, and the guy was there. I said I want some pinstripes on my guitar. He said oh yeah, OK – he's laughing – just lie it down here. I says where; he says right here, on the concrete floor. Sure enough, he did it really neat."

The guitar survives in pinstriped form to this day, although not with its first owner. "It's in California," Gibbons reports, "and the guy won't sell it. I know the guy. I'm working on him."

Somewhere along the way, Gibbons acquired a white Fender Jazzmaster. "So there was no turning back. We started a band, down at the same end of the street, across the way, The Saints. Three guitars and drums, no bass," he smiles. "Then it was The Coachmen, and later on Billy G & The Ten Blue Flames – we added three saxophones. We'd seen Little Richard, his band was from Houston, the Grady Gaines Orchestra, and he had guitar, bass, drums, three saxes, and Richard on piano."

By now it was the mid 60s – how time flies when you're a slave to the frets – and Gibbons was playing with some high-school chums. Then a band called The 13th Floor Elevators made the scene and, according to our Texan guide, coined the term psychedelic. "Their first record, in 66, was The *Psychedelic Sounds Of The 13th Floor Elevators*. I said oh my god, that's it. These guys were completely off the wall. We started a band called The Moving Sidewalks."

Now he was playing a Telecaster. In 68 he discovered Hendrix and, like many a budding guitarist, moved over to the Jimi-favoured Stratocaster. "Lo and behold, we had put out a couple of records that caught on, one called '99th Floor', and a crazy completely psyched-out version of 'I Want To Hold Your Hand'."

They toured with Hendrix. Correct: *they toured with Hendrix*. A certain guitar player was, as you might imagine, beside himself with excitement at these astonishing developments. "It blew my mind. It was like, wow! Every day I learned something new. Hendrix liked what we were doing. I'd tiptoe into his room. 'Yeah, come on in man.' He was listening. In those days a record player was the size of a Buick automobile, and what was funny was that every day we'd take a hotel room, and he'd find a couple of guys to drag up this record player. It was one of those big old console jobs; looked like a piece of furniture.

"Hendrix was playing the first Jeff Beck Group record, *Truth*. Rod Stewart on vocals, Nicky Hopkins on piano, Mickey Waller on drums, Ron Wood on bass, and Jeff playing guitar. And of course we were studying, man. We knew all about Jeff Beck. I said wow, dig those sounds. And Hendrix said, 'Yeah, he's playing a Les Paul, man.' Sure enough we started seeing pictures of the Jeff Beck Group and Jeff had a Les Paul sunburst."

It was soon after this that Gibbons discovered the John Mayall *Blues Breakers* album with Clapton. "I'd seen pictures of the Les Paul but they were so rare. I started asking around, and there was this buddy of mine, Reid

Farrell, a white guy that played in this black group called Archie Bell & The Drells. They had a big hit called 'Tighten Up'. We'd known each other since high school. His slang name, I guess hanging around all the black guys, was Red Pharoah, which was a cooler sounding name."

One day Reid – or rather Red – called. "He said, 'You've been looking for one of those Les Pauls, right?' And I eagerly says yes man, what you got? I said it doesn't have to be a Les Paul necessarily, that old style, but I suspect it's something to do with those two big pickups. I didn't even know what they were called. He said well, I've got a guitar that has those pickups on it and I'll sell it to you."

This turned out to be a 1958 Gibson Flying V. A guitar even rarer than a sunburst Les Paul. But everything is somewhere, and this one was with Red. For now. "He brought it over. I said what is that? But I said I don't care, it's got those pickups. So I bought it for 300 bucks. And sure enough, man, we stepped up to the land of humbucking. It was really wicked. Hadn't really given humbuckers much thought because I was on this Hendrix trail, but here we were in the land of fat."

Not content with opening for Hendrix, the Sidewalks lined up a support slot to The Jeff Beck Group. "That's when I first made pals with Jeff. He was still playing his sunburst, the only guitar he had. I was playing the Flying V. I was really flamed on about getting the Les Paul sunburst. Jeff said yeah man, you can't beat this combination. By this time Marshall had started to manufacture the double-cabinet stack, the 100-watt head with two 4 by 12 cabs. I was hearing Jeff every night, and Ron Wood was playing through the same rig, two each. And … it … was … wicked. That did it."

The Moving Sidewalks were putting out records on a small local label out of Houston, and one of their labelmates, The Magic Ring, had a Rickenbacker 12-string player name of John Wilson. He called Gibbons one day and said he'd heard our man was looking for one of those old Les Pauls.

Gibbons replied casually in the affirmative. Wilson said that a cattle man with a big ranch just outside the Houston city limits had one of those things.

"Keep in mind," says Gibbons, "that to get around town we had secured a 1936 Packard automobile. It was a beater. But it was running and it was big. We could pack gear in like you can't imagine. An artist buddy of mine would loan it us, and eventually he just gave it to me. We had a girlfriend, Renee Thomas, a friend of the band. She made fringed leather vests and our guitar straps. She had an opportunity to audition to win a part in a movie, but she had to go to California."

How was Renee to get from Texas to California? It seemed unlikely that Greyhound would take handmade leather items as payment. So the kindly band gave her the Packard. Off she went. She got the part. She sold the Packard. She sent Gibbons the cheque. "I think it was $350," he recalls.

Gibbons insists that the cheque arrived in the mail, accompanied by a very sweet letter, exactly at the moment that John Wilson pulled up and said hey, let's go see about that guitar. This they did. You can almost see them through the dust as they roar away toward the cattle and the city limits.

"And sure enough there it was," says Gibbons. He picks up the empty Coke bottle again, holds it up to the light, between finger and thumb, examining another shining achievement in modern American design. "The guy pulled out a sunburst Les Paul from under the bed. He said to me yeah, I tried learning on this damn thing, but I can't make heads or tails of it. He said you want it, then you can have it. I said how much you want? He says how much you got? I pulled the cheque out and says I just got this today, 350 bucks. He says I'll take it. So I took off with that guitar."

This is the famous Pearly Gates that Gibbons would go on to play with ZZ Top, the instrument that would make his name. It was, to say the least, a momentous day in the history of Billy F. Gibbons. "I'll tell you, man, that is some kind of guitar. This was 1968, right after summer, probably the last of August. The weather was hot, it was the summer of fun. And I played that guitar." He did, too.

Why 'Pearly Gates'? He replaces the Coke bottle on the table one more time. "We had named that car, the Packard, Pearly Gates, because it not only got Renee to California but it got her the part. And we thought that the car must have had divine connections. When she sold the car, I called her back. I said Renee, I got this guitar with the money. She goes well, we're gonna call that guitar Pearly Gates and you're gonna play divine music." He did, too.

Gibbons had happened upon a wonderful example of the 1959 sunburst Gibson Les Paul. It's the sort of thing that makes you consider your place in the universe. He laughs. "Yeah, I've wondered along the way why this particular example of the Burst is so robust. Really, the only explanation is that it just happened to be put together on the right day. The particular day that all of the disparate elements came together was just that magical moment, I suppose. It was all guess work back in those days.

"These instruments were not intended to be world-class works of art, these were utilitarian forms of ... well, you were meant to just go out and play them and then throw them away some day. But I was most fortunate in being able to acquire that one, and brother, my world turned upside down. It was just fierce, that and a Marshall."

Has he ever been close to losing this precious piece of Gibson magic? "Nearly. We were in Fort Worth, Texas, played the Panther Hall. We had come off stage and it was during the blow-off, the gear was being put out, and I rarely let that guitar out of my sight. I wouldn't let it out of my hand. I stopped at the bottom of the stairway and laid it down. The hallway was a bit narrow. I stepped just to one side, and turned my back for a split second. Fortunately, the door guard saw the guitar case in the wrong hand, and he put the roadblock up, said uh-uh. I turned around and there was the guy smiling. He said, 'You looking for this?' I said yeah, I sure am."

That did it for Gibbons: that brief flutter of the heart caused him to wonder what he would do if the guitar ever did go AWOL. "The character of that instrument really personalised the sound of the early days of ZZ Top," he says. "That and the Marshalls. What would I do if that thing ever went south? Thought I'd better look for a spare."

This was around 1971, 72, and his recollection is that nobody much cared about Bursts back then. He started his search for something of equal character. It wasn't easy. If you wanted a red SG, no problem, but the sunburst Lesters were hard to find, even then.

"I managed to rack up a few in the collection, but I didn't find a single example that … well, I take that back. After years of collecting these things, I'd get 'em, but I'd put 'em in the closet. We'd use them every now and again, just for a bit of a different foray into something."

The only other instrument that could meet on Pearly's ground belonged to a fellow in Victoria, Texas, "way down in the desert". He had a 58 Explorer. After years of constantly checking in – "Hey, you want to sell that thing?" – Gibbons got lucky and the deal came through. That Explorer, he says, is on a very close par with Pearly. "And again, what makes them the way they are? Well, no one knows."

I wonder aloud what his $350 investment back in 1968 might be worth now. Much more than a thousand times that, surely? Back when Gibbons bought his, they were within the grasp of players. They aren't now, or very few are. What does that tell you? "That they've become badges of honour," he says. He stops to think. "A badge of shall we say legitimacy. To see one, even it's hanging under glass on a wall, you know that you're in the presence of someone who has a deep appreciation of the finest of the fine."

It doesn't strike you as wrong that a potentially fine musical instrument might be under glass? "These things were made to be played. They were not thought of as classic instruments. These were made to make loud noises, irritating sounds. That's my view."

And while we're on the subject, does it seem odd to Gibbons that people might play Les Pauls because he happened upon one? "Yeah. There's a Pearly Gates fan club, there's a number of guys that have approached me, and, you know, very honestly, they say I'm playing because of you and that crazy guitar. In the beginning I thought it odd, yes. However, with the growing demand and interest, which doesn't seem to be flagging in the least, it's actually downright flattering."

We chat on for a bit, but I know the man has to get to the studio, to do to his Les Paul what every vintage Les Paul should have done to it. I laugh out loud when he tells me that he was so in thrall to the legend of the Clapton/Mayall *Blues Breakers* album that he got himself a subscription to the *Beano*, the British comic that Clapton is seen reading on the front of the album. "I tracked it down and they sent it every week. People would look … what is that?" Was this the only man in late-60s Texas who received the *Beano* in the mail every week?

OK, off you go and play some guitar, Billy. Just before you get up, though, describe what it is that's special about the sound of Pearly. "That sound? God. I'd have to search for a string of words. It would be a whole chapter in itself."[1]

5. HEARTBREAKER

How Jimmy Page, Peter Green, and Jeff Beck established the Burst

Eric Clapton's startling performances with the John Mayall band, from the time he joined them in April 1965 to his departure in July 1966, captured the imagination of many a budding British blues guitarist lucky enough to catch them at a club date. Young white guitarists were discovering the blues, creating what we now call the British blues boom. Not everyone was impressed with spotty youths singing about their tough lives on the Thames Delta, and a group called The Liverpool Scene managed to satirise the genre and its leading bands with a song that sported the rousing chorus: "I've got the Fleetwood Mac, Chicken Shack, John Mayall, can't fail blues."

Some of the blues-boomers were inspired by the guitars used by their black American influences, but through Clapton's inspiration some of the better (and better-off) guitarists discovered that a Gibson Les Paul with humbucking pickups, wound up through a powerful tube amplifier, produced a magnificently rich and emotive sound that was well suited to this musical setting.

Peter Green was one such young Londoner who came under Clapton's spell, and a player so good that he would sweep away any notions of satire or poking fun. He first saw Clapton with Mayall's band in May 1965 and returned many times to drink from the well. Green was in no doubt what it meant for him as an up-and-coming musician: he should move from playing bass to the guitar, and he should get a Gibson Les Paul.

"I decided to go back on lead guitar after seeing Eric Clapton," he remembered later. "I'd seen him with the Bluesbreakers before he considered singing, and his whole concentration was on his guitar … and it was really impressive. … All music that you'd ever heard was washed away by this group of guys that were letting Eric Clapton take the floor."[1]

A few months later, probably toward the end of 1965, Green found a sunburst Les Paul just like Clapton's. "I stumbled across one when I was looking for something more powerful than my Harmony Meteor," he recalled later. "I went into Selmer's in Charing Cross Road and tried one. It was only £110. It sounded lovely and the colour was really good."[2] He had it in time to join his first proper band, Peter B's Looners, run by keyboardist Peter Bardens. Green was playing in Bardens's band by December 1965, Les Paul in hand.

Another version of the story has Tony Tyler selling Green his Les Paul. Tyler was a semi-pro keyboard player and occasional guitarist, and later became a journalist on *New Musical Express*. He worked at several music stores in London, presumably including Selmer. It's not clear if Tyler might simply have sold it in his capacity as a shop assistant or acquired the guitar himself before selling it on to Green.

Whatever the circumstances of the purchase, Green bought the Les Paul. The guitar would serve him well during his golden period, from the time he permanently joined Mayall's band in July 1966, replacing Clapton, to his tenure at the helm of Fleetwood Mac, from 1967 to 70.

In my view, Green was the best of the British blues-boom players. I'm not alone in this view. But for me, when I hear him today on record, he speaks with a consistently clear, direct voice that is emotionally charged and equally able to communicate delicate grace or moving power, as appropriate. It is a joy to behold.

What I also like about Green is that he is not merely a blues player. When someone plays blues guitar badly, it's full of clichés, boring, and very, very repetitive. Over the years, too many second, third, even tenth-rate blues bands have considered it enough to launch headlong into a blues in E and hope for the best – despite being in possession of precisely zero ability for improvisation and a similar amount of imagination. Plodding blues hell is the result.

Green, on the other hand, was a wizard. He memorably ventured into pastures new and was rarely dull or uninspired in his home territory of the blues, as on the impressive 'Black Magic Woman'. But when he conjured up a 'Man Of The World', I was even more in awe of his assured abilities. Blues-inspired, certainly, but to me this was moving in a much more mature and individual direction.

Mark Knopfler heard something inspiring and fresh when Green pitched an orchestral backdrop against his Les Paul in 1968. "I've always loved the sound of Gibson guitars with strings,"[3] says Knopfler. "Remember 'Need Your Love So Bad', that sort of stuff? It always stuck with me so much, that combination of sounds: a Les Paul and orchestral strings."[3] That particular Fleetwood Mac cut stayed in Knopfler's mind at least until the mid 80s when he recorded 'Brothers In Arms' with Dire Straits, deploying the gorgeous combination of Les Paul and strings.

Peter Green is still around today but, as I'm sure you know, he is not in great mental health. 'Drug casualty' is a term bandied about with little precision but it really does seem to fit Green. The story is often told how he took acid, fried his brains, and never quite re-entered the real world. He left Fleetwood Mac, in personal disarray and amid a good deal of confusion, in 1970. A few years later, he passed his Les Paul on to Gary Moore.

It's terribly sad that one of the greatest guitarists of our day seemed to halt his own creativity in this way. And if his suffering really was down to some bad acid trips, then at least it's one of the best anti-drug ads I can think of.

For now, let's be content to listen again to some of his great recorded works. And great they certainly are. Author Christopher Hjort dug deep into the Green legend for his *Strange Brew* book about the British blues boom. I asked Hjort to single out some highspots, and he did his best at narrowing it down.

"Green's legacy of studio recordings in the years from 1965 to 70 amounts to roughly 150 tracks," Hjort calculates, "with John Mayall, Fleetwood Mac, his solo album *End Of The Game*, sessions for Eddie Boyd, Otis Spann, Memphis Slim, and others, and the two dozen Fleetwood Mac live tracks now available officially on CD. With rare exceptions, he used that same Les Paul for all of this studio and live work."

Green's great strength lay in his restraint, suggests Hjort. The guitarist recognised and exploited the rarely-used power of holding back, leaving the listener on the edge of his seat. "He was an out-and-out blues player, yet he could also conjure up the unexpected. On 'The Super-Natural', from the February 1967 Mayall album *A Hard Road*, he defined a new school of guitar playing with beautiful legato phrasing on his Les Paul – a lesson Carlos Santana surely took to heart," says Hjort.

There are countless examples of pure Peter Green blues. No doubt you have your favourites. Hjort picks a couple, almost at random, starting with a satisfyingly smooth shuffle, 'Watch Out', from 1969's *Blues Jam At Chess*. "And then there's the hair-raising 'If You Be My Baby', from Fleetwood Mac's second album, 1968's *Mr. Wonderful*, which sounds as if he can barely keep his Les Paul on a leash. At times he simply stops singing and just lets the guitar rip.

"His 1970 solo album *The End Of The Game* is demanding but rewarding for listeners who care to dig in for a bit of Green's most exploratory jamming. Try the funky opening cut, 'Bottoms Up', where he wrings extraordinary sounds from a wah-wah pedal and his Les Paul."[4]

Back again to the mid 60s, and to the time when Jeff Beck had just replaced Eric Clapton in The Yardbirds. Clapton had been playing a Fender Telecaster, owned by the group's management, and Beck inherited the guitar briefly when he stepped into Clapton's shoes in February 1965. He dumped that axe – "a terrible guitar" – and then sort of permanently borrowed a very good Tele from a friend. In April, he added an Esquire (effectively a single-pickup Telecaster) to complete his brace of Fenders.

Beck is a completely different guitarist from the blues purists. His roots lie more in rockabilly and rock'n'roll and he has an experimental frame of mind. He would take the electric guitar way beyond any notion of blues rules. His great canon of Yardbirds recordings – including 'Heart Full Of Soul' and 'Shapes Of Things' – seem almost to merge into one mind-bending demonstration of the most out-there and inventive use of electric guitar in the mid 60s. Beck bought his first Les Paul at the end of February 1966, a few weeks after returning from a gruelling six-weeks-plus US tour with The Yardbirds.

I first met Beck back in 1993 when he graciously allowed us to photograph some of his instruments for my first Les Paul book. We went to his astonishing Elizabethan mansion in Sussex, and while the photographer did his thing, we spent a happy hour or so nattering over some tea in the kitchen. I've interviewed Beck on a couple of other occasions, too, and what follows draws on a mix of those three conversations.

Beck says he saw Clapton, early on, playing a Les Paul with the Mayall band. He made a mental note. Clapton's guitar "sounded great" remembers Beck. "I already knew Les Pauls sounded good because Jimmy Page had a Custom. They had this deep sound, and I really needed that power in a three-piece, to help fill out the sound.

"So I went sorting around. There was a guy at Selmer's shop in Charing Cross Road, I think it might have been Mickey Keen, he worked there but he said he'd got a good one at home. It was him or one of the others who worked there – that was the shop to go to. So this guy said yeah, meet me at so-and-so and I'll bring along the guitar." Beck says this first Les Paul, to which someone had added a black pickguard, was a 1959 model and cost him about £175.

"I've always been fascinated by the classy look of a Les Paul," says Beck, "the way they were finished – they always looked more classy than a Fender Strat. A Fender Strat always looked very rude, you know? Vulgar, with those two horns. So I thought, well, that's rock'n'roll. When you look at the violin shape body on the Les Paul, it was like you were getting more for your money," he laughs.

"On the Les Paul, there was the beautiful way the pickguard was mounted, just the feel of it – you couldn't ignore it. You plugged in, and it was an instant disappointment ... unless you had actually listened to Les Paul himself and started to mimic him. Then you'd have fun with that.

"But it was far too expensive to just have fun with it. I wanted a guitar where my heart was, and that was the [Gene Vincent's] Blue Caps thing. But hearing Pete Green and Eric use it, it just changed my opinion about it. I still stuck with a Tele – I was on a Tele at the time – but when you turn up the Les Paul to ridiculous beyond-all-belief distortion and make use of it to feed back, well, that's when I was swayed away."

Beck immediately began gigging with his new acquisition – and even managed to record with it before Clapton got to Decca in May 66 for the *Beano* sessions. "The Les Paul stuff I did on 'Over Under Sideways Down', that was the last stages of my involvement with *The Yardbirds* ... that was all Les Paul." The band recorded that single and The Yardbirds album, commonly known as *Roger The Engineer*, between mid April and early June, and Beck's Les Paul is indeed all over the recordings.

Christopher Hjort again acts as our trusted guide through these sessions, this time based on the author's detailed research for *Jeff's Book*. Hjort says that the *Roger* album offers a brilliant mix of Beck's maverick musical approach. "Compared to Clapton's distorted high-volume punch, Beck drew many shades of sound out of his Les Paul. Beck of course came from a rockabilly background and had little if any respect for the purist approach. By that point, his style was in full bloom."

He points to tracks as diverse as the simple blues-derived 'The Nazz Are Blue', where Beck pumps along with power and aggression, and 'I Can't Make Your Way', which sounds almost as if the guitar had been recorded underwater. "The deftly executed riff in 'Over Under Sideways Down' sounds like a deranged fiddler," marvels Hjort, "given the right kick by a fuzz box between Les Paul and amplifier. And on both 'Lost Woman' and 'Rack My Mind' his guitar tone blends so perfectly with Keith Relf's harp and vocal that at times they're indistinguishable."

Hjort is amazed not only at how Beck handled his Les Paul but how he really could sound like Les Paul, the actual living and breathing guitar player. "The swinging 'Jeff's Boogie' is quite mind-boggling. In a little over two minutes, it's a lesson in how many sounds can be extracted from one Les Paul, one amplifier, two hands, and the twisted imagination of a guitar master."[5]

That first Les Paul of Beck's was soon in the wars, smashed almost fatally during The Yardbirds' fourth US tour, in late 1966. "I've sad news to report this month," he wrote in a regular magazine column. "I've smashed my Gibson Les Paul, and what is more, it wasn't an accident. I picked it up, swung it by the neck above my head, and smashed it on the floor."[6] A few months later he reported: "Yes, the Gibson Les Paul is repaired now. It's as good as new. Well, almost."[7]

Beck, out of The Yardbirds by the end of 66, put together The Jeff Beck Group the following year and continued to play his almost-good-as-new Les Paul, now with twin white-bobbin pickups revealed after the pickup covers were removed during the repairs. Beck removed the finish from his guitar early in 68. "I saw a pale guitar in a 50s book," he recalls, "so I stripped off the sunburst to make it look like that. I went to a carpentry shop in Nine Elms [south London] and bought some paint stripper. I'd been a painter in the car business, so I knew what I was doing. I didn't want it to look shiny."

He used his Les Paul to great effect for the superb *Truth* album, recorded in April and May 1968 with Rod Stewart (vocals), Ron Wood (bass), and Mickey Waller (drums), plus Nicky Hopkins and John Paul Jones (keyboards). He'd cut one track, the remarkable 'Beck's Bolero', back in May 1966 with Jones on bass, Hopkins on keys, Jimmy Page on 12-string, and Keith Moon on (yes) drums.

That guitar suffered more damage – "some idiot knocked it off a stool," says Beck, "the headstock snapped off and it cracked near the body" – and the instrument was the victim of some ill-conceived restoration, which Beck rightly describes as "revolting". He still owns that guitar today, but back in October 68 he needed another Les Paul.

He bought his second one, possibly a 1958 model, from Rick Nielsen, later of Cheap Trick and a noted guitar collector. "Mickie Most was coming over to the States," says Beck, "and he got this chap from somewhere, came out with 40 Les Pauls or something. It was just before a gig, and I played the guitar that night, right out of the box."

Hjort reports that this second Les Paul was a beautiful specimen, distinguished by an impressive figured top. "The pickup covers had again been taken off, this time revealing a white back pickup and a zebra (black-and-white) front pickup. Unfortunately, Beck's second Les Paul was never preserved properly on record. When it was time for The Jeff Beck Group and Rod Stewart to make a second album, *Beck-Ola*, in the spring of 1969, Beck was favouring a Fender again. Sadly, the fate of this particular Les Paul is not known, but I believe it was stolen in New York City in August 1969 and never recovered."[8]

Beck's third Les Paul came along in late 1972 when he formed the power trio Beck Bogert & Appice. At first using a Stratocaster, he called again on the "deep sound" of a Les Paul to fill out this new three-piece. This time, in Memphis, he bought a converted mid 50s Goldtop, modified by the Strings & Things store with two humbuckers to replace the original P-90 pickups and a heavy dark-brown refinish to the body. Beck himself calls it an 'oxblood' colour.

Despite a growing dependency on Strats, Beck used his oxblood Les Paul for some of *Blow By Blow*, the excellent jazz-rock album he recorded with producer George Martin toward the end of 1974. "I was divvying about between Strat and Les Paul. The Les Paul is more attuned for jazz-rock, and it was partly because of George Martin that I used it: his ears were having a bit of trouble handling the raucous screaming that I was doing," he laughs.

"George would flinch and start walking around and making tea and things. He likes good mellow sounds. So I thought well, there's no point in making the guy suffer. I may as well play melodically. And then maybe I'll come back one night and scrub over it with the Strat. Eventually, when I started to do 'Freeway Jam' and stuff like that and needed to go crazy, I decided the Strat was more my tool, you know?"

Beck took the oxblood Les Paul on the road when he toured the US and

Japan in 1975 to promote *Blow By Blow*, but since then his loyalty has switched almost entirely to Fender Stratocasters. "With the Les Paul, I'd put it down carelessly," says Beck. "They weigh a ton, and if you snap the head off one of those you're in big trouble. You can't bolt another neck on. So I got fed up of having to have repairs made, and I suppose I turned to a Strat in an emergency one night. And I just never went back."[9]

And so we leave Jeff Beck to his Fenders. Meanwhile, if Eric Clapton is god, then to many Les Paul fanciers Jimmy Page is some higher kind of deity. Buddah, perhaps. For many years of his illustrious career with Led Zeppelin, Page played a sunburst Les Paul. And that crazy double-neck, for a bit. And that duotone Danelectro. And he did have a few more Les Pauls. Yes, this is going to be a tricky one. And Les Paul fanciers do love a tricky one.

As we've already learned, Jimmy Page was an early adopter in the rediscovery of old Les Pauls in Britain. He owned and played a three-pickup Custom in the early 60s, before most people even knew that such a guitar existed. Page worked his way through The Yardbirds, arriving as a bass player to replace the outgoing Paul Samwell-Smith in June 1966 but soon switching to six-string – using a Fender Telecaster – to play in a dual-guitar frontline with Jeff Beck. He became the sole guitarist when Beck left in November.

Next, of course, he formed Led Zeppelin. You'll know the story about The Yardbirds disintegrating and Page viewing the project as a sort of New Yardbirds, and how he then settled on a line-up with vocalist Robert Plant, keys and bass man John Paul Jones, and drummer John Bonham. Zeppelin played their first gigs in September 1968 and later that same month started recording their first album. Page was still playing the Tele he'd used with The Yardbirds, but the following year, probably in April, he acquired his first Burst.

However, there were a few early near-misses. An intriguing photograph appears in an issue of Gibson's house magazine, The *Gibson Gazette*, that shows Page, still in The Yardbirds, clutching a sunburst Les Paul at what looks like a backstage gathering. The caption links the picture to a gig where The Yardbirds had "rocked the foundations of the Alexandria, Virginia Arena", which dates it to September 9 1966.

That was toward the end of an interesting couple of weeks for The Yardbirds, because Jeff Beck had temporarily departed the band, allegedly ill but apparently off to see his girlfriend in Los Angeles. Page looks disgruntled in the picture: perhaps because he's had to pose for yet another backstage snap; perhaps because he's fed up with Beck's antics. But clearly Page did get to play Beck's Burst while the other Yardbird guitar man was away.

The guitar is the sunburst Les Paul that Beck had been playing since he'd acquired it earlier in 66. The guitar is only partly visible in the *Gazette* picture but clearly shows the nut area in some disarray: it looks as if Beck had taped around the neck here, probably as a temporary fix for some damage. Other shots of Beck himself playing the guitar at the time also reveal this treatment.

Another photograph, from The Yardbirds' *Little Games* studio sessions, recorded around March to May 1967, shows Page with a Bigsby-loaded Burst. Some have speculated that this is another sighting of the Keith Richards Les Paul, on loan to another pal, just as it may have been to Eric Clapton the previous year. Stones sideman Ian Stewart played some piano at the sessions, so perhaps he brought the guitar along. And if it is that instrument, Richards must have been tiring of it, because he would sell it to Mick Taylor, the latest of John Mayall's talented guitarists, that September. If it was already considered for sale, perhaps Page was trying it out – and if so, he decided to wait. But the right Burst wasn't too far away.

Joe Walsh apparently took a sunburst Les Paul along to one of the Led

Zep's US dates in the first half of 1969, showed it to Page, and Page bought the guitar. It's said that he paid Walsh $500.[10] Walsh, who would join The Eagles in 1975, was in The James Gang at the time. Like many things associated with Page's guitars, the evidence for the exact date of the transaction is not clear.

Page was asked in 2004 about the circumstances. "Joe brought it for me when we played the Fillmore," he said. "He insisted I buy it, and he was right."[11] The earliest photograph I've seen of Page playing his sunburst Les Paul on stage in 1969 is from a gig at the Rose Palace in Pasadena, California, on May 2. So Page's "when we played the Fillmore" could apply to eight potential dates in Zeppelin's itinerary, from January to April. During their first US tour they played the Fillmore West (in San Francisco) for a four-date run, January 9 to 12, and the Fillmore East (New York City) on January 31 and February 1; on the second American tour, they appeared at the Fillmore West on April 24 and 27.

It's likely that Page would have wanted to play this great guitar as soon as he got it, so the most likely time for the sale is one of those last two Fillmore West dates: we can assume that he acquired it at the end of April, and then he's pictured playing it on stage a few days later. (The Rose Palace pictures also have Page playing the Tele, so it seems he was still getting used to the Les Paul. But the Tele all but disappeared after that – although, famously, Page would later pull it out in the studio for the 'Stairway To Heaven' solo.)

However, there is an intriguing bit of stage banter from Robert Plant during the Fillmore West gig on January 11, captured by a bootlegger, that temporarily throws a string-winder in the works. Evidently there were equipment problems during that show, particularly with Page's set-up, resulting in some delays between songs.

During one of these lulls, Plant says to the audience: "Has anybody got a Les Paul? Jeff who? Tell him to bring it here then!" Why would he mention a Les Paul if Page wasn't playing one? But maybe Plant was just teasing Page: if only he had a Les Paul like Jeff Beck's, then maybe he wouldn't be having these problems.

Or perhaps – just perhaps – the sonic problems were linked to Page wrestling with a newly-acquired guitar? No photos have come to light from this concert – and there are no pictures of Page with a Burst until that concert on May 2 – so for now we are left guessing.

Other evidence indicates that Page's road-weary Telecaster was coming to the end of its days. Zeppelin manager Peter Grant said later: "San Francisco was the first show that Jimmy played the Les Paul guitar on stage. He was playing a Fender before that. He'd had it for years, from being in The Yardbirds. There was something wrong with the pickup, and I remember every night he was there with the soldering iron, soldering the guitar."[12]

Whatever the circumstances and the time-frame, when Walsh showed Page the Les Paul, Page's first reaction was a loyal one, that he'd stick with his trusty Telecaster. "But as soon as I played [the Les Paul] I fell in love," Page recalled later. "Not that the Tele isn't user-friendly, but the Les Paul was so gorgeous and easy to play. It just seemed like a good touring guitar."[13] And what we know for certain is that Page was using his sunburst Les Paul on stage with his band by the first week of May 1969.

Obviously the guitar wasn't only suited to touring. Page would have wanted to become familiar and comfortable with the instrument because he knew that Zeppelin would be starting work on their second album at the end of May. There are pictures from the sessions that show him using it. "I first used it on *Led Zeppelin II*," he said later, "and I immediately started using it live, as well."[14]

Page's first Burst remained his favourite guitar throughout the Zeppelin period and eventually came to be referred to as Number 1 after he acquired others. In 1977, Page tried to describe what he liked about the guitar. The interviewer asked if his playing changed when he moved from Telecaster to Les Paul.

"Yes, I think so," said Page. "It's more of a fight with the Telecaster but there are rewards. The Gibson's got all that very stereotyped sound, maybe, I don't know, but it's got a really beautiful sustain. I do like sustain. It relates to bowed instruments. Sustain speaks for itself, that's the whole thing. It's the whole area that everyone's been pushing and experimenting in, once it became electric, if you think about it – it was mainly sustain."[15]

I was lucky enough to see Page's Number 1 Les Paul up close in 1993 when we photographed it, along with two other Page-owned instruments, for another book. I went to a house Page owned at the time in southern England, in Bordon, Hampshire. It was a lovely place, and even though Page himself was away, I began to get a sense of the owner.

As I wandered around while the photographer set up and Page's tech, Carter, scurried around to fetch guitars, I spotted a favourite pre-Raphaelite picture on a wall. What a nice coincidence, I thought, as I walked over to it: Page likes this one too and we both have the same print. When I got closer, however, I had a shock. This was the real painting. Page does not seem much interested in replicas; he goes for the real thing.

His Number 1 Les Paul was certainly the real thing, but it had seen some work over the years. I picked it up: no serial number, indicating repairs to the neck or headstock or both; bridge pickup cover off, showing double-black coils, but not an original pickup (apparently the original was replaced on an Australasian tour in 72 after it failed); a push-pull modification to the bridge tone knob, "for in or out of phase" according to Carter; a gorgeous honey-like colour to the top, and the wood without much figure; tuners changed for Grovers; and, to me at least, a rather unusual neck shape.

"Yes," smiled Carter, amused by my evident fascination with this historic instrument, "it's Number 1. The most beaten-up one." Hardly beaten up, I would have said. Well used, certainly, but in pretty good nick considering.

Someone who made a much more scientific assessment of the guitar than me was Edwin Wilson, the Historic Program Manager, Engineering, at Gibson's Custom Division. He found himself at another of Page's properties in England after Page had agreed that Gibson should make a limited run of exact copies of Number 1 in 2004.

The first thing Wilson noticed, like me, was that the guitar wasn't as dilapidated as he'd imagined it might be. Asked in the late 70s if much had been done to the guitar, when it was still being regularly gigged, Page said: "Yeah, it's been resprayed, but that's all gone now, it's all chipped off."[16] All those years later, Wilson was pleasantly surprised. "I would have expected it to be very, very beat. But it wasn't. It had a lot of checking on it and a lot of ageing, it had some wear, but it was still in relatively good shape. But the most interesting thing was the neck."

Ah, the neck. Walsh seems to be the culprit here, if that's the right word. Page was asked recently if he had the guitar's neck refinished. "No," he replied. "When I acquired it from Joe it had already been refinished. It's possible that one of the reasons he wanted to sell me the guitar was that it didn't feel the same to him when he got it back from the shop." And the neck was already sanded down when Page got it? "It came as it was with the shallow neck. The only thing I did was change the tuning machines to the sealed Grovers, which I was familiar with from my Les Paul Custom. With a three-piece band like Led Zeppelin, you couldn't have slipping machine heads."[17]

Without a serial number, it's not immediately obvious which of the three production years Page's Number 1 comes from: 1958, 59, or 60. But that hasn't stopped years of speculation about something that can never be decided with 100 per cent accuracy. And then Page asked Wilson the dreaded question: "What year do you think it is?"

"That put me on the spot," says Wilson, with what I can only assume is Southern understatement. He admits that there are people out there who look at vintage Bursts all the time and probably know more than he does on the subject. The received wisdom among Burst folk is that 58 necks are generally the chunkiest, with the same big fat style of the preceding Goldtop, that in 59 they become a little slimmer, and that later in 1960 they become positively thin. Though nothing like Page's "shallow" neck. And all of that is said while bearing in mind that with a neck shaped by hand in a busy factory, there can never be absolute rules.

Anyway, here was Wilson in close proximity to the great guitar, and with permission from the owner to do whatever necessary to assist in the production of the modern Gibson copies. And with a question to answer for the owner. "I was looking at the guitar from the standpoint of somebody who works with tooling for making these things, who has dealt with tooling and production on many different levels," says Wilson. He looked hard and long at the neck, from all angles, turning it this way and that, measuring and taking notes.

It looked to Wilson as if the person who had sanded down the neck – Walsh, his repairman, whoever – had not had enough wood there in the first place for the guitar to have been a typical big 58 neck. "It would have swollen up more around the heel," he says. "And if it were a 60, I don't think the heel would have been shaped as it was. If it were a late 60, where the neck was real thin, there wasn't enough wood there. So I said to Jimmy, to me it looks like a late 59 or maybe an early 60."

While he was examining the neck so closely, Wilson became increasingly impressed by its current state. "What's real interesting is that the neck is as stable as it is given how thin it is. In the middle section, it's sanded really strangely. It's right on the truss-rod, you know?" The truss-rod is the strengthening metal bar that runs inside the length of the neck. "I think you could probably take a pocket knife and shove through that thin section there and you'd hit the truss-rod, there's that much wood gone out of there. It's amazing to me that the neck is as good and as playable as it is. The neck felt comfortable on his guitar and the guitar felt comfortable: a good weight."

The frets were very low on the guitar. Page has said: "The frets were that way when I got the guitar. If any of them started to show signs of extreme wear, I'd replace them individually. I don't like to totally refret a guitar." Asked about the push-pull bridge-pickup tone knob, he replied: "I wanted to be able to reverse the phase of the pickups to get a close approximation of the sound Peter Green got."[18]

Green in turn had been in search of the sound of his hero: he was trying to get near to Eric Clapton's tone and, noticing that Clapton used mainly the bridge pickup, he simply and rather dramatically removed the neck pickup from his Les Paul. When he decided to put it back, probably early in 1967, he mistakenly positioned it 'backwards' – in other words with the polepiece screws nearest the bridge – and apparently connected it out-of-phase.

This is often offered as the explanation for the Green guitar's unique sound. Of course it also had a great deal to do with Peter Green himself, just as the sound of Jimmy Page's guitar – a Les Paul probably more speculated upon and picked over and wondered about in the ensuing years than any other – had a great deal to do with the musical ability in the head and heart and hands of Page himself.

Page has owned other Les Pauls. In 1993, Page's guitar tech Carter told me his boss had about 70 guitars in total. Page's original Les Paul Custom, the one he bought in the early 60s, went missing on tour in the early 70s. Or, as Page described it with tongue rather painfully in cheek, the guitar was "lost by TWA".[19] Page was clearly heartbroken by the loss of a guitar that meant so much to him: he even placed an ad in *Rolling Stone* magazine seeking its return, unfortunately without success. Eventually, he got a little compensation in 2008 when Gibson made another limited run of replicas, the Custom Shop Jimmy Page Les Paul Custom.

Page got another sunburst Les Paul in the 70s, often known as Number 2. This one is serial-numbered and therefore clearly identifiable as a 1959 model. He mainly kept it as a back-up to Number 1, although he seems to have used it at least for 'Kashmir' on stage around 1975, and it has turned up here and there on later projects. At some point, Number 2 had multiple pickup-switching controls added by a studio maintenance engineer, Steve Hoyland. Hoyland told me he probably made the modifications in the late 70s. "The guitar never sounded very good originally," reckoned Hoyland.[20]

Page also acquired a cherry red 70s Les Paul Standard, another backup guitar, and in the early 90s he had Roger Giffin build him a replica of Number 1. Giffin had a good reputation in Britain as a guitar maker, and in 1988 he moved to California to set up a satellite workshop for Gibson on the West Coast, next door to the company's artist relations office – at first with fellow maker Rick Turner, later for a while with Grover Jackson.

"Players got to know about the place and what they could do here," Giffin told me at the time. "They could come in and order something a little different. That was my prime idea, to be able to make one-offs."

Giffin made the copy of Page's Number 1 in 1992. It has "J PAGE" on the rear of the headstock where the serial number would normally be. "It's a nice guitar, but plain as hell, hardly any figure in it," Giffin said of the original. "Odd neck shape: it's had a re-shape at some time in its life, which made it fairly asymmetric, like a section through an egg – deeper on the bass side than the treble. Very comfortable, actually, and he obviously got used to it and decided he wanted a copy of that. He loved it, and I made the copy exactly the same as the original."

So it was a road version? "Basically yes," said Giffin in 93. "I don't think he's going to take the old one out on the road any more. I refinished the neck for him because all the lacquer had come off and it was sticking in his fingers every time he played it, just flakes of lacquer."[21]

In interviews, Page would usually be asked at some point about his influences – evidently a stock question for some writers – and would talk of rockabilly and blues, but often the subject would turn to Eric Clapton. "Eric was the first one to evolve the sound with the [Les Paul] and Marshall amps," he declared in 1977. "He should have total credit for that."[22]

Page took that evolution further, putting his ex-Joe Walsh Les Paul to remarkable use during Led Zeppelin's time at the very top of the rock tree in the 70s, on stage and in the studio. He used other instruments from time to time – most distinctively a black-and-white Danelectro Standard 3021, which he'd had since his session days, and a Gibson EDS-1275 12-string/six-string double-neck, acquired in the early 70s. But it's the Burst with which he'll always be most associated.

"The second album was done on the Les Paul," said Page, "and I stuck with that all the way through. Then again, I'd bring in other guitars because of their sonic quality. In a way it would have been a good idea if I'd have got into Strats, but the reality was that I loved the sound of the Les Paul. I just found that I could get so much tonal quality out of it."[23]

What sort of quality, exactly? I asked Dave Gregory, former XTC guitarist, to guide us through some Page-and-Burst highpoints. He found it hard to keep the *Led Zeppelin II* vinyl off his turntable and argues that the record set a fresh benchmark for rock, due in no small part to the sound of Page's new guitar-shaped acquisition. "It's heavily influenced by Jeff Beck's tone on the *Truth* album of a year earlier," says Gregory. "Page has this barking, wailing tone-monster of an instrument that was just impossible to ignore. It was like a dark, irresistible power."

Gregory selects 'What Is And What Should Never Be' for special analysis because it shows off a number of the Burst's different qualities in Page's hands. "He starts with thumbed chords – neck pickup – then introduces the choruses with notes and chords played on the harder-sounding bridge pickup, slipping gently back into the verse section.

"Next, with pickup switch centred and both pickups active, Page plays a graceful slide solo before switching back to the bridge pickup for that more aggressive chorus section. It all ends with an arresting chordal thing – paired 16th-notes and muted chops – coughed up from the bridge pickup and panned back-and-forth left to right in the stereo picture behind Plant."

The second *Led Zep II* track on Gregory's hit list is 'Moby Dick'. Yes, the drum solo. But listen to that intro and outro either side. "Those 50s Bursts do not twang," explains Gregory by way of introduction, "and they're not particularly suited for jazz playing. However, the thick but light mahogany bodies and necks give a specific mid-rangey tone – aimed squarely at the solar plexus. Perhaps that's why the sound they produce is so appealing to males of a certain age! Add in humbucking pickups and a Tune-o-matic bridge, and there's a brightness and definition to the tone that's lacking in the earlier P-90 Goldtops."

He suggests that the opening guitar riff of 'Moby Dick' provides a perfect demonstration of the sound of the instrument's bridge pickup in all its naked glory (even if double-tracked). "Page has tuned his low E-string down a whole step, to D, and you can hear it knocking against the top of the pickup as he cranks out the big riff, throwing in bluesy comments on the upper strings. Maybe he tamed the brightness of the pickup slightly by rolling the guitar's tone control back to 6 or 7. But it's a lovely tone here, helped by Page's fine technique, and it proved beyond any doubt that blues and heavy rock were exactly what these guitars did best."

Page probably left his Les Paul at home during Led Zeppelin's Welsh holiday in 1970, Gregory suggests, because the guitar didn't make its presence felt again in a big way until the release of the band's fourth album, the following year.

Opening track 'Black Dog' has a snarling double-tracked riff that provides a stomping counterpoint to Plant's vocal angst. 'Rock And Roll', which follows, finds Page applying the 'Dog' set-up to a motoring 24-bar groove powered by a full-tilt drum track from Bonham – and it appears yet again, later, in the unusual 'Four Sticks', says Gregory. "Not much of a song – but what a great noise!"[24]

The long-awaited fifth album, *Houses Of The Holy*, closes with 'The Ocean' and another classic Page riff, locked tightly into Bonham's merciless drum track. The guitar, reports Gregory, sounds bright and snappy – but it retains the unmistakable Gibson honk.

Not only did Page and Burst create a revered and unforgettable on-stage image, but in the studio the Zep guitarist reminded a generation of guitarists and guitar fans just what a Les Paul sunburst model could do in talented, imaginative hands. For many, this would remain unsurpassed as the definitive combination of player and instrument, a 70s pairing to rival Clapton and Burst in the 60s Mayall period.

Of course, other players were drawn to the sunburst Les Paul in the wake of its headline use by Clapton, Page, Green, Beck, and the rest. Some, however, did not get on with the guitar.

Tony Hicks of The Hollies found one in a pawn shop while shooting a television show in the States, probably late in 1966, and the TV company coughed up the necessary $80. "But I've never loved those guitars," he says. "I'm just not happy with humbucking pickups." His main guitar remained a Gibson ES-345, with its filter switch able to provide him with something closer to a single-coil sound when he needed it. "I just prefer more of a single-coil sound for rhythm, and then hit the humbucker for a solo on overdrive."[25]

Others felt like they'd come home when they landed on a Les Paul. Paul

Kossoff came to prominence in Free in the late 60s. He was a passionate Burst player, often able to say in a handful of notes what many would waste dozens attempting. "You don't play a billion notes, but you play a few goodies, hopefully, like Freddie or B.B. do," said Kossoff. "I like to move people; I don't like to show off. I like to make sounds as I remember sounds that move me."[26] Now, regrettably, all we have is the records; Kossoff died at the age of just 25 in March 1976.

We only have the records that Duane Allman made to remind us how great a player he was, too. He used a couple of Bursts. First up was a regular sunburst one that he acquired in summer 1970 by trading his humbucker'd Goldtop plus $100 or so. Legend has it that before he parted with the Goldtop, he made sure to swap over the humbuckers he loved so much from that guitar into the 'new' Burst – which he used on some of the *Layla* album with Eric Clapton, as well as with The Allman Brothers Band.

The following year, Allman got a Burst with a darker 'tobacco' sunburst, nicknamed Hot 'Lanta. He used it on classic Allmans recordings including *At Fillmore East* and *Eat A Peach*. The guitar – its sunburst a little faded today – was the basis for a Gibson Custom Shop limited-run in 2003 and is today owned by his daughter, Galadrielle, who has loaned it for exhibition at the Rock & Roll Hall Of Fame & Museum in Cleveland, Ohio.

Allman died in October 1971, aged 24 years. By that time, even Gibson could not ignore the wave of interest in their old-style Gibson Les Pauls. The question was, were they in a position to do anything about it?

6. VINTAGE

The notion of collectability takes hold in the 70s and 80s

Gibson had not manufactured its old-style Les Paul models since 1960. Toward the end of that decade the company was still touting various SG models as its prime solidbody guitar – the design that, as far as Gibson was concerned, had replaced the old-style single-cutaway Les Pauls. Many guitarists thought otherwise.

Gibson was changing. Revered company president Ted McCarty and his number two, John Huis, left in 1966 after buying the Bigsby musical accessories company of California, which they re-established in Kalamazoo – where Gibson continued to produce instruments at the Parsons Street factory. Early in 68, after a number of short-stay occupants in the chair, Stan Rendell was appointed president of Gibson. Maurice Berlin, head of Gibson's parent company CMI, told Rendell that they were "not doing too well" with Gibson. "They had lost a million dollars at the factory for the two prior years," recalls Rendell, who faced the usual brief handed to incoming presidents: make sure you improve the company's fortunes.[1]

Guitarist Bruce Bolen, born in England and raised in Chicago, joined

Gibson in 67 to organise and perform promo shows as a sort of travelling representative player for the company. "One of the reasons I was hired was because Gibson's electric sales were floundering," he says. "All we had in solidbody electrics were SGs, plus the archtop and thinline instruments, and they weren't selling all that well. The mainstay of the company at the time was the flat-top acoustics. So I was hired basically to go out and sell electric guitars."

He found that management at Gibson and parent CMI were generally unaware of the growing fondness among rock guitarists for the original 58–60 Les Pauls. "I was just a punk kid, and most of the people there were in their fifties or older," Bolen recalls. "I don't think they had a great grasp on how important that guitar was becoming once again. The Mike Bloomfields, Eric Claptons ... they'd found it to be something really precious that offered a sound that was very conducive to their form of music."[2]

Those original Bursts were beginning to attract a premium price when used examples came up for sale, reportedly going for anything from a couple of hundred bucks to as much as $1,000.

Gibson finally woke up to this interest and decided to do something about their deteriorating position within the electric guitar market, and specifically about the increasing demand for instruments of the old Les Paul design. Gibson brought Les Paul himself back from semi-retirement and made a new endorsement contract with him. By the time Rendell became president of Gibson the decision to start making reissues of old-style Les Pauls had already been made by CMI.

At the Gibson plant in Kalamazoo, Rendell and his team faced their own difficulties. He recalled the position: "We had all kinds of quality problems. We had production problems. We had personnel problems. We had union problems. We had problems that wouldn't end."[3]

Bruce Bolen, meanwhile, had a showstopper for his Gibson promo gigs.

He'd taken out on the road a prototype of the forthcoming reissue Les Paul Custom, as far as he can remember by very late 1967. "People were just falling apart about it. They couldn't wait to get one."[4]

But the fact that he had a black Custom to show off should have sounded an alarm bell. When it came to it, Gibson reintroduced the wrong models. At the June 1968 NAMM trade show in Chicago they officially launched two new-old Les Pauls, with the man himself there to play them. The new releases were the relatively rare two-pickup Les Paul Custom, at $545, and the Les Paul Goldtop with P-90 pickups and Tune-o-matic bridge, at $395. Nothing particularly wrong with either of those guitars in themselves, but they were not what players were getting most excited about. Where on earth was the humbucker'd sunburst that everyone wanted?

Gibson's ad for the revived guitars, headed "Daddy of 'em all", admitted that the company had been forced into the move. "The demand for them just won't quit. And the pressure to make more has never let up. OK, you win. We are pleased to announce that more of the original Les Paul Gibsons are available. Line forms at your Gibson dealer." It would have been more accurate if they'd said: "We are pleased to announce that two models you don't really want are now available."

Gibson's ownership shifted in 1969. The new owner, Norlin Industries, had recently been formed upon the merger of CMI and ECL, an Ecuadorian brewery. 'Norlin' came from combining the names of ECL chairman Norton Stevens and CMI founder Maurice Berlin. Norlin was in three businesses: musical instruments, brewing, and what was described rather loosely as 'technology'. The takeover was formalised a few years later and Berlin, a man widely respected in the musical instrument industry, was moved sideways in the new structure, away from the general running of the company.

Many people who worked for Gibson at the time have said how, when these changes happened, a new breed of employee began to appear. The most common description – and indeed the most polite – is of a Harvard MBA with suit, slide-rule, and calculator at the ready. To translate, that's a Master of Business Administration graduate from the Harvard Business School, armed with the tools of his trade. Or as one long-serving Gibson manager of the time put it to me, on condition of anonymity, "I'd think about people, about machines, about parts – and these new guys would 'solve' all the problems with a calculator. They had nothing to offer other than that they were looking for a place to invest their money and gain a profit. That was their motivation."

Many Gibson people felt that there was a move away from managers who understood guitars to managers who understood manufacturing. Some of the instruments made during the years that followed Gibson's takeover have a bad reputation today. The new owners are generally felt now to have been insensitive to the needs of musicians.

Another insider, again anonymously, said: "Up until about 1974 everything was hunky dory, and then it began to change. Too many people were doing too few things, too much money was being spent on too little, and it started to affect the infamous bottom line."

Gibson was not alone in smarting from the effects of these new management methods. Two other big names in American guitar-making had been taken over during this period: Fender, by CBS in 1965, and Gretsch, by Baldwin in 1967. Clearly this was a sign of the times as economic analysts advised large corporations to diversify into a range of different areas, to pour in some money – and to sit back and wait for the profits.

The shift toward what was called a 'rationalisation' of production meant that Gibson made changes to some of the guitars built during the 70s (and, to some extent, into the 80s). Generally, Gibson made these alterations for three reasons. First, to save money. Second, to limit the number of guitars returned for work under warranty. And third, to speed up production.

Most players say that Gibson Les Pauls from the 70s are relatively heavy compared to examples from other periods. And an old Les Paul is never a very light guitar. The weight of 70s examples was partly due to an increase in the density of the mahogany that Gibson was buying, but also to a change in body construction, because they started to use what's now known as a 'pancake', layering multiple maple and mahogany slices. This lasted from about 1969 to 1973.

Gibson also changed the way they made guitar necks, starting around 1969. They moved from the traditional one-piece neck to a stronger three-piece mahogany laminate, and around 1974 to three-piece maple, intended to provide even greater strength.

From about 1969, Gibson also added a 'volute' to the back of the neck, just below the point where it becomes the headstock. This was a sort of triangular lump that reinforced this notoriously weak spot. Another change made at the time to minimise problems in the same area came with a slight decrease in the angle at which the headstock tipped back from the neck. Such practical changes did nothing to enhance Gibson's reputation among those who liked the older guitars. For them, these changes emphasised the differences between old and new.

The same year, Gibson dropped the recently reissued Goldtop model and replaced it with the Les Paul Deluxe. It was a further example of the newly corporate Gibson still apparently not able to respond to what players were screaming for. Give us the old-style sunburst Les Pauls with humbuckers! Gibson heard half of the message – and still managed to screw it up.

The Deluxe had humbuckers. But – and this is a big but – they were mini-humbucking pickups, apparently used as a way of soaking up some old stock. At first the Deluxe was only available in Goldtop look, but gradually sunbursts and other colours were introduced (and a shortlived revised Goldtop came along in 71, with wrapover bar bridge). The Deluxe had its own sound, but the model was by no means a proper humbucker'd Les Paul. Gibson was apparently unable to provide the obvious guitar – a reissue of the sunburst model with full-size humbuckings – so some hip dealers began to take matters into their own hands. And prices for the originals began to creep up. Demand outweighed supply.

Chris Lovell had set up the Strings & Things store in Memphis, Tennessee, in 1971. They made some oddball guitars for name players and became known as the place for the more crazy stuff. Jeff Beck got his third Les Paul there, the 'oxblood' brown one, in 72. Strings & Things soon tried to do something about the lack of new sunburst Les Pauls from Gibson. "As far as I know we were the first to order them from Gibson," explains Lovell. "Everybody was playing Les Pauls but you couldn't get any. We'd had Clapton and now Page and Walsh and Beck – and there weren't any of *their* models available at the stores.

"Then Gibson actually reissued them – and they reissued the wrong things: the black Custom 'fretless wonder' with no frets and the Deluxe with those goofy baby humbuckers. And we're all looking at each other, like, *what are they doing?* Clueless! How can you aim at a bullseye and miss it that much? They redid everything that no one wanted."

At first, Strings & Things would take a new Deluxe and re-cut the pickup holes, or routs, to take big proper-size humbuckers. "We would modify the Deluxes into Standards," says Lovell. "Then we decided to just call Gibson and see if they'd be able to field us the right guitars."

This was 1974. Lovell called Gibson. They said, oh, call our custom shop. Lovell called the custom shop. They said really? Well, OK, came the hesitant reply, we'll make you two guitars just like you say – you really did say flame top, cherry sunburst, mahogany backs, no volutes on the headstock, small headstock, right? We'll make them and send them on over directly. Thank you so much for your order.

"They made two and sent them," says Lovell. "They were all wrong. The cutaway was just totally whacked-out. I called this guy back at the custom shop – he sounded like more of a regular shop guy and not a guitar guy. I said these Les Pauls, they look beautiful, but the body shape is all wrong. He didn't want to go for that. So he says he'll mail me the blueprints of the original Les Paul."

The blueprints for the Les Paul arrive in the mail. That's right: valuable Gibson history with a ten-cent stamp to cover it. Lovell takes one of the two guitars that Gibson had sent him and lays it on top of the blueprint. Guess what? "It's wrong. So I call him back and tell them we've got to try it again. They built six at that point, which were the first six we got. I don't count those first two because we didn't keep 'em."

Lovell tells me a funny story at this point that you'll want to hear. Strings & Things were getting a name as the store to visit in Memphis if you wanted good service and something a little bit different. They got to know quite a few bands, as you might imagine. Including the guys in Kiss. Lovell does not relate if he considered makeup as a sideline for his store.

Anyway, first time through Memphis, Kiss had played a small gig; next time around they came back as stars. They dropped by the store. They were very keen to show Lovell and the guys at Strings & Things a couple of really cool Les Pauls that Gibson had given them. You know what's coming, right? "They open the cases up – and it's those two Les Pauls that are just goofy," laughs Lovell. "They can't tell the difference, so we didn't say anything. We said oh, those are just great."

So, back to our main story here. How did they get on with the first 'proper' six sunbursts that Gibson sent them? Lovell says they were much better, although Gibson couldn't get the cherry sunburst right at all. They got the cherry backs and back of the neck dead right. But not the top colour. What to do? Strings & Things asked Gibson if they'd send further orders unfinished, but not surprisingly they said no. So Lovell asked for them to be just natural-finished, with a simple coat of clear lacquer over the bare wood. Gibson agreed. Strings & Things would strip off the clear and refinish the guitars in their own shop, bringing them to what Lovell describes as "killer looking sunbursts".

Who was buying them? "Just local players and people who heard about them," says Lovell. "Basically, Gibson built them for us for $750 apiece, if you can believe that. We sold them for $1,500, not a penny more or a penny less. Which we thought was a ton of money at the time."

In fact, that's about the price that an original 1958–60 Burst would have sold for back then. Lovell agrees, but says he noticed them taking a bit of a lift around 1978 and 79. "I saw a buddy of mine spend $2,500 for a real Burst and I told him I thought he was crazy for blowing that kind of money."[5] Hollow laughter. Many people have a story like this. If only they'd recognised that this was not a stupid purchase that their friend was making, it goes, but had shelled out some money of their own on one. Or six. They'd be rich! Then the hollow laughter. Repeat to fade.

As we know, players and collectors were beginning to take a real interest in the original sunbursts. Real as in spending their money. Spending as in not small amounts. Today – when the search for a million-dollar Les Paul is no joke – we would call these people early adopters. Among other things. Some might also say lucky devils. Shall we settle on calling them men of taste and foresight? Much more polite, I think you'll agree. And, in fact, more accurate.

First, I want you to meet Vic DaPra. He first got turned on to what a good Les Paul can do by his older brother, a drummer. This was in the late 60s. "My brother Val was in college and I was still in high school in Canonsburg, Pennsylvania," DaPra recalls. "He was bringing back Fleetwood Mac albums, Michael Bloomfield things, and Cream was out, and a bit later Led Zeppelin.

I had an instant attraction to all of that. It's difficult to say who it was that *really* did it for me, but I'd have to go between Jimmy Page and Peter Green."

DaPra got his first Burst in 1972. "A girl actually bought it for me as a gift, from Guitar Trader in New Jersey. I think it was maybe $1,800 or so. I'd wanted one for a long time. I can't even put into words my thoughts when I opened the case for the first time. And when I got that one, I had to have a second one." Why? DaPra laughs: "Because Jimmy Page had two. So I bought another, took a loan out for it, that was in 73 – cost me $1,600."

He's been a collector ever since. "Playing was always important to me, but the collecting thing was an addiction. Still is. No doubt about it." He doesn't have either of those first two Bursts any more, but today he's ended up with eight of the things. "Through the years you naturally want to trade up, trade up, trade up. Back then you could: it was easy to trade into a better guitar. There was always another one available."

This is such a common experience with Burst collectors. Other guitar collectors might settle down once they have this or that model, but with Bursts, each one is subtly different in looks, and the temptation very often is to want to find a better one. You know you have acute Burstitis when, no matter how many you have in your collection, you still need to search further for *that guitar*, the one that gets you just a little bit closer to the perfect Burst you have in your mind's eye. It's out there somewhere. I know it is.

"There's no two of them the same," says DaPra, with that hint of wonder in his voice that grips the Burst collector when they talk of this magical, almost mystical aspect of their collecting mania. "If you buy a Les Paul Custom, it's black with three pickups. And that's it. But with a Burst, every one is different. Each one has its own little nuance: the fade; the colour; the top."[6]

I'd also like you to meet Tom Wittrock. He too was an impressionable youth absorbed with music and in thrall to his favoured guitarists. He too was lucky enough to have an older brother who would share passions and discoveries. "Bart was a guitar nut before me and was into the sunburst Les Paul and other vintage instruments," recalls Wittrock. "This was in Houston, Texas, where I grew up, and where he had a music store, Rocking Robin. He was able to point out that these guys I liked so much were playing this particular guitar. Bart got a conversion around 1970."

A 'conversion' is a Les Paul that has been converted from one specific model to look and play like another, usually a Goldtop to a Burst. As you might imagine, this is the direction in which the work usually goes. No one is going to make a humbucker'd sunburst into a trapeze-tailpiece Goldtop, now are they? In other words, no one is going to mess up the most desirable one to make the least popular one. No, the most common job is of course to take a mid 50s Goldtop and 'convert' it into a Burst lookalike.

This can involve relatively simple operations (a 57 Goldtop already with humbuckers need only have the top 'revealed' to sunburst), or more complex jobs (early Goldtops need more work to cut out wood for the pickups and to reposition the neck). A skilled workman can make an excellent job and produce an instrument that looks more or less like the real thing. An unscrupulous workman can make a very good fake this way. A poor workman will make a botch of the job and ruin a perfectly decent guitar. It's been happening since the late 60s, although today the quality of workmanship is more often in the 'very good' category.

Done in good faith, then, conversions offer the means to play what is a little closer to your ideal guitar but without the enormous price tag of a real one. Done in bad faith, or passed on later without true origins explained, they are fakes. Of which more later. But back in Houston in the early 70s, Wittrock's brother had an excellent good-faith guitar.

There were other benefits to growing up in Houston. "One of the very first guitarists I would go see playing a Burst was Billy Gibbons," says

Wittrock. "But I didn't get really hip to music till I was in my late teens: a lot of other people were into it much younger. I started seeing a lot of people I was listening to on records who were also playing this very particular model of guitar: Duane Allman; Eric Clapton not so much by that point; Peter Green in a big way. I also saw that a number of players had used the Goldtops and the other 50s Les Pauls.

"So my interest in those original Les Paul models was real strong between 1970 and 72," he continues, "but the direction of the sunburst was the strongest. My brother was already using a conversion and telling me about it. And my heroes were playing Bursts, not just any old Les Paul."

He got his first Burst in 1975, soon after moving to Springfield, Missouri. "The guitar came into a local store as a trade-in. A friend of mine told me there was a sunburst Les Paul down there and that I should go see it. He knew I was interested in these guitars – because I already talked about them too much," laughs Wittrock.

"It was a very clean late-1960 model and they wanted $2,000. My experience at that point already told me that was a very fair price. I'd seen them advertised up to $2,500, at places like George Gruhn's GTR store in Nashville. Anyway, I made arrangements to secure it while I gathered the money to pay it off. I saw how great it was, heard how great it was, and said to myself yes, this is worth all the effort it's going to take to get it. Even then, for a lot of people $2,000 was quite a bit of an effort."

The sunburst Les Paul was already priced ahead of many other desirable old electrics. For example, Wittrock recalls buying his first vintage instrument, a 56 Stratocaster, in 1972 for $475. He got hold of a few others, too, around the time of his Burst, all for well under $1,000, and closer to 600 bucks.

"When I heard of this Burst, I was just growing into the mindset of guitar collecting and dealing, rather than just gee, I want to own a Burst and keep playing this kind of guitar. I already had a 68 Goldtop that was stripped and sunbursted and cut for humbuckers, because I knew that was the lowest-priced way to get that type of guitar."

Not that there was much competition in sunny Springfield at the time. He says the vast majority of people had no idea there was even such a guitar, let alone be willing to pay very good money for them. "When I bought that Burst for $2,000 I was literally the talk of the town," he smiles. "They'd say: there's the guy who spent $2,000 for a used guitar! I'd be at a party and I'd hear people talking about this guy, didn't even know who it was. I'd say, you want to know something even funnier? I'm the guy! Most of them would just laugh at me. One or two would take it further and ask what would possess you to pay that much for that guitar. And when I told them, some of them would listen to me. There's a passion here that's more than just money for craziness."

Wittrock has been evangelising for the Burst more or less ever since. You might say he's the daddy of all Burst collectors. And he seems to have kept it more or less in perspective. "It was a fortune I paid for the guitar at the time – and it's worth a much bigger fortune today. But if it was still worth $2,000 I'd still be happy I had the guitar. I didn't buy it for its potential dollar value. I bought it because it was the guitar I was dying to own. And once I got one, I wanted more."

There's the familiar story again. It does not end with buying a Burst. Quite the opposite: that is only the beginning. It is a quest, and a quest that has no discernible end. The Knights Who Say Ni! are lucky: they only demanded a couple of shrubberies. Had their quest been for Bursts … well, they'd still be looking now for one with a slightly nicer split-level top.

Meanwhile, Wittrock started trading guitars and acquiring a few more Bursts, helped by his brother and the Houston store. It slowly grew into meeting other people who were also Burst collectors and people who were interested in Bursts, he says. He came to realise that there was a wider passion for this guitar. The enthusiasts began to see a vintage market growing around them, gradually spreading worldwide, as the interest widened to create something well beyond local sales.

"I would go to functions as they started, like the very first Dallas guitar show," he recalls. "I was there as much as an observer as anything. I didn't have my own booth: I was in with my brother, just to learn. And I walked out with the only Burst that was sold at that show. That was the second one I actually owned."

Dallas, Texas, has hosted a guitar-collector show since 1978. The idea is simple and effective: dealers, collectors, and other guitar nuts gather to buy, sell, and trade instruments, and – some might say of even greater importance – to gossip about this or that deal and who shouldn't have sold what to whom and why and where that better deal could come from and did you see the beauty I just picked up? The other big show, also in Texas and now touted as the biggest in the world, has been staged at Arlington since 1986.

Some of the conversations and arguments that began as the natural currency of the big Texas shows, and seemed just as valuable as the dollar bills that changed hands, have inevitably shifted in more recent years to the various guitar-collector forums on the internet. These are much like the internet in general: delightfully informative one moment and irritatingly vacuous the next. They certainly have their uses, but there's nothing quite like meeting up in person at a guitar show every year. And no one (yet) has found a way to play a guitar online.

I ask Wittrock if it's possible to articulate what it is about the Burst that attracts such adulation among its collectors. He pauses and thinks. "Part of it," he says, "boils down to my opinion and the opinion of so many other people that the Burst is the finest example of the Les Paul ever made. It is pretty well established as a great guitar – and it's hard to dispute that, even if you don't like it. That in itself made me feel like I'm looking at something that is truly supreme to begin with. But the final kicker for me was the beautiful maple that they put on the top of some of them."

It was this individual character and splendour that drew Wittrock, as it has subsequently drawn so many other guitar collectors, to want to seek potentially more attractive examples of the instrument. Some call it grain – technically it is figure – but this pattern in the maple that varies from example to example, and which in extreme cases can be spectacular, is a large part of what drives collectors. We will return to this subject again.

"It's what motivated me to choose which ones I wanted," Wittrock agrees. "And the Burst was the one I wanted to play, not just own, but to actually play. I preferred it over Fenders, over other models of Gibson. So when it came down to collecting, the final part of my interest came down to the wood grain, all other things being equal."

Wittrock has been collecting Bursts since the 70s, more than 30 years now. He's had time to consider all the factors that stir his fellow collectors of the instrument. "We all pretty much agree that we collected these guitars merely because this was the model of guitar that really moved or motivated us emotionally more than any other. And we still have that feeling. That's what got us into it and that's what's kept us into it."[7]

7. RESTRUCTURE

Dealer specials and one-off replica Les Pauls

Back in the mid 70s, while discerning players and collectors were hanging on to the original sunburst Les Pauls they could find, Gibson took enough notice of the handful of custom 'dealer specials' they'd made for Memphis dealer Strings & Things to mention it in passing to the press.

Roger Matthews of Gibson said in 1974: "We are producing a Les Paul Standard model which could be related to the instrument produced in the latter part of the 50s. The limited edition that is now in production has the large humbucking pickups and is available in sunburst finish."[1]

Gibson opened a new factory in Nashville, Tennessee, in summer 1975 and for the time being ran it alongside the operation that continued at the old Kalamazoo building. Nashville was set up to produce very large quantities of a handful of individual models, while Kalamazoo was more flexible and had the potential to specialise in small runs. Nashville was therefore the obvious choice to produce the highest-volume models in Gibson's solidbody line at the time – the Les Paul Custom and Les Paul Deluxe – along with various other solidbody models.

Gibson finally gave way and – at last – introduced the Les Paul Standard in 1976, as a Nashville production model listed in catalogues and pricelists. The guitar came complete with – at last – a cherry sunburst top and proper humbucking pickups. The Standard name, you'll remember, was the one Gibson had given the sunburst model in its 1960 catalogue.

Against that background, it seemed to Strings & Things that there was now little need to have Gibson continue to make sunburst Les Pauls for them. The store's founder Chris Lovell says they received 28 special orders from Gibson between 1974 and 1977. Four were lost in a store fire, making a total of 24. "We did it for almost four years — and it took Gibson that long to figure out that this guitar was what people wanted, whether we asked them to do it or not. They should have figured that out a lot quicker." Those 24 instruments are now known as the Strings & Things reissues, and they too have become collectable. Look out for a 70s Burst with what Lovell calls a "cock-eyed" hand-stamped serial number.[2]

Strings & Things wasn't the only dealer in the 70s to notice that some guitarists were thinking older instruments often seemed more playable and sounded better than new guitars. That feeling was exemplified by the hunt starting up for old electric solidbody Les Pauls. Some players of acoustics had felt this way for a while, and a small number of specialist dealers had grown up in the States since the late 40s to cater for the demand. Harry West in New York City and Jon & Deirdre Lundberg in California had been among the first.

But now older electrics, too, were being sought, and the Les Pauls were near the top of many a wish-list. Stephen Stills of Crosby Stills & Nash had amassed a collection of about 70 guitars by the middle of the 70s. Touring with his solo band at the time, he needed two dressing rooms: one for himself; another for the 17 guitars that accompanied him. Included was a 1960 Burst. Like collector Tom Wittrock, Stills was an old-guitar evangelist. He had the advantage of being in the public eye. "I don't think they've built anything new that's worth a damn since 1965," Stills said in 76. "It's all mechanised."[3]

Charlie Daniels too had a chance to air the feeling that was spreading among musicians when he was interviewed for a guitar magazine. "If a guitar sounds good and plays good, I don't care if it's a 58 or a 75. It just happens that most guitars that sound good and play good are old ones."[4]

Maybe the image of Clapton with his Burst on the 66 *Blues Breakers* album really did start the vintage-guitar trend. But by the mid 70s, what with Stills and Daniels and others articulating what many guitarists were thinking, it seemed that a trend was settling in. Somehow, went the vibe, only old guitars were worthy of attention by 'real' players.

On the face if it, this is a non-argument. Good guitars have been made today, last week, 30 years ago, 50 years ago, whenever. In the same way, poor guitars also turn up in every period of production – decades ago, a while back, recently, or right now. But if you know the context of a guitar's manufacture, it can give clues as to the chances of it being a better one or a not-so-good one.

At certain periods, the combination just clicks. The factory gets into its groove, the materials come together, and a series of great guitars is the result. But you can never really know until you sit down with the actual guitar, plug it in, and turn up the amp. Wood varies, and you cannot predict exactly what it will do in combination with the other materials to hand. Whatever the resulting guitar's vintage or reputation.

And how come this word 'vintage' started to turn up in conversations about old guitars in the 70s? As a word to describe something old, it certainly has positive associations. Vintage wine, for example, is the kind you sip in rarefied circles with others who appreciate the finer things in life. And who have the cash to pay for them. The first ad I've managed to find with the word 'vintage' used for guitars was for a firm called Guitar Resurrection in Berkeley, California, late in 1973, but I bet there are earlier examples.[5] Once upon a time, old guitars were called secondhand or just plain used. Now they were turning into vintage pieces. Salesmanship can make anything sound that little bit better with the right jargon attached.

The first published attempt to sort out the various Les Paul models and their dates of manufacture came in Tom Wheeler's *The Guitar Book* in 1974. Les Paul said at the time: "If I'd known in the beginning that the guitars were going to wind up as collectors items, I'd have kept a more detailed history as it developed."[6]

Nashville-based dealer George Gruhn wrote in *Guitar Player* the first serious magazine piece about the new collecting trends, published in the first months of 1975 and grandly titled 'The Art And Science Of Guitar Collecting'. Gruhn emphasised the desirability of old Les Pauls in the article. "There are currently more people looking for Les Pauls than for any other electric guitar," he reported. The 1958–60 Burst, he said, "is today probably the most sought after of the Les Pauls, and has become the standard by which other guitars are judged, at least on the current market".[7]

As we've seen, Gibson had finally added the sunburst humbucker'd Les Paul to its contemporary pricelist of new models. They called it the Standard, at $649, but still the company seemed to ignore the precise requirements of vintage fans. Meanwhile, down at the low end of Gibson's market in the 70s, oriental makers were competing with well-priced copies of many classic American guitar designs, Gibson Les Pauls included.

Some of the Japanese copies were cheap both in price and quality, but brands such as Ibanez began to appear on decent instruments. By the end of the 70s, a Made In Japan label was no longer the sign of an also-ran, with the best makers slowly turning the oriental guitar into a well made, competitive instrument on the world market.

It was Ibanez, Electra, Aria, and Tokai who made the most notable attempts to copy Gibson Les Paul designs, although there were others. Ibanez guitars were made at the Fuji Gen Gakki factory in Japan; Electra and Aria at Matsumoku; and Tokai at their own factory in Hamamatsu. During the 70s, these brands took a great deal of time and effort to copy mostly Gibson and Fender models, especially Les Pauls and Stratocasters.

In some Eastern countries, copying is a culturally acceptable process, in contrast to the view in the West where the law values ownership of designs through copyrights and trademarks. The Japanese motor-car industry, for example, started by more or less copying Western designs. As with the early Japanese guitars, however, the copies were hardly exact, and had a style of their own. They didn't necessarily work the same, but they (kind of) looked similar.

Gibson's parent company, Norlin, was probably not much detained by sitting around and considering cultural differences. Instead, it took legal action in 1977 against Ibanez's US arm, Elger. The action had to be focussed on an area of the copying that infringed a trademarked part of the design. This was rather more grown-up than shouting across a crowded courtroom: "You stole our guitar!"

Norlin's lawyers highlighted the way oriental makers had copied Gibson's distinctively shaped (and trademarked) headstock – apparently without noticing that Ibanez had moved to a different shape in 1976. There was a settlement out of court, with Elger promising not to copy Gibson. Ibanez at least began to concentrate on a series of original designs. Ironically, these became popular, and Gibson, among other big US makers, suffered as the oriental makers gained ground.

Since then, many collectors have used the term 'lawsuit' to describe any oriental copy guitar of this period, whether or not the brand suffered legal action. Gibson filed more suits in the years following the Elger action, but none got as far as the courts until the much more recent Gibson vs PRS case. This concerned the inspiration for the design of the PRS Singlecut model, which PRS won following an appeal.

The so-called 'lawsuit' guitars have their fans, too. Michael Wright, author of several guitar books and the overseer of a fine, large guitar collection that feeds his wide knowledge of the subject, has an Electra Les Paul copy of which he's especially fond.

"One evening in a local used guitar shop in a seedy Philadelphia neighbourhood," Wright recalls, "after several glasses of Scotch with the owners, I saw some guy come in with a Les Paul, a Standard from the 70s as I recall, and an Electra. While the owners oohed and ahhed over the Gibson, I calmly walked out with the Electra for $350. It has deeper flame in the maple than any guitar I've ever seen, and it has those killer St Louis Music humbuckers. Let someone else pay a fortune for the Gibson name!"[8]

Back at Gibson, Tim Shaw joined the company in 1978, having worked in California and then locally in Kalamazoo as a guitar repairer and maker. His first few months with Gibson were spent in the pickup plant in Elgin, Illinois, but by early 1979 he was working with Bruce Bolen in R&D at Kalamazoo. Together with Chuck Burge and Abe Wechter, Shaw built prototypes and artists' instruments and worked on new designs, one of which turned into Gibson's first proper attempt at an authentic remake of the 58–60 Burst.

"I had a lot of fun there," says Shaw. "It was frustrating in some senses, because we knew what the product was supposed to be and we were trying to be like the spirit of the old guys. We worked in the basement of the old building, the Gibson factory that you see in all the old pictures.

"You could say there were ghosts looking over our shoulders. You could go to those places in the factory where, for example, Lloyd Loar had his picture taken, the section on the second floor where all the mandolin stuff used to be, like in the 20s catalogue with all these guys and the big belt-driven machines. You could go and find those places. So we had a real appreciation of the history of the company, because we were in a building that had been in existence for 70 years. And we took that real seriously."

Shaw remembers the new Heritage 80 series Les Pauls as their first stab at asking questions like: What's the best that this guitar ever was? Are we building it like that now? And if not, why not? "Management didn't want to hear about it at first," says Shaw, "so we had to fight tooth and nail to do it."

The R&D team used a 1954 pattern sample to provide the carving of the Heritage's body top, and disposed of current production oddities such as the volute below the back of the headstock, while moving a little closer to older pickup specifications. Pretty, figured timber was selected for the tops.

Bruce Bolen, head of R&D by then, managed to persuade Norlin to put the vintage-flavoured Heritages into production – not as standard Les Pauls, however, but once again as separate, premium items, touted as 'limited editions' and not included on the company's regular pricelists. Launched in 1980, the various Heritage Series Standard 80 models lasted in production for just a couple of years.

Perhaps as a result of those models, Gibson began to move away from some of its production quirks of the 70s. The volute was removed, and gradually there was a change back to one-piece mahogany necks. In 1982, the Kalamazoo factory put out the limited-run Les Paul Standard 82, yet another stab at a modern Burstalike, distinguished from the Heritage Standard 80 primarily by its one-piece neck and the fact that it was made in Kalamazoo.

Kim LaFleur, whom we'll meet again later in the book, remembers buying one of these. "I was in Rainbow Music in New York in 1982 and they had at least seven or eight real Bursts on the wall in the back room, in the vintage section, running around $6,000. I was playing in a band and really didn't have enough money to get a real one. Gibson had just reissued the Heritage series, and the last hurrah from Kalamazoo was the Standard 82. So I got one of those at Jerome Sound in Albany. But I'll tell you what – I couldn't use it. It was just so wrong! None of the appointments were correct. Nice looking guitar, but I traded it back and got my workhorse, a Standard with a Nashville bridge, and carried on playing that."[9]

Meanwhile, another specialist dealer in the USA began to wonder if Gibson might be able to make something even more like an original Burst than the efforts so far. The Guitar Trader store in Red Bank, New Jersey, had been set up by Dave DeForrest around 1970. Timm Kummer joined as manager later in the decade.

Kummer says that someone from Gibson R&D had been out to Guitar Trader to measure a bunch of 1958–60 Bursts. The result was the KM model of 1979. "Which," laughs Kummer, "had a maple three-piece neck, a huge volute, and a headstock the size of a heliport. No dish to the top. I believe the fella that did the research probably lost his job there. We couldn't sell 'em. Very few had any flame in the top. Customers were a little too fussy."

Maybe Guitar Trader's customers were fussy – or perhaps it was just that they, like many others, thought that Gibson ought to be making guitars like they used to. Specifically Les Paul sunbursts. It couldn't be too hard, surely? It was obvious to everyone else what was wrong with the current Standard, the Heritage 80s, and the one-offs like the KM and the Standard 82. Not enough attention to detail!

Kummer sums up the feeling: "Everything was falling on the deaf ears of those people who were running Gibson, which was Norlin at the time, and CBS, who were running Fender. They were pencil-pushers and they just didn't get it."

So Guitar Trader struck a deal to do the research, to give Gibson the specs they needed to make what they hoped would be a proper Burst reissue. "We thought we had an exclusive with them," says Kummer, "although they started selling these specials to other dealers, like Jimmy Wallace in Texas and Leo's out in California." As with the earlier Strings & Things custom jobs, the specials that Gibson made for Guitar Trader and others were turned out in relatively small numbers. Kummer's best guess is that Guitar Trader ended up with 53 reissues.

A typical ad for them came in the store's May 1982 newsletter. "Guitar Trader and Gibson Guitars announce the ultimate Les Paul reissue," claimed the blurb, alongside a repro of the original Standard entry from Gibson's 1960 catalogue. A list of features followed: "Dimensions as per 1959 model shown; 'painted-on' serial number; original style bridge; two-piece highly figured tops personally selected by our luthiers. These instruments will be produced in strictly limited quantities at the original Gibson factory in Kalamazoo, MI, and represent a special investment value."

Guitar Trader added that if you ordered your '59 Flametop' immediately for summer 82 delivery, they would install original 50s pickups, subject to availability. Kummer reckons that happened for the first 15 lucky customers. The price (with case) was $1,500, although it later crept up to $2,000. In the same newsletter, Guitar Trader was happy to offer an original and entirely real 1959 Burst, with "tiger-striped curly maple top", for $7,500. By the end of the year, Aerosmith's Brad Whitford was pictured taking delivery of his Guitar Trader Flametop. "Hasn't felt this good since '59," he reckoned.

Gibson's plant manager at Kalamazoo, Jim Deurloo, recalled that the dealer specials were selected from the production line at Gibson but were custom-built to some degree. "It was at a time when we weren't making a vintage-looking instrument," he said. "We were making what was in the catalogue at the time – and not the guitar with the washed-out top. I remember that Guitar Trader selected each top, and they were very picky about the colour."[10]

Kummer reckons they would go to the factory and select particular planks of wood, before they were cut to size, and photograph them. Customers would select which planks they wanted their instrument's top to come from by looking at these pictures that the Guitar Trader guys brought back from Kalamazoo. "I guess the biggest risk was what it was going to look like once the finish was applied. Because a bare piece of maple, even though we intensified the effect by wetting it with some fluid, well ... you can never know exactly what you're going to get."

Guitar Trader's deal with Gibson lasted only a couple of years. Who bought them? "A lot went to guys who couldn't afford the 5,000 or 6,000 that a real burst was. Brad Whitford, who was on a sort of hiatus from Aerosmith at the time, was a good customer. But he was probably the only name player. I don't know if his endorsement did a whole lot. That's a tough thing to gauge. Guys who bought them were running restaurants, they were dentists, players, every walk of life. These were certainly not cheap guitars."[11]

Back in the management boardrooms around 1980, Norlin had started to consider selling the Gibson company. The following year, Norlin suffered substantial losses in its music divisions, and the firm sold its profitable technology and beer divisions in 82. As well as Gibson and Gibson Accessories, Norlin's music divisions included Lowrey organs, Moog synthesisers, and a 'band and orchestral' section.

Gibson sales fell by 30 per cent in 1982 alone, to a total of $19.5 million compared with a high in 1979 of $35.5 million. Gibson was not alone in this decline. The US guitar market in general had virtually imploded, and most other American makers were suffering in broadly similar ways. Their costs were high, economic circumstances and currency fluctuations were against them, and Japanese competitors increasingly had the edge.

Norlin relocated some of its sales, marketing, admin, and finance personnel from Chicago to Nashville around 1980. All of the main Gibson production was now handled at the Nashville plant, while Kalamazoo had become a specialist factory making custom orders, banjos, and mandolins. Then, in July 1983, Gibson president Marty Locke informed plant manager Jim Deurloo that the Kalamazoo operation would close. The last production at Kalamazoo was in June 1984, and the factory closed three months later, after more than 65 years of worthy service since the original building had been erected by Gibson. It was of course an emotional time for the managers and workers, many of whom had worked in the plant for a long time.

One employee said that people there knew the closure was inevitable. "You added it all up, and the Kalamazoo factory was falling apart. It was a very old building, steeped so heavily in tradition and history. The Nashville plant was brand new, in 17 acres, a very beautiful facility. What it boils down to is that the business could not support the two facilities, and there was really only one choice." This same observer noted that the business was easier to sell, too, now that it just had the Nashville plant with its more amenable labour relations and lower costs.

Some of the key people were offered positions at Nashville. But Jim Deurloo, together with Marv Lamb, who'd been with Gibson since 1956, and J.P. Moats, a Gibson employee of equally long standing, decided to leave. They rented part of the Kalamazoo plant and started the Heritage guitar company in April 1985. They continue that business today, with a line of 24 models. As Lamb put it: "We all grew up building guitars and we didn't know too different. We could have searched for another job, but we wanted to do what we know how to do best."[12]

By the summer of 1985, Norlin had found a buyer for Gibson. In January of the following year, Henry Juszkiewicz, David Berryman, and Gary Zebrowski completed their purchase of the entire Gibson operation. They paid an undisclosed sum, now generally thought to be about $5 million. By this time Norlin's main business was in printing, and Gibson was the last part of its once-large musical empire to be sold off.

Juszkiewicz, Berryman, and Zebrowski had met while studying at the Harvard Business School in the late 70s. Since then, Juszkiewicz had been in engineering and investment banking, Berryman in accountancy, and Zebrowski in marketing. Crucially, Juszkiewicz was an enthusiastic guitarist who loved Gibson instruments. The three had gone into business together, teaming up in 1981 to turn a failing Oklahoma electronics company into a successful operation. When they bought Gibson in 86, Juszkiewicz became president and Berryman vice-president of finance and accounting, while Zebrowski continued to run the trio's electronics business.

The most immediate effect of the new ownership was that a lot of people were fired, including the plant manager, the quality control manager, and many others. This was hardly likely to be a popular first move. Juszkiewicz said early on that he was in the process of 'restructuring' Gibson's production operation. He said that the new Gibson set-up would be extremely aggressive in developing and introducing new products, and insisted that they would be more creative in merchandising and marketing than Gibson had ever been, with a more competitive pricing policy.

As far as the ever-popular Les Paul models were concerned, Juszkiewicz's position was that he had inherited a poor relationship between Gibson and Les Paul himself. "Les obviously had a proprietary interest in the success of his guitars, and they'd killed them, so he was pretty annoyed." Juszkiewicz reckoned that Les, who lives in New Jersey, was constantly courted by the New Jersey-based maker Kramer. "He even did an MTV video saying how nice Kramer guitars were. So I established a rapport with Les early on, and that seemed to solve the problem," says Juszkiewicz. "I listened to what he had to say. He wanted to see a lower-cost Les Paul instrument in our imported Epiphone line, for example, and we ended up doing that a few years in."[13]

There were several changes to the roles of some key Gibson guitar-design people around the time of the change of ownership. Tim Shaw moved from the Custom Shop and R&D to an international role, travelling often to Korea to help expand the Epiphone lines. He left Gibson in 1992, after 14 years service with the company, and currently works for Fender in Nashville.

Gibson's new Reissue Outfits, effectively an attempt to recreate more accurately the old-style Burst and Goldtop, had been in production since 1983, driven by the persistent demands of customers seeking perfect duplication of the hallowed 50s instruments. The Heritage models had turned out to be a half-hearted attempt at a proper reincarnation of the most celebrated old Les Pauls.

These Les Paul Reissue Outfits were the next steps – backward and forward at the same time. They came in Curly Maple Top or Gold Top, and when they appeared on pricelists in 1985 were pitched at $1,599 and $1,299 respectively. Regular production models retailed for $999. There was some way to go before detail-conscious customers would be happy with the reissue models, but Gibson had at least made a start.

Changes in fashion among guitar-players and guitar-makers were not kind to Gibson during the 80s. Some of the key musicians who had been allied closely to the original Les Paul had moved on to other models. At a charity benefit show in London in 1983, Jeff Beck, Eric Clapton, and Jimmy Page played together on stage. Beck played Fender Stratocasters. Clapton too played a Strat and, for one song, a Gibson Firebird. Page mainly played a Fender Telecaster, although he did use a Burst briefly. Beck and Clapton would go on to work with Fender and produce signature models a few years later.

The new guitar-making trends of the 80s were moving away from the Les Paul style of solidbody. There were fads for odd-shaped and 'headless' guitars as well as synthesiser hook-ups. Fender's Stratocaster was the flavour of the decade, and an offshoot, the so-called superstrat, attracted many of the high-octane players who might otherwise have been naturals for a Gibson Les Paul.

The superstrat was largely developed by the American maker Jackson from the Stratocaster. It offered more frets, deeper cutaways, a drooped pointy-shape headstock, modified pickup layouts, a high-performance vibrato system, and bright graphic finishes. In many ways it was the antithesis of a Les Paul Burst, and it came to define the mainstream rock guitar of the 80s.

Jackson and the related Charvel brand attracted important players, not least the highly talented Eddie Van Halen. But Ibanez too had a highly visible line of superstrats, especially the RG series, and did much to popularise the style. Key 80s guitar heroes Steve Vai and Joe Satriani opted for Ibanez models and helped to design new instruments. In a 1989 interview, Satriani summed up the way many players and makers were trying to synthesise the best of several instrument styles into a new kind of guitar. "I've tried to get the ultimate Strat sound and the ultimate Les Paul sound from one guitar," said Satriani, "but it's like a jinx."[14]

Of course, some players kept the faith. You would hardly expect such a passionate Les Paul fan as Joe Walsh, for example, to switch allegiance. He'd joined The Eagles in time for their huge *Hotel California* album of 1976, stayed until they disbanded in the early 80s, and would return for the recent reunions. In 88, Walsh still defined his all-time favourite guitar set-up as a vintage Les Paul through a pair of Fender Super Reverb amps. "I'm partial to a 59 or a 60," he said. "It depends … 58s are fun too. Les Pauls just really make it for me. I do also love Strats and Teles, though."[15]

When Gibson stumbled on old hand Gary Richrath of REO Speedwagon, who still relied on an enviable collection of old Les Pauls, they got him to endorse the company's attempt to jump on the superstrat bandwagon, the US-1 model. The resulting 87 ad displayed Richrath among his vintage collection of seven Bursts, a Goldtop, and two Customs – but there he was holding the incongruous looking US-1.

Gibson was experiencing a problem that has never been too far from the company's door ever since. Players want Gibson to be traditional, to make good modern versions of their innovations from the 50s. But if the company tries to innovate now or to run with new trends, well, that's just un-Gibson, and not to be tolerated. The US-1 did not last long in the Gibson catalogue.

Among all the new shred players lining up for their new superstrats, along came Guns N' Roses to redefine hard rock – and, no doubt to Gibson's delight, guitarist Slash used mostly Les Pauls on which to unleash his aggressive blues-laden licks.

Slash had been influenced to take up Les Pauls by Jimmy Page and Joe Perry. As Guns N' Roses began to sell millions of albums, he assembled a fine collection of guitars, with a good showing of vintage Les Pauls (including one of the earliest-numbered 1958 Bursts). But the guitar he was most often seen with on stage was a regular late-80s Standard, and the one he used to record the band's first hit album, 1987's *Appetite For Destruction*, wasn't a Gibson at all but a replica.

"I'm really attached to my guitars," Slash said recently. "Everything I have in some way, shape, or form is a favorite. I'm partial to Les Pauls, of course. A couple of them are replicas, and one is very dear to me because it's the guitar that really cut the ties between me and any other sort of guitars. It was built by Chris Derrig, and I got it through Guns N' Roses management when we were doing the basic tracks for *Appetite For Destruction*."

Slash said he was experimenting with guitars but didn't have much money, and so he couldn't just go pick up anything he wanted. Being in the studio for the first time, he realised that he had to get a guitar that sounded really good. "I'd been using Les Pauls, but they'd get stolen or I'd hock them. So Alan Niven, the band's original manager, gave me this hand-made 59 Les Paul Standard replica. I took it in the studio with a rented Marshall, and it sounded great. And I've never really used another. It has zebra-striped Seymour Duncan Alnico II pickups.

"I ended up in the studio with the Les Paul replica," said Slash, "and that was my main guitar through the beginning of the first Guns N' Roses tour. I later got another replica made by someone named Max [Baranet]. I had those two on the road for the first year. Then, when Gibson gave me a deal on two Les Paul Standards, I put away the replicas because I'd banged the crap out of them."[16]

The irony is that the guitar that more or less brought the Burst back to public consciousness wasn't made by Gibson at all. But for most collectors, the real thing had never gone out of fashion anyway. In fact, for them it was still the most important guitar in the world.

8. WORKMANSHIP

Was the 50s Gibson factory making guitars or conjuring up miracles?

As more players and collectors discovered the 1958–60 Les Paul sunburst model for themselves, and Gibson tried to make a modern version of that instrument, so the original guitars came under closer inspection. What was it about them that was so special? Were they different back then? Could the same qualities be matched now?

It's clear that a solidbody electric guitar is not simply one thing. In fact, it's a system of various components that, ideally, should work well together in order to provide the player with a blissful experience to help him create a glorious noise. And those disparate systems do not become a guitar until they are assembled. The best instrument makers understand this, and occasionally they achieve a great instrument as a result.

Or, as Jeff Beck once told me: "I think the pickup picks up whatever character is in the acoustic sound of the string, and that's going to vary according to every single facet of the guitar: the thickness of the body; the resonance of the wood; all the rest of it. All that is definitely going to make a difference – otherwise every electric guitar would sound pretty much the same."[1]

Many would argue that the solidbody electric as a system reached its historical peak in the 58–60 Burst. Max Baranet has been a repairman and has made replicas of Gibson instruments, so, naturally enough, he's made close studies of historical construction methods. He says this peak of which we speak is more like an X. Beg pardon? Explain please.

"If you draw a big X, you can think of the bottom of the X as the early development of the electric guitar, with all the different factors coming in from different points," says Baranet. "Well, the top of the X is where we are now in the early years of the 21st century. And that junction of the X, right where the lines cross, is the 1959 Les Paul. Various factors all came together at that point for that one year. And then they started to diverge again. But for that particular tone, it was all perfect at that one point."[2]

Let's focus in on the junction at the centre of that X. The sunburst Gibson Les Paul consists of three main systems that, as with any solidbody electric guitar, have to successfully co-exist and harmonise as a whole in order to make a potentially good model into an individually great guitar. Those three systems are the woodwork, the electronics, and the hardware.

The woodwork is the body, neck, and fingerboard, and also includes the finish. The electronics takes in the pickups, wiring, and controls. And the hardware is all the other odds and ends that are fitted to the instrument.

In the beginning was the wood, and the wood was with Gibson. But how much wood, and what kind exactly? The 58–60 Burst has a three-piece body consisting of two bookmatched halves of carved maple on top, glued to a thick mahogany base. Bookmatching is a technique where a piece of wood is sliced into two and then opened out down a central join, like a book, and sometimes this can provide symmetrically similar patterns on the wood's surface.

Gibson had used this kind of look – bookmatched maple, sunburst finish – on a handful of models before the Burst, including a couple of solidbody electric steel guitars: the relatively broad-bodied Doubleneck Electric Hawaiian back in the 30s, and the Royaltone, produced for a couple of years from 1950. The backs of Gibson's archtop hollowbody guitars were regularly made from thin, carved, bookmatched maple, often using spectacularly beautiful timber.

The woodworkers at the Gibson factory in Kalamazoo used solid mahogany not just for the body base but also for the neck of the Burst, which they glued to the body with the aid of a tight mortise-and-tenon joint. A rosewood fingerboard was glued to the neck, over a strengthening truss-rod in a channel in the neck. White plastic binding was glued to the front edge of the body and to the outer edges of the fingerboard.

The necks varied in profile during the years of production: generally they were quite large in 58, moving to a smaller but still rounded profile into 59, and then slimmer and flatter into 60. The metal frets on the fingerboard were generally medium-sized in 58 and became larger during 59. But of course, with a semi-handmade product, there are always exceptions and anomalies.

The Brazilian rosewood fingerboard has been the source of much fuss since, mainly because the wood is now a controlled species and rarely available to present-day makers. Thus grows another part of the myth: if you can't get something easily, well then, it stands to reason it must be good. In fact, there's no doubt that Brazilian rosewood is a good fingerboard wood – but so are other rosewoods and a number of similar woods.

The glue that Gibson used back in the 50s was probably hide glue, which, as the name implies, is a substance that is made from animal products, in contrast to the various synthetics used more commonly in recent times. "Hide glue really soaks into the wood," says Baranet. "It leaves a minimal film between the parts, and when it dries it crystallises, like glass. Tap a pane of glass and it will vibrate. If you use epoxy or aliphatic resin, that always stays gummy to a degree and doesn't soak in as well. It effectively leaves an insulating layer between the two pieces of wood.

"Obviously, you don't want to do that at the three important joints in the Les Paul – fingerboard to neck, neck to body, and body to top – because it will kill the tone. Hide glue helps the tone, whereas if you use the synthetics, that is the end of your tone. It will just be mush."[3] Presumably some kind of special training would be required for those guitar players who wish to hear the sound of a particular glue.

In general, Gibson sourced its maple from relatively close to the factory, while the mahogany came from British Honduras (now Belize) in central America, and the rosewood from Brazil. When Tim Shaw was at Gibson researching construction for the Heritage Standard reissues of 1980, he studied the wood used in the original Bursts.

Shaw discovered that pretty much all the maple Gibson used was hard maple from northern Michigan. And the mahogany? "That was central American, from Honduras. They used to favour what was called 'pattern grade' mahogany, although that is no longer a Lumber Association grade. They tended to get mahogany that grew in well drained areas.

"The extremely heavy mahogany that we see these days," says Shaw, "is a result of growing in ground that is not well drained. The tree sucks up water and a lot of minerals from the soil. You can be on a hillside, and up the hill is a mahogany tree with completely different mechanical properties than down the hill. In the old days, they went for more of the 'uphill' stuff."[4]

This combination of woods – mahogany neck and body base, split maple top, rosewood fingerboard – was what Gibson had used for the Les Paul since its introduction in 1952. Remember, the maple top had only become visible since the finish was changed to sunburst during 58; it had always been there before but was hidden under the gold paint.

A relatively small percentage of Bursts display astonishingly patterned maple. The woodworker's term for this pattern in timber is figure, but guitar people generally call it flame. (Grain is something different, usually the lines in the wood that travel 'across' any figuring, depending on the type of cut.) Any tree can potentially provide figured timber, but it's actually an unpredictable fluke. Some trees will have it; others will not. Figure is caused by a genetic anomaly in the growing tree that produces ripples or rays in the cells of the living wood.

The visual effect of figure is also determined by variations in the colour and density of the tree's growth, the effect of disease or damage, and the way in which the timber is cut from the felled tree. Quarter-sawing – which means cutting so that the grain is generally square to the face of the resulting planks – often provides the most attractive figured wood, sometimes giving the illusion of roughly parallel rows of three-dimensional 'hills and valleys' across the face of the timber.

Edwin Wilson, currently the Historic Program Manager, Engineering, at Gibson's Custom Division, explains how the method used to cut the wood affects the resulting figure. "If it's quarter-sawn, the result can be really intense, like a hologram," he says. "If you tilt the resulting board to and from you and look at it, it's like a 3D effect. Whereas if it's flat sawn or if it's rift sawn, then you'll get real thick, wide flame on it, and as you turn it, not only does it have a hologram effect but the figure moves from left to right also."[5]

In extreme cases, figure in maple can look dramatic – like a hologram, as Wilson describes it. And for many collectors it is this drama that is at the heart of the attraction of the original sunburst Les Paul guitars.

Clive Brown is a specialist in vintage guitar restoration based in northern England, and he says that figured or flamed wood was not universally prized at the time that Gibson was using it for guitar-making in the 50s. "The furniture industry didn't want it," explains Brown, "because for them it was unstable. The flame goes one way and the grain the other, and that causes an instability.

"It's OK on a Les Paul, for example, because you're gluing the maple to a lump of mahogany that isn't going anywhere. But the furniture industry wouldn't use it for table legs or chair legs or anything like that, because it has a tendency to twist. And that made it a cheaper wood. Furniture people would use straight-grain or other more stable wood, and they only used flame in veneers. Of course, Gibson used it for the thin backs of their archtop guitars, too, where the struts make it stable. But sometimes you can even see movement in that maple."[6]

Wilson occasionally finds the same attitude today. "Sometimes when I enquire about buying some figured woods – curly maple and so on – they say, actually, we burn that stuff, it's just garbage. Some people are still of that mindset."[7]

No one knows exactly how Gibson approached the job of allocating the maple to the various Burst tops in that period between 1958 and 60. It's not clear if there was somebody in charge of picking wood to bookmatch and if there was any kind of selection process. A good guess is that they used what was available at the time and did the best job they could.

A question we can get nearer to answering is why Gibson chose to use this particular mix of mahogany and maple. We know now, of course, that it was a happy combination. We think the mahogany does most for the tone of the Les Paul and that the maple probably adds some bite. But Gibson had no precedent to consider at the time: when they developed the Les Paul in the early 50s, Fender was one of the few companies making solidbody electrics, and they used ash for bodies.

When I asked Ted McCarty about his memories of the Les Paul's birth, when he was president at Gibson, he told me about the experiments they tried with different materials. "One of the things we did was to take a piece of iron rail from the railroad track," he said. "We put a bridge and a pickup and a tailpiece on it, and tested it. You could hit that string, take a walk, come back, and it would still be ringing. The thing that causes it to slow down when you use wood is that the wood 'gives' a little bit, you know?

"We made a guitar out of solid rock maple. Wasn't good. Too shrill, too much sustain," continued McCarty. "And we made one out of solid mahogany, but that was too soft a sound. Didn't quite have it. So we finally came up with a maple top and a mahogany back. We made a sandwich out of it by gluing them together.

"Then we wondered about the shape. We really wanted something that wouldn't be too heavy. The Fender was a larger guitar. So we made ours a little smaller bodied, in a traditional shape."[8] The Les Paul shape may have been partly based on the existing ES-140 electric archtop model that Gibson had introduced in 1950.

And then there's the carved top of the Les Paul, something that would mark out the new solidbody guitar as a Gibson, in contrast to the flat and relatively simply-produced competition from Fender. The maple was carved in the factory to produce the distinctive 'belly' in the bridge and tailpiece area – giving a similar look to Gibson's established archtop instruments and familiar to many players, but here done in solid wood. Tim Shaw thinks that Gibson probably used the same machine to carve the belly of the Les Pauls as they did for the archtops.

Some players and collectors have acquired a skewed impression about the workings of the Gibson factory back when these now-hallowed guitars were made. They seem to think that the workers were doing what they did for the benefit of later generations of guitar fans who want to carefully and methodically map out the chronologies and sequences of events. Not so. They were factory workers who were proud of their work, but who nevertheless needed to meet targets and get the product out of the door. Especially on Friday afternoon.

Max Baranet again: "I get a lot of people thinking that the details on these guitars are supposed to be exactly a certain way. Like the idea of the classic 59 top carve. Within reason, yes, there is a 59-style carve that is definitely different from what they started doing later when they reissued them, when they made that flatter. Every time I got a Burst in my shop, I would cut a template across the top to see what the contour looked like. They never came out the same. They wander to the left, they wander to the right; it was higher, lower, it was all over the place."

Many people – players, collectors, makers, restorers, wizards – are in awe of what is generally called (hushed tones, now) *old wood*. Baranet: "If you're spoiled by knowing a real 59 tone, you have to have the old mahogany to get it. If you haven't played these old guitars, you're not really going to miss it. I think that's why it's mostly us old-timers that are driving these prices sky high."[9]

Others think it's all part of an overplayed myth. Brown: "Any tree out of which you can get a Les Paul body, which is 14 inches across, has to be 28 inches in diameter, because you lose half the wood in bark and sapwood. A 28-inch tree is an old tree. They didn't give a damn about it being old wood in those days: it was wood. It was all around them and it was cheap."[10]

Once the wood shop at Gibson had worked its magic – or had simply done its job, if you take a more pragmatic view – then the paint shop got hold of the instrument. The new sunburst finish that Gibson began to apply to the maple top of the Les Paul in 1958 was unlike the sunburst they traditionally offered as an option on most of their archtop models, acoustic or electric.

A sunburst finish is supposed to conjure up the real thing: colour is added to the guitar's top to create a bright centre that darkens toward the edges. It's an attractive look when done well, and you could argue that it's not just an allusion to the visual qualities of a real burst of sunlight, but also a hint at the sonic qualities of a good instrument, where sound radiates from the guitar in beautiful waves. Or something like that.

Anyway, traditionally, Gibson's sunbursts were darker than the type they introduced on the 1958 Les Paul. For Gibson, sunburst as we know it had begun back in the 20s when a gifted designer at the company, Lloyd Loar, developed a quartet of acoustic instruments known as the Master Series. Launched in 1922, Loar's guitar, mandolin, mandola, and mandocello were full of innovation – and they came with what was called a 'cremona' finish, a shaded brown sunburst. Gibson would use variations on this look for years to come.

Now, for the Les Pauls, Gibson used two colours, red and yellow, to create a bright and cheerful sunburst. How exactly did they achieve this finish? Yet again, no one knows for sure, but educated guesses make for a reasonably clear picture.

Clay Harrell is a guitar collector who has studied finishes and paint techniques, and he offers a comprehensive guide to what may well have happened at the Gibson shop in Kalamazoo around 1959 when a worker came to paint a Les Paul sunburst. The sequence of events was probably: add red pore filler to back and sides of body and back of neck and headstock; apply clear lacquer; spray or stain yellow colour on to front; apply clear lacquer; spray red colour on to front; apply clear lacquer(s).

If you take a look at the mahogany back of the body and neck of a Les Paul sunburst model you'll notice that classic cherry finish; sometimes faded now, sometimes not. The 'pore filler' is what the worker would use to prepare (and dye) the mahogany. "Because mahogany is an open-pore wood, you have to fill the pores," explains Harrell. "Lacquer will always shrink, so if you don't fill the pores with something, then the finish sinks down into the pores and you don't get that nice smooth look."

The pore filler was largely silica, like fine sand, mixed into a turpentine-like base and, in this case, a red aniline dye was also added, all mixed up to the consistency of mud. The worker would brush on the red mud, let it dry, and then scrape it off, leaving the silica in the pores of the wood and a red-dyed mahogany. "Then they shot clear lacquer over the top of that," says Harrell. "That's the way it looks to me."

There was no need to pore-fill the maple because it is a closed-pore wood and offers a smooth surface to take the finish. So next comes the yellow 'middle' of the sunburst on the front of the guitar, achieved with dyed lacquer.

"Lacquer is a clear coat," explains Harrell, "like the film that ends up on the top of the guitar. But you can tint the lacquer different colours and use it that way, adding either a translucent or an opaque colour. The red in the sunburst, for example, is a translucent alcohol-based aniline that you can mix directly into the lacquer. Lacquer is full-bodied, maybe the consistency of cooking oil, where the alcohol-based aniline is the consistency of water."

Significantly, the lacquer that Gibson used in the 50s and into the 60s was nitro-cellulose based. Gibson's supplier was probably Forbes Finishes, a Detroit-based automotive and industrial coatings manufacturer. This kind of paint was relatively dangerous – the clue is in the 'nitro' of the name – and so today, while it is still available, it is less widely used. The nitro-cellulose formulation available today is different, too. Harrell says it has more plasticisers now, designed to prevent checking and crazing.

There is some debate about how the first yellow lacquer was applied to the maple top of a Les Paul. Was it 'shot' (sprayed) or 'stained' (brushed or rubbed) on to the maple? Harrell thinks brushed. He has looked closely at chips and dings in the finish of original Bursts and noticed that the wood surface looks yellowish. "That isn't 100 per cent proof that the wood was stained yellow, because wood over time goes yellow from UV light. But to me it looks like the wood was stained yellow."[11]

Restorer Clive Brown reckons they used both methods. "For the first ones, in 58, I think they were spraying on coats of yellow lacquer until they got the desired yellow. By 59, they'd gone to dyeing the wood yellow. I don't know why they changed, but it was probably down to cost. You have to guess at those things now. Dyeing the yellow was probably a bit quicker: you can just brush it on or rub it on with a cloth."[12] A bonus of adding yellow to the maple was that this would enhance and animate any figure in the wood. That's because alcohol-based aniline dye is absorbed inconsistently. "In a piece of figured maple," says Harrell, "the areas that have flame are a different hardness than the surrounding maple. These will absorb the dye differently, and that's how you get that on-fire look. The dye absorbs differently into the different fibres of the wood – and you end up with better flame.

"You can pick up a piece of raw maple and say, oh, this wood is not very flamey. Then you wipe it down with some yellow aniline dye, and all of a sudden you'll be saying: wow! It really brings out the figure in the wood."

With the yellow in place, the sunburst effect was completed with red-tinted lacquer, and there's general agreement that the guy at the Gibson paint station would probably spray this on.

At times, Gibson also made some Bursts with a darker 'tobacco' sunburst, using a slightly different colour at this stage. There is speculation that it was done to guitars that had any faults or anomalies at the edges of the top. Duane Allman's second Burst, nicknamed Hot 'Lanta, is a well known example of a tobacco sunburst (sometimes known now as a darkburst). "To finish," says Harrell, "there would be a couple of coats of clear lacquer over the colour. Result: one Gibson Les Paul sunburst."[13]

These original colours can fade over time. In particular, the red element in the sunburst fades. "The first Les Paul sunbursts, in 58, seem to keep the colour rather better," says Brown. "But Fender and Gibson had the same problem: from about late 1958 through to the end of 59, the red pigment is prone to fade out, apparently through exposure to natural daylight. The dye they used then wasn't colourfast."[14]

Gibson were certainly aware of this soon after introducing the new sunburst look, because they sent a note to store owners, which read: "In order to preserve the delicate coloring of this beautiful Gibson instrument, avoid displaying in show windows where it will be subjected to direct or excessive sunrays." No doubt the Gibson dealers in California were more exercised by this notice than those in, say, Michigan.

The red-fading effect can lend an attractively aged quality to a Burst, sometimes in combination with a yellowing of the top clear lacquer, to create a look quite different from how the instrument started life around 50 years ago. Collectors have concocted names for the colour of faded Les Paul sunbursts – they might call this one a teaburst or that one a honeyburst in an attempt to describe the effects. Some guitars can fade so far they have a sort of green, or gold, or even grey look. It's another factor that adds to the notion that each Burst is a unique instrument with its own character and appearance.

During 1960, Gibson appears to have changed the red colour quite dramatically, and some Bursts from that year have a distinctly tangerine look. Colours will always vary, even when they're supposed to be uniform, as anyone who has bought paint at a professional supplier will know, or anyone who has bought carpet. When the paint or carpet store guy tells you he can't guarantee the colour from tin to tin or roll to roll, or from numbered batch to numbered batch, just imagine that problem magnified to industrial levels.

You'll have noticed that there are various items fitted to the body and neck of a sunburst Gibson Les Paul. While we're here, we ought to make a quick inventory. There are two plated metal strap buttons. There is a plastic pickguard, which is fitted to the body with a screw at the neck and a screw into a metal bracket, down near the bridge pickup, that in turn is screwed to the side of the body.

There are two plastic plates on the back of the body, held in position with screws. The larger one covers a pocket containing the electrical components and wiring. In there are four CTS potentiometers ('pots'), a couple of capacitors, a couple of ground (earth) wires, some braided and shielded connecting wires, and military-spec solder joints to hold it all together. The small round plate covers a hole that contains the body of the selector-switch mechanism. There is a metal output jack (socket) on the side of the body, below and behind the control knobs. It has a plastic cover secured with four screws.

There are four clear plastic control knobs on the front of the body, with gold-painted bases that make them look gold-tinted. Each is attached to the top of one of the shafts of the four pots. The knobs are known now as bonnet, bell, or top-hat types for their shape in profile, and each has a small metal pointer-dial fixed underneath. During 1960, a metal cap was added to the top of each knob.

Looking down as you play the guitar, the knob nearest the tailpiece is for neck volume, and to the right of that for neck tone. The two knobs below are bridge volume (left) and bridge tone (right).

There is a nickel-plated zinc-alloy Tune-o-matic bridge, Gibson's model ABR-1, with six brass saddles and two plated zinc adjustment wheels, and a separate nickel-plated aluminium tailpiece that locks on to two mounting studs. There is a three-way pickup selector switch with plastic tip and a surrounding plastic ring (nicknamed the 'poker chip') that has Rhythm and Treble printed on it. In the Rhythm position the switch selects the neck pickup, in Treble the bridge pickup, and in the centre both pickups.

There are pearloid plastic position markers, of trapezoidal shape, inlaid into the fingerboard at the third, fifth, seventh, ninth, twelfth, fifteenth, seventeenth, nineteenth, and twenty-first frets. These are known now as crown markers because of their shape. There is a hard plastic nut at the top of the fingerboard, which stops and spaces the strings here.

There are six Kluson tuners fitted to the headstock (or peghead). They each have a closed metal back and a plastic acorn-shape button on a thin metal shaft. This plastic darkens with age and is notoriously prone to shrinkage. An extra ring was added to the existing one at the base of the button late in 1960. There is an inked-on serial number on the rear of the headstock, under the clear lacquer. The first digit – 8, 9, or 0 – indicates the year of production – 1958, 1959, or 1960.

There is a two-ply black/white plastic cover on the headstock fixed with two screws, to hide the truss-rod adjustment channel. There is a 'Gibson' logo and a 'Les Paul Model' logo on the headstock. And there are twohumbucking pickups.

Ah yes, the humbucking pickups. If the body and neck of the Les Paul sunburst model imply some kind of corporeal entity, with the finish its skin, then the pickups are without question this guitar's heart. These two humbucking pickups link to the Burst's controls and feed the signal out to an amplifier. They are probably more bound up in myth and half-truth and speculation than any other component of this already enigmatic guitar.

But first, let's consider some pickup facts. A humbucking pickup is intended to reduce the hum and electrical interference that afflicts regular single-coil pickups. The ability to 'buck' or cut this hum provides its name.

The relatively simple secret that turns a pickup into a humbucker is that it has two coils wired together electrically out of phase and with opposite magnetic polarity. The result is a unit less prone to picking up extraneous noise, and incidentally providing a tone that some players have come to love.

There isn't much to a Gibson humbucker when you look at in isolation. The two bobbins inside are wound with 42-gauge plain enamel wire. One has slugs, the other adjustable screws with a tiny metal keeper bar underneath. There's an Alnico magnet of type II or V, depending on what Gibson's suppliers had available. There's a piece of wood acting as a spacer. There's a baseplate and a cover. There's a plastic cut-out to hold it to the body. Plus a little wiring. That's about it. Simple but effective. Who better to talk to about all this than Seth Lover, the inventor of Gibson's humbucking pickup? I was lucky enough to be invited to Lover's home in Garden Grove, California, back in 1992. He lived up to his name. He was a lovely man: unassuming, friendly, and bright as a button. He was 82 when we met. I was very sad when I heard of his death five years later.

At home in Garden Grove, I sat with Lover at his dining table. He told me how he'd worked in radio and electronics in the 40s – occasionally for Gibson, occasionally for the US Navy. As a Kalamazoo native he was well aware of Gibson, and eventually, in 1952, he joined the company's electronics department full-time, working alongside Walt Fuller. Lover stayed there for 15 years until he moved out to California when Fender offered him a job.

While Seth scurried off to his workshop at the side of the house to find what he called "some of my old stuff", his wife Lavone – and there's a name, Lavone Lover – said that she rather wished that her husband had stayed in the Navy, because she adored travelling. She bemoaned the attitude that deemed people over 65 automatically useless. "When you're 64 years, 11 months, and 29 days you're fine," she said. "Next day, you're too old."

Seth at 82 was quite clearly still buzzing with ideas and schemes. He returned from the workshop with a couple of pickups. First, he showed me the Alnico pickup he'd designed for Gibson, the one it used in the neck position on the Les Paul Custom in 1954. Gibson had made pickups since its first electric guitars appeared in the 30s, with the single-coil P-90 model one of its best.

Lover put down the Alnico and picked up the other unit he'd set on the table. This, he said casually, was a sample he'd hand-made to show Gibson the design of his humbucker. I pinched myself. There it was, fitted into an old cut-down P-90 mounting ring. Pickup history of the most exciting order. I was not dreaming.

Did someone at the company want him to design a humbucker, to get rid of the hum problem of single-coil pickups? "Oh no," said Lover. "Ted McCarty just wanted me to build a new pickup. And I thought, well, why don't we get an improvement? Because every time you got a regular guitar near an amplifier, you had to twist yourself to get away from the hum. I knew there were humbucking choke coils, so why can't we build a humbucking pickup?"

A choke coil, he told me, is where you have two coils "wound and connected just right" to eliminate any hum pick-up. "We used it in audio amplifiers at Gibson in the early 50s, where we had a tone choke. If you put an ordinary single-coil in there it would pick up hum from the power transformer. I didn't want that. So I had them make me a humbucking choke coil."

I asked Lover how he developed the humbucking pickup from this prototype, the one he was toying with on the dining table here. "Well, we never sold any like this," he laughed, pointing at the two rows of crude circular indentations in the top. Gibson's sales people asked Lover if he could put some adjustment screws on the top of the pickup, so they would have something to talk about when they came to introduce it to music-store owners. He dutifully added them to the production model.

So these six adjustment screws were not a practical requirement, then, but a sales point? "They weren't really necessary," said Lover, "because this pickup was very sensitive. You could pull it up close to the strings, so long as when you picked on the strings they didn't buzz against the cover. I set the pickups in the guitar with the screws of one pickup toward the bridge and the other toward the fingerboard. People wanted to know why I did that." Presumably some technical reason? "I did it for decorative purposes," explained Lover, laughing again.

Lover said he originally started work on his humbucker design in 1955. Across their dining table, Seth's wife Lavone smiled, no doubt thinking back to happy times in Kalamazoo. Gibson's new humbucking pickups began to appear on instruments during the early months of 57. The Les Paul Goldtop switched from P-90 single-coils to humbuckers that year. The new pickups were in place on the model when the finish was changed to sunburst the following year. On those sacred guitars, they conjure up one of the most appealing and conducive guitar sounds ever.

I asked Lover if he was aware of the trend that started in the 60s with players removing the metal covers from the humbuckers, thinking it would give them a better sound. The question kept Lover in a jovial mood. First, he told me how he chose the material for the cover. "That pickup had a good treble," he said, "because of the type of cover material. If it was brass it would deaden it, and aluminium too would have deadened the high end.

"I went through the chemical handbooks and looked at metals that had a high resistance, not low resistance. And I found that non-magnetic stainless steel, which this sample happens to be, has high resistance. Only thing was, you can't solder to it. Nickel silver has high resistance, and I tried different covers to see what effect they would have. Nickel silver and stainless steel did not affect the high frequency response. So I picked out the nickel silver because you could solder to it." Nickel silver is a silver-coloured alloy of copper and nickel, nothing to do with real silver.

And what about the players who take off the covers? Lover said that gold-plated covers would also damp the high frequencies, because gold is a good conductor. "I think one of the reasons why, all at once, the guys started taking the covers off the pickups is that, somewhere along the line, someone had a gold-plated or a brass cover on his, and when he took it off he noticed that difference in sound. So he left it off."

And everyone else started taking them off – even if, technically, there should be very little effect on the sound if their Burst came with the regular nickel covers. No matter what they thought they heard. "The only difference is that a nickel-silver cover helps to prevent pick-up from fluorescent and neon lamps. That was my reason for using a cover," said Lover.

I asked him what he thought of a couple more bits of folklore surrounding the now revered early models of the Gibson humbucker. Once the covers came off the pickups, it became evident that the butyrate plastic used for the two bobbins inside might be coloured black or white or a combination of the two. Some guitar nuts even became convinced that this could indicate better tone, rating them (in descending order of desirability): double-white; zebra (one black bobbin, one white); and double-black. "I don't think that had a darned thing to do with it," laughed Lover.

"We used to buy our pickup bobbins and covers from a company over in South Haven, Michigan, called Hughes Plastics. They ran out of black material but they had white. We were not going to stop production just for that. So we got white bobbins – and I couldn't see any difference one from the other. I think white was a better colour for winding, because you could see the wire in there a lot easier than you could with the black. The wire was dark brown enamelled wire, and number 42 was the standard wire size for years."

The other matter I brought to Lover's attention was the decal with 'Patent Applied For' that was stuck to the base of Gibson humbuckers from 1958 for about four years or so. These pickups are now known among collectors and players as PAFs and are considered by some as the best-sounding examples.

"They put that decal on," he explained, "because they started making humbuckers before they actually got the patent – so the patent was 'applied for'. Gibson didn't want to give others any information as to what patent to look up to make copies. I think that was the reason for it, because they carried on for quite a while."[15]

Lover said that as far as he knew there were no significant changes made to the pickups immediately following the move from the PAF decals to the patent-number decals. And the patent number quoted was 'mistakenly' that for a tailpiece and not the humbucker. So even then, Gibson managed to continue to baffle potential copyists. The patent-number pickups lasted from about 1962 to 64 or 65. After that, aficionados say, the pickups changed and are not worth getting up for. Although, of course, many players have found them more than acceptable.

They can be remarkable, the original humbuckers – PAF or patent-number. In the Burst they seemed to find a fitting home – and only about a year after they had been introduced. It was almost as if Gibson in general and Lover in particular had known precisely what would be needed.

Looked at from where we are now, we have to consider all this in the context of the evident contrast between the guitar industry in the 50s and what we have today. Now, there are dozens of different kinds of pickups to tease the imaginations of players, and many, many makers who offer everything from regular, basic models to highly developed devices that are said to offer great tone, low noise, high power, or whatever combination provides this month's fashionable flavour. The vintage tone of a Gibson PAF or patent-number humbucker remains a measure for some players against which newer pickups are measured. Other musicians don't even consider the old styles and instead want a modern tone from a modern pickup. There is no shortage of choice.

One of those makers, who naturally has to consider such things on a daily basis, is Jason Lollar. He set up Lollar Pickups near Seattle, Washington, in the mid 90s, although he's been making pickups since the 70s. He offers about 35 pickup models – for six-string, bass, and steel – and makes three variants on the PAF-style humbucker. Those old 'uns are obviously an inspiration for any pickup maker.

"Absolutely," says Lollar. "They generally have a good sound and a real clear tone with some detail at the high end. They tend not to be as muddy sounding as a lot of humbuckers, but mostly it's this real clear harmonic structure that marks them out."

He says that everything in an original humbucker has an effect on the tone, that different materials used for the metal parts, including the screws and slugs and so on, will make the pickup sound brighter or smoother, make it distort a little bit faster, make it cleaner, whatever. Lollar has taken apart old Gibson humbuckers, made new pickups with old parts, tried every combination of old and new materials, all to see if he can hear or measure any differences. Mostly he trusts his ears rather than what measuring tools might tell him. And there are differences, he's decided.

"We're talking split hairs, right? But the thing I discovered is that a lot of the sound is in the materials they used." So if you could duplicate the old materials – and that's actually a very big if, full of complications and contradictions – but if you could copy them, you could duplicate the old sound?

"I don't know if you'd get exactly the sound," he smiles, "but you'd get something that was close. I've done that using old parts and there's a distinct tone to it. But that's not something that everyone wants. There are a lot of guys who will try to copy the exact details, but they miss the overall picture. I use my ears more."

Something that Lollar has analysed with machines are the Alnico magnets Gibson used in their old humbuckers. To destruction, in fact. His conclusion is that, back then, there were more impurities mixed in with the basic Alnico metals – aluminium, nickel, and cobalt – than there are in modern Alnico magnets.

"Those differences have an effect on the performance and outcome. I don't have enough samples to know whether or not that varies between every batch of magnets that Gibson bought back in the 50s. But you can determine that they're a little bit different from the magnets you get today."

How close are Lollar's humbuckers he makes today to a good PAF or patent-number Gibson humbucker from the late 50s and early 60s? "They have many of the same characteristics," he says. "But … the only way to get a PAF is to go out and buy a PAF." He laughs at this statement, knowing that it's just as well he doesn't work for a big corporation with PR people and suchlike. They would have just disappeared out of that open window over there. Three floors up.

"On my stock Imperial humbucker," says Lollar, "the bottom end is a little tighter than a PAF, which I think is a good thing. It has some of those extended overtones, but they are a little bit smoother. So they're similar. But they're different."[16]

Let's call on a few more views on the ancient art of humbucking before we draw this section to a close. I know some of you will be suffering from technical overload, and that is never pretty.

David Wilson is the man who since 1999 has run *The ToneQuest Report*, a subscription-only magazine that describes itself as "the player's guide to ultimate tone". In a couple of recent issues he organised an in-depth investigation into Gibson humbuckers.

Wilson and his team did this by spending a day with a collection of six original 1959 Bursts, intently listening to musician Jonn Richardson playing them, as well as examining, testing, and listening to multiple sets of PAF and patent-number humbuckers. "Even more so than the physical attributes and the variations," says Wilson, "we wanted to totally digest the sound of those guitars and pickups and how they varied one from the other."

I wondered if Wilson had become more or less in awe of Gibson's classic humbuckers after doing all that work. "I personally am more," he says. "My case leans to their clarity and extraordinary string definition. They have a great deal of presence in the bridge position, and there isn't anything 'warm' about them, as some people say. The highs aren't rolled off and they aren't midrangey. In the neck position, it's even more startling how bright and snappy those pickups are. Clarity is the big underline every time, where every string blooms on its own, where there's a dynamic response to pick attack instead of this flat, linear thing that you get with many modern pickups. But it all comes down to personal taste."[17]

Clive Brown puts it like this: "Normally with humbuckers, you find in your neck position it's muddy and in your bridge position it's a bit clangy or nasally. But when you plug in a good one, the pickups are balanced great and everything works together. Wow!"[18]

Wilson continues: "People will say ah yes, but these pickups have aged, and that's why they sound the way they do now. Well, most of the seminal albums that we know and love that have PAFs on them, dating back to the Clapton *Beano* album, featured guitars that were barely ten years old. So how do you explain that?"

Wilson says that he has heard what he describes as "stellar examples" of Gibson humbuckers from the PAF and the patent-number periods. "We heard some pickups – a few – among those six 59s that lacked a little something. I can't tell you whether that was attributable to the pickups more than the guitar: who knows? But I don't think you have to have a PAF rather than a patent-number pickup to get the sound.

"I couldn't tell you whether the Bursts we favoured in our tests were stand-outs more because of the pickups or more so because of the happy accident of the way the guitar came together," says Wilson. He shrugs, as many do when confronted with the mystery of these instruments. "We'll never know."[19]

You'll remember that Tim Shaw at Gibson investigated the old Bursts for some of the early reissues from the 80s. He soon heard about the way things were back in the 50s and 60s. "When I got there in 1978, low seniority in the factory was 18 years. So at that point, everyone I knew in the building had started in 1960 or earlier. Obviously processes evolve, but in any company there is an institutional mindset, and there are some things I saw that were obviously pretty much unchanged, and with no reason to change them."

Shaw made the working assumption with pickups that there were no exotic or unusual materials involved back around 1959. "I assumed that everybody did pretty much the same thing: you bought something you can get relatively easily and you use the hell out of it. So any 'magic' that exists is accidental magic."

Shaw is an ideal guide because – as you can tell from what he said just there – he is enamoured of the sound of the old guitars but entirely down-to-earth, and well informed, about how it all happened. It's as well to have such a clear head on our side in these matters.

I ask him my favourite to-the-nub question. If his time machine was jammed on the "1959, Kalamazoo" setting – a known fault for the model available to my interviewees – then what would he go looking for in the Gibson factory? Shaw knows guitar factories inside out; he's been all over them, right around the world, since the 70s. But if he could hang longer in one spot during this time-machine visit, he decides, it would be in Gibson's pickup area.

"Just because that's where a lot of the voodoo creeps in," he explains. "I would want to see if they magnetise them. That to me is just the biggest weird question." This is pretty technical stuff. It has to do with isotropic materials – those that have a preferred direction of orientation – and it has to do with the efficacy of the resulting pickup. Suffice to say that Shaw has a suspicion that Gibson magnetised the humbuckers before rather than after assembly, but he'd really like to know which.

He would also want to drop by the area in the factory where the pickups were wound. He is not alone is this desire. The women who did this work at Gibson in our preferred period have become legendary. They were responsible for operating the machines upon which the pickup bobbins were wound with wire.

"I'd walk over to the coil winders and see what the tension was," says Shaw. "There are a bunch of apocryphal stories about all that. Seth Lover was once asked what the winding spec was, and he said they wound them until they were full.

"Now then, that's not really much of a spec! Five-thousand turns of plain enamel wire is the spec – because 10,000 turns of plain enamel is what went on the P-90 pickup, and they just cut it in half for each coil of the humbucker.

"With plain enamel wire, 6,000 turns pretty well stuffs them to the gills – you can't get more on them. And if you look at them, they're not stuffed to the gills. With 5,000 turns they look pretty good."[20]

ZZ Top guitarist Billy Gibbons took a visit to the Gibson factory. Not by time machine but in the actual year of 1971. Not exactly golden period, it's true, but six or seven years after the end of the great pickup era is closer than most guitar nuts have managed to get. "It was dead of winter, snowing like crazy, but we got the 50 cent tour, the whole bit, top to bottom," reports Gibbons.

"We went up to the room where they were making humbucking pickups. We saw the original machine that the famous PAFs were made on. Three ladies were operating the machine. It was a long rod, running left to right, with three wrapping points: one on the left end, one in the centre, and one on the right end. These ladies would slide a pickup bobbin down to the centre and put one on either end."

The winding women would use .42 gauge enamel wire on a spool under a glass dome, Gibbons remembers from his early-70s visit. The wire was fed through a hole in the top of the dome.

"They would put this wire on to each bobbin," Gibbons continues, "and they had something like the winding stem on a wristwatch, connected to a counter. You could set how many turns you wanted the motor to spin. Once the wires were in place, they'd hit a switch, the motor would start spinning the rod, and the bobbins would be flying, dragging the wire off the spool.

"There was a guide that went left to right, much like a fishing rod has, allowing the wire to be laid into the bobbin in a fairly sophisticated way, left to right, right to left, and so on."

Gibbons says that when the clicker hit the defined number of turns, it would trigger the off switch. "What I noticed – and this is probably why some humbuckers sound different, with more oomph or power – is that the ladies had a footbrake, a long bar.

"When the motor stopped, it would make a noticeable click, so that they knew that particular bobbin was complete. They would step on the brake and it slowed the turning mechanism. And if they were talking, well … when we were there, we noticed they didn't always step on the brake straight away, so another couple hundred turns got put on the bobbin. It was not an exact science."[21]

It was not an exact science. This might well be the catchphrase that sums up the entire story of the guitar we have under our microscope. Science is, anyway, something of a misused term when it's related to guitar-making. Certainly there is some science involved – inevitable when you're dealing with the physics of a musical instrument, especially an electric one – but an individual maker is more inclined to be concerned with the art of guitar making. Big companies like Gibson, however, need to come up with a way of combining the two, of merging a little art into a little science, all in the cause of producing a good instrument that players will want to buy.

The inexact science Gibson employed explains why the sunburst Les Pauls from 1958–60 are individuals. It is also why some are better than others. And it is why collectors who acquire one of these often remarkable guitars will usually find themselves soon wanting another example: perhaps it will be better; certainly it will be different.

That is why Tim Shaw says that the Gibson factory at the time was made up of decent, solid Midwestern folks trying their best to do a good job.

"But, with the best will, they were not guitar people. Players came in and said gee, it would work better if you did such-and-such. Now, in terms of all the structural stuff, in terms of all the engineering stuff, nobody had an idea that 50 years or whatever later, here we would be with people going wow, I wonder why they did *that?* They must have *known something.*"

He laughs out loud at the idea. "They didn't!"

Gibson, says Shaw, was a pretty disciplined organisation back around 1959 or so. They had access to the best woodworking materials and machinery in the world. They had a lot of pride in what they were making. "Because they firmly believed they were making the best guitars in the world."[22] And very often they were.

9. REISSUE

Gibson gets really serious about recreating its valuable past

Before we get going here, onward into our quest to find a million-dollar sunburst Les Paul, let's briefly recap the story of this instrument so far – from the manufacturer's point of view. Over to you for a few moments, Gibson.

OK, we launched our debut solidbody electric guitar, the Les Paul model, in 1952, about two years after Fender's industry-first. Changed the pickups to humbuckers in 57 and the finish from gold to sunburst the following year. We dumped it in 60, after sales were still sluggish, and replaced it with the modern SG solidbody. Then – what do you know? – guitarists started rediscovering the old-style Les Pauls, and we were forced to reissue it in 68. Apparently we didn't reissue the right versions.

So, we stumbled through the 70s, and still with not-right reissues, according to the vintage guys. But we did knock up some custom jobs for a handful of specialist stores who seemed to want Les Pauls just like we made 'em in the 50s, sunburst top and all. No idea why, but business is business.

These guys wanted what they called the 'correct' narrower headstock, the 'correct' thin binding in the cutaway, the 'correct' shape of top carve, and, oh, a ton of other tiny details. In fact, they wanted a Les Paul just like we used to make. By 76 we even had one of our own on the pricelist, the Standard. Still not right! screamed those damn vintage nuts.

Come the 80s, well, we figured, maybe there really was a market for good new versions of the old 'uns. So we made some Heritage Standard models, and quite a decent stab at a reissue they were, if we say so ourselves. More store guys lined up wanting the old look and feel, so we made a few more of those. About 83, we introduced some Burst-like guitars that we officially called reissues. But it would take another ten years to get properly into all that.

Recap over. Gibson gets back to work. J.T. Riboloff joined the company in 1987, moving to Nashville from his home in California where he'd worked as a guitar maker, repairer, and restorer. He was hired for Gibson's Custom Shop and soon became involved in work on new designs and reissues. "When I went there, the Les Paul reissue was basically a regular Standard with a flame top," he says. "Slowly but surely, they let us get away with a little more."

Tom Murphy was another important addition to the team that developed the reissues. He'd been at Gibson since 89, and a few years later he moved from the finish repair department to the Custom Shop. As a player, he'd been attracted over the years by several of Gibson's attempts to recapture past glories.

"I'd owned two of the reissues made for Texas dealer Jimmy Wallace, for example," Murphy recalls, "and I would fantasise that I was getting a real good copy of an old Les Paul. But I'd soon get disenchanted and wonder why I thought they were going to be anything close to the original. They never cut it!

"Without having any vast knowledge of construction, I found that something just wasn't right with the overall feel. I wished someone at Gibson who knew would fix it. Don't they have any old Les Pauls they can look at? Then I thought, well, I guess mother nature never intended for us to have those guitars again. These days, I don't know why I thought it was that complicated."

Once at Gibson, Murphy began to appreciate the practical – and the political – considerations necessary to produce a good, acceptable reissue.

Riboloff had found that a lot of players who asked him to build special one-off Les Pauls were requesting the slimmer-profile neck associated with the 1960 Burst. Gibson boss Henry Juszkiewicz couldn't help but notice a loud E chord of excitement when a sample was shown at a trade show, and he told Riboloff to start work on a production version. This appeared in 1990 and was called the Les Paul Classic. "One of my main things," says Riboloff, "was to try to get the stock instrument as cool as the custom ones. That's how the Les Paul Classic came about."

Juszkiewicz decided that the Classic had to stand out from the rest of the line and insisted on a bold '1960' logo on the guitar's pickguard, emphasising the inspiration for its slim neck and 'correct' headstock size.

Riboloff's original intention had been to make the Classic with a relatively plain top and faded finish, resembling some of the less visually spectacular old Bursts that players like Jimmy Page would still occasionally take on stage. Later variants with more extreme figured tops were added, such as the Classic Premium Plus. But among all this retrospection, the sound of the Classic was definitely modern thanks to some very powerful coverless humbuckers.

A year later, in 1991, the Burst reissue was revised and split into two models, effectively the Standard 59 Flametop Reissue and the Standard 60 Flametop Reissue. This is where the proper, modern reissue started. Those guitars adopted the 'correct' details of the Classic model as well as more traditional-sounding humbuckers, as developed by Riboloff.

Juszkiewicz and his colleagues had owned Gibson now for several years. You'll recall that they had bought it from owner Norlin in 1985. They seemed to have a better awareness of the company's historical importance and recognised that many players and collectors placed a high value on some of the old achievements.

Beginning in 91, Riboloff worked on some commendable reissues of Gibson's oddball 50s solidbodys, the Flying V and the Explorer, as part of the company's Historic programme. Many people still use the Historic name as an all-purpose umbrella to refer to any of Gibson's reissues, no matter what Gibson called them at any particular time. The accuracy of Riboloff's work with the V and the Explorer set Tom Murphy thinking that perhaps the same thing really could be done with the Les Paul models.

"Early in 1992," Murphy recalls, "dealer Norm Harris ordered a more accurate Les Paul for his knowledgeable clientele. I fielded that order, and I told him what could and could not happen. Through that year, he received guitars that were really beautiful, with great tops. I did a few things to the body: flattened out the belly a little, for example. But no carving was re-established, no new body thickness, no new routing of the back – we would just give TLC to those orders.

"There were several other orders from stores all over the country for custom orders of Les Pauls," says Murphy. "I would paint them with a faded sunburst, or the lighter colour on the back. But the feeling was: when are we going to admit it and totally re-do the reissue Les Paul?"

As it turned out, it wouldn't be too long. He points to the significant arrival of A Marketing Manager Who Actually Owned A 1960 Burst. And, for once, one who understood the arguments. "He spoke the language," explains Murphy, evidently surprised by this trait in a marketing gent.

Murphy was invited to plant-management meetings. He presented a list of around 25 important changes that he said should be made to the reissue.

Gibson people set to work in an attempt to replicate more closely than ever the magic of an original sunburst Les Paul. Management supported the costly experiments. The 'new' reissue would have more accurate body carving, the smaller-size vintage-style headstock, a retooled fat neck-profile, holly veneer for the headstock face with a silkscreened logo, the most attractive figured maple for the top, a slight reduction in neck pitch, proper routing of the control cavity, an early-style Tune-o-matic bridge, and the reinstatement of a longer, wider neck tenon (or tongue) at the neck–body joint.

"It was a matter of retrieving all those things," says Murphy. "It was almost as if they'd been thrown out and scattered across the plant floor, swept under a table. They were here – somewhere. I won't take credit for designing the 59 Les Paul," he smiles. "That was done when I was nine years old. But I will take credit in unearthing and finding some of these key old things."[1]

Matthew Klein in the Custom Shop helped to establish the new shape for the body carving – the form, as it's known – by measuring every hundred-thousandth of an inch of the carving on a bunch of original Bursts and constructing a grid from which the production form was developed.

J.T. Riboloff reckons he examined maybe 25 different Bursts from the 1958–60 era. "They were all different," he laughs, pointing by way of example to the fact that no two headstocks were anything like the same. "The machine heads would be slightly further north or south, the scroll was shorter, and the logo would be different," he says, clearly exasperated by any attempt to find rules or uniformity among the output of the Kalamazoo plant in the late 50s.

"They were soft-tooled back then," explains Riboloff, meaning that the machines and tools and fixtures used to build the old guitars could be modified and adapted at will, as the circumstances dictated. "And so every guitar is different. Really, there is no super-correct one to reissue. Anyway, with these 25 to hand, we took the best attributes of each instrument – cosmetics, carving, and all – and combined them."

Riboloff explains that the escalating retail price of the reissues was another factor in concentrating the team's efforts at Gibson. "It got to the point where we wanted it to be more of a replica rather than a reissue," he says.[2] Keith Medley in R&D built the prototypes, and the results were proudly displayed to the public for the first time at the 1993 NAMM musical-instrument trade show. The 'new' revised and improved Les Paul Standard 59 Flametop Reissue had arrived, along with a similarly ravishing 60 (and a new Goldtop 57 Reissue).

I talked to British guitar-maker Roger Giffin at the time. Giffin had moved to California in the late 80s to set up a satellite workshop for Gibson on the West Coast, specialising in one-offs and artist instruments. This meant he had an interestingly detached-but-attached view of Gibson back then. "They're trying to resurrect as many of the original designs as they can," he said late in 92. "One or two people over in Nashville have gone to the trouble of finding things like original moulds to make pickup rings and all the original metalwork to make parts as they were made."

But, said Giffin, his experience indicated that Gibson simply didn't have very many of the original bits and pieces any more. "I asked them on numerous occasions what happened to the original tooling for this or for that, and they said, oh, it's at the bottom of Lake Michigan, used as boat anchors. They just dumped it. All the tools to make the tailpieces, vibrolas, whatever – all scrapped. Unbelievable! A total lack of foresight.

"Of course, the guitar nuts around the world all want Gibson to do accurate reissues, but they don't understand the problems there are in running a company of that kind," Giffin concluded. "Especially when they didn't keep all the old stuff to refer back to. All they've got is pictures and descriptions and occasional blueprints."[3]

Tim Shaw, who worked in Gibson R&D at the time, remembers that the company was intent on making the revised 93 reissues better all round. "At that NAMM show they finally said to the team OK, just go and do whatever you've got to do to get it right. For example, the early reissues still had the rather conventional one-inch-wide neck tenon that terminates short of the fingerboard end, where the new ones had the inch-and-a-half tenon that goes straight into the pickup pocket."

Shaw reports that Gibson had already started to re-establish good relations with its wood vendors, which he says had "slackened off" during the last years of Norlin, and now pushed to get those relationships fully up to speed.

"Gibson started buying decent curly maple again," says Shaw, "both the northwest type, which is the big-leaf, more brownish stuff, and the eastern maple, mostly still from northern Michigan, which is whiter and tighter-grain. Elsewhere, there was a general conscious attempt at Gibson to get as close as the technology of the time would permit, including getting a new carver and working hard at getting to the 'correct' arch on the top."[4]

Further improvements were made following that serious fresh start in 93, since when reissue Bursts have been in and out of the Gibson line with various model names. Usually there's a 1958, 1959, and 1960 model, sometimes with options on quality of top figure and aged finish.

Over the years, the Historic reissues have been continually and gently tweaked in the Custom Shop to bring them closer than ever to the original instruments of those hallowed three years. No detail has been too small for attention.

Take the serial number, for example, which on original-period Pauls is ink-stamped on to the rear of the headstock. As any Les Paul forger will tell you, it is very hard to get close to the typeface and style and ink-colour of the original numerals. Gibson faced the same problem. Tom Murphy, who worked at Gibson on the reissues in the early 90s, takes up the story. "At first, back then, I'd asked our normal stamp supplier for a smaller typeface, because we'd had odd-shaped, bulky numbers through the 80s," he says.

"We ended up realising that the original-style number was not produced any more, so we went 'below' it: smaller, with a more aesthetically pleasing look, in the right style but not the right size." That wasn't received well by the real buffs, says Murphy. "So we fixed that. We stumbled on a way to put those numbers on a stamp, in another configuration. From 1999, the number style changed again, and we were very happy with it. It wasn't exactly perfect, but it was in the right font, of the right height and the right width."[5]

Another strand of Gibson's relatively recently discovered interest in selling its illustrious past comes in the shape of so-called signature models, which means making copies of famous guitars owned by celebrity players, usually but not exclusively in limited Custom Shop runs. This was particularly appropriate for the Les Paul models, because the Les Paul Model itself had been the original signature solidbody electric guitar.

Not that anybody really bought a Les Paul guitar because they wanted to sound like Les Paul the musician. Depending on your viewpoint, you might say that's a sad fact. But Les's jazz-flavoured style – whether on his layered guitar-orchestra hits on Capitol (with and without Mary Ford), on his earlier Decca trio work, or even on the two entertaining duet records he made in the 70s with Chet Atkins – none of that admittedly good music is going to make you want to rush out and plug a humbucker'd Burst into a Marshall.

Les himself had endorsed Gibson's very first solidbody electric upon its launch back in 1952. But since then, no other musician's name had ever appeared alongside Mr Paul's on a production Gibson Les Paul. Arch-rival

Fender had re-popularised the idea of the signature model, starting with the Eric Clapton Stratocaster in 88. Gibson followed up by going for arguably the biggest name among the legion of famous Les Paul players, honouring Led Zeppelin's Jimmy Page with the first signature-edition Les Paul, launched in 95.

This first Page Paul lasted in the line for four years and accommodated the guitarist's request for an unusual neck shape and fret height. Page wanted the feel of his favourite Burst, known as Number 1, which meant low, low frets and a neck profile thinner at the seventh fret than the first, then fattening again toward the 12th. Visually, the guitar appeared as a basic Burst with a lightly-figured top, gold-plated hardware, and Page's which-way-is-up autograph logo on the pickguard.

The pickups were the powerful ones that had been used for the Classic, combined with a push-pull switch on each of the four control knobs (as on Page's Number 2 original). Depending on your requirements, this could seem like a wonderfully expansive range of tonal possibilities – or just too many choices.

In this way, the 95–99 Page Paul neatly highlights the major advantage and disadvantage of any signature instrument – whoever the artist might be, whoever the manufacturer is. The advantage for a fan is that, if you like the player concerned, you might feel a little closer to his style by owning one of these guitars.

The disadvantage for a musician is that it's unlikely that one player's specific requirements will match your own. It goes back to Les Paul himself, who constantly modified the guitars that Gibson would sent to him. As players, we adapt instruments to suit our own quirks, quite rightly oblivious of what anyone else might like or might think we should do. This is known as the artistic temperament. It is what drives artist managers mad. But that's another book.

More signature Burst-style Les Pauls have followed the original Jimmy Page model, named for Gary Moore (2000), Gary Rossington (02), another Page, more closely replicating his Number 1 (04), Slash (04), Duane Allman (06), and Warren Haynes (06), with an upcoming model in progress at the time of writing for Peter Green/Gary Moore.

Tom Murphy left Gibson in 1994 to set up his own Guitar Preservation company, specialising in guitar restoration, and now combines that with work for Gibson as a freelance. At his own workshop he developed his skills for refinishing and restoring old guitars. He found that it seemed natural to 'age' the finished job, blending in the new areas to sit more comfortably with the original worn guitar.

He wasn't alone in developing this technique, but many found him to be among the best. Some guitar repairers had, like Murphy, been using a version of the idea in their own work, making good after visible repairs to merge them into the overall look and feel of an older instrument. But why has it become so popular in recent years?

Murphy thinks it's down to the scarcity of vintage guitars. Years ago there was a good supply of original instruments about. "If a guitar was refinished because of someone's ignorance," he says, "like I had to do many times, or attempted as part of a repair, it denigrated the guitar. But back then there was an alternative. In those days there would be an original instrument available at a reasonable price."

Back when a particular original vintage model might sell for, say, $400, while a refinished one was just $100, it was an easy and relatively cheap decision to go for the original. Even when the original became $2,000 and the refinished one $800, you'd probably still want to buy the original.

"But as the availability of the original instruments diminished and the prices skyrocketed," says Murphy, "the viability and the option of restoring an old one has now become more necessary, out of practicality. And it's more accepted, because we've all had to say, well, it's not that big a deal if the paint has been redone on a Strat body or whatever. I'm a purist as much as anyone else. I'd rather they were all original guitars. But you can't always have that now."

So Murphy developed his ability to make a guitar look 'right' that had been repaired or restored by using ageing techniques. Fender introduced its aged Relic series in 1995 after Keith Richards complained that some replica guitars made for him by the company's Custom Shop for a Stones tour would look better if, as he put it, they "bashed them up a bit".

There followed a line of new Fender Strats and Teles with wear-and-tear distress marks added to the finish and the hardware to make them look as if they'd been knocked around on stage and on the road for years. At first this work was outsourced by Fender to Vince Cunetto. The success of Fender's Relic scheme popularised the general term that's now used – it's known as relic'ing. The technique did not go unnoticed at Gibson HQ in Nashville.

Murphy was doing the same thing to selected models in the Les Paul reissue line. He prefers to call it a 'broken-in' feel rather than an aged look. "I do whacky things to the finish that simulate things that old guitars encounter over the years," says Murphy, "like heat, cold, scratching, dinging, all that kind of stuff. It somehow emulates all that."

The first to benefit was the Standard 59 Reissue Aged model, which officially started life as part of the Custom Shop line in 1999. The paint colours were made to appear faded. The nickel parts on the instrument, such as the pickup covers, were realistically tarnished. The lacquer 'skin' was checked and effectively dulled. Remarkably, the guitar really did look old and worn.

Gibson has used different names at different times for the ageing process – Custom Authentic from about 2001, and Vintage Original Spec (or V.O.S.)

from 2006 – but the idea remains the same. Like Fender and its Relics, Gibson aimed to recreate the almost indefinable attraction of an old vintage guitar but in a new instrument – and at a stiff price, of course.

Murphy tells me that the aged reissues profit from a combination of techniques that he reached to simulate wear on small areas of the guitar. But what's the secret of getting the aged look? "I can't tell you that," he laughs. "I can tell you it's done by hand, though – but that's just because it's the only way it can be done. I swear that if we could do it with a laser we'd have the laser version and the hand-done version. But we can't.

"It would be great if we had a magic box to put them in," says Murphy, "a time machine or something where we could just switch it on to, let's say, winter in Minnesota, 1959. But we can't do that."[6] Not yet, anyway.

A true cynic might even question Gibson's right to make reissues of old Gibson instruments at all. What's the connection, in fact? Gibson has been sold twice since the famed 1958–60 Bursts were made, and the company now resides in Nashville, many hundreds of miles south of Kalamazoo. Surely today it's just a brand, with no physical or practical links to the old factory and its workers and managers and production methods?

The Gibson company of today, with its headquarters in Nashville, naturally sees it differently. Perhaps it considers its Historic reissue programme as some kind of recompense for the imposition of owning the Les Paul name and yet not benefitting from any of the millions of dollars that have changed hands over the years for its old vintage collectables.

It's a bit like the idea that Bill Weasley tried to explain to Harry Potter in one of J.K. Rowling's books. "To a goblin, the rightful and true master of any object is the maker, not the purchaser. All goblin-made objects are, in goblin eyes, rightfully theirs. They consider our habit of keeping goblin-made objects, passing them from wizard to wizard without further payment, little more than theft."[7]

Leaving the goblins aside for a moment, we can see clearly that the lure of history is strong within the 21st century Gibson operation, despite the company's regular development of new models and original ideas. Even such an apparently modern phenomenon as the remarkably popular *Guitar Hero* video game – which has sold over 14 million copies since its launch in 2005 – features an unmistakable Les Paul-like wireless controller.

Edwin Wilson is the Historic Program Manager, Engineering, at Gibson's Custom Division, and he is precisely the person to tell us how the reissue programme is faring today. So it's there I go to meet him, at the Custom Shop, just along from the main Gibson building. He says that things have changed tremendously since the fresh start for reissues that happened in 1993, eight years after he joined the company.

"In 93, we were having to get production and manufacturing at Gibson to understand all these pretty major structural changes," says Wilson. "It was a 100 per cent improvement over previous guitars. There were some things about them that maybe weren't right, but that was the year of the learning curve on those guitars. The guys in production had to get used to doing things different to how they had in the past."

Wilson explains that it is often difficult to communicate to a Gibson factory worker the importance of what must seem like insignificantly tiny details. "A lot of the people that they hire are not really guitar aficionados, so when you say that you need to make a heel *this* shape, they don't really know what they're going after. You're trying to explain something without pictures.

"That part of it is still difficult. But they're all very willing to learn, as they were in the beginning. If they had been guitar collectors and really enthusiastic about it all, they would have looked at it and gone, well, yes, of course, I know what you're trying to do."

Wilson is very aware of the demand from reissue customers for what we might call 'vintage correct' details. And yet there is widespread disagreement on the details – not least because the original guitars do vary, one from another. Wilson, who seems like a patient man, sighs and tells me the current example.

"The latest thing I hear about is the material we use for our nut blanks. Before that it was the fingerboard inlays. And there's two questions I get asked most about the guitar itself. One is about the top 'dish' shape, and two is about the neck profile. Maybe guys own an original 50s Les Paul. The neck feels a certain way, and that's what they're used to. And then they buy one of our guitars and, naturally enough, it doesn't feel exactly like their own guitar."

There are several things that the Gibson Custom Shop does in construction of the reissue instrument that are 100 per cent period-correct, says Wilson. "If we didn't go out and get an original guitar and copy it identically, then we did go and look at several guitars and we came up with the sum of all those guitars."

So it must be frustrating when, say, someone approaches Wilson at a guitar show and complains that – what shall we choose? – when they complain that the dot on the i of the Gibson logo is in the wrong place. I should point out that I am not teasing Wilson here. This has been a genuine complaint. "At times it is frustrating," he smiles. "Not to hear someone say that, because I know that it's not in the right position. I'm one of them! The frustration can be to get some of those changes to happen here in our building at Gibson. That's my challenge, every day, 24 hours a day."

Sometimes, Gibson can get too close to the original specs for comfort. Several years ago, Wilson was talking about one of Gibson's original plastics vendors with a senior member of staff who had been with the company since the days of the original Bursts. Wilson was pleased, because he had managed to track down the vendor and was about to order some original plastic. And the senior man said no, that would not be a good idea.

"I asked him why. He says it's because we constantly had fires with that material. He told me they'd get it and put it up in the stockroom, it would sit around, and it got so hot up there that when you'd go up you'd see this stuff smoking."

That kind of information makes you think twice about replicating the past, says Wilson. "There are some things that I would have a very difficult time getting approved. Too much of a fire hazard! In order to do it right and get in the quantities that we'd need, we'd have to build a separate building and store that material in there – and that is just not practical."

How important is the Historic reissue business to the company now, I ask Wilson? "Gibson, as far as the guitars go, is a very diversified company," he says. "On one hand we have new technology, like the robot guitars, where we try to move ahead and take guitars to the next level. At our main plant I know they are experimenting with different types of neck joint, trying to progress that science, for example.

"But it's also very important at my end, in the Historic Program, because this is what Gibson is known for. This is something that has been around for well over 50 years. When someone says a Gibson, they know it's a Les Paul. And the iconic guitar for the company today is the flame-top Les Paul. It's all-important."[8]

Gradually, then, Gibson people have sifted through the old achievements, re-introducing old-style parts, tightening up on original dimensions, getting closer to the grail. Inevitably, the process has been a slow one to advance. Some collectors take the view that it is only in the most recent years that the Burst reissues have come anywhere near the originals they are meant to replicate.

Mike Slubowski has not only written about the reissues but has a fine collection of them alongside his three original Bursts. "That's really where I started with Les Pauls," he says. "I bought a couple of Standards and then quickly moved into the Historics. And they in turn probably drew me to think, well, maybe it's time for a real Burst.

"In 1999, when Gibson did the major upgrade to their Historic line and tried to make them more historically accurate, they made a couple hundred aged guitars by Tom Murphy, and I purchased one of those. That first year, they were marketed exclusively through Vintage World, a store in Rhode Island that is not in business any more."

I presume that Slubowski, who now has more than 25 reissues in his collection, rates Gibson's recent productions almost as highly as the originals. "I think, especially in these last few years, that they are making some superb instruments. I don't know why that is. I have a 2006 and it's probably my main stage guitar. They are pleking all of them now, so they come perfectly set up, and that one in particular rings like a bell." Pleking refers to the use of a Plek Pro machine at Gibson's Custom Shop that provides a more accurate finishing of an instrument's frets and nut, something a player is likely to appreciate almost immediately.

Slubowski's main criticism of the current Historics is a common one. "They've never gotten the necks right on them. The shape is just not like a 59 or 58," he says. "They're still making them too big, most of them, too rounded in the shoulders."[9]

Joe Ganzler, who runs a business authenticating original Bursts, is a fan of the earlier reissues. "I really like the early 90s ones from 93 and 94, the first Historic reissue, if you will. I grant you that the details are certainly far from the mark, but the thing that I like about those guitars, and especially the 94 Murphys, is that there was that level of care and attention and detail. Those guitars were literally handmade, but handmade with a care that just seems to be lacking in the last decade of manufacturing."

Ganzler visited Gibson's Custom Shop in 1995 and was blown away by the dedication and loyalty of the team. "It was like a little skunk works," he recalls. "They were off to the side, building these guitars. There was a little bit of arrogance, a lot of pride, and just a hell of a level of detail. That's what I see in those early Historics. Sure, they're dimensionally wrong, the routs are not correct, the pickup placement is not spot on. But the quality of the wood and the finish work is phenomenal."[10]

Tom Wittrock we've already met. He's been collecting Bursts and dealing in guitars for decades. "Most of the time when I see reissues, it's at the large guitar shows, where there are millions of guitars of all types. And most of the reissues that I have put my hands on, the necks do not feel like 50s necks at all," he says. "Still Gibson makes them this way, and apparently the buying public is happy with them this way. For me, they're not the same experience as the originals, but they are exceptional guitars – better than Gibson's production stuff. Close enough that the average great player would not care about the differences."

Wittrock has noticed the trend at some workshops to take a reissue Gibson and rejig it so that it might play or feel different. And, ideally, so that it sits a little closer to the original vibe. It is, he says, something we all hoped relic'ing would provide – not just to make new guitars look older, but to make them feel more comfortable, more broken-in. Like a favourite pair of shoes.

"Shoes don't feel as good new as they do when we've worn them for a week or two," says Wittrock. "People are having this done to reissue Les Pauls, quite expensively, and when it's done, the guitars feel and play drastically better, at least to my hands."[11]

Kim LaFleur heads up Historic Makeovers, one of the companies offering reissue upgrades. Together with Dave Johnson, LaFleur aims to turn a Gibson reissue into an old pair of shoes. Figuratively speaking. He has played guitar for more than 40 years and has what he describes as "a good size collection" of 50s Les Pauls. The idea for Makeovers came late in 2006 when someone showed him one of the latest Goldtop reissues by Gibson. "I had eight 50s Goldtops of my own. I said, well, there's always something about these Historics – they get it to a certain point, but then they don't follow through on a few appointments. And then, afterward, I got to thinking more about it."

LaFleur called Johnson, a guitar restoration specialist, with a specific query: if he sent over a Historic reissue, could Johnson remove the neck 'shoulders'? "That was the one thing that bothered me the most about the Historics," says LaFleur.

"All the 50s Les Pauls I own had a different feel as far as the depth of the neck goes – some bigger, some thinner – but they all felt better than the Historics, which felt awkward. So I thought we could improve the Historics by shaving the shoulders off. This wouldn't take anything away from the width or depth, but at the bottom of the binding we would start rolling away immediately, instead of going straight down and then rolling."

From that basis, LaFleur and Johnson added more modifications that they thought would improve a reissue. They ended up with a short but significant checklist: replace fingerboard with Brazilian rosewood board; replace truss-rod with 50s style; re-glue fingerboard with hot hide glue; replace inlays with 50s style; refret; replace nut with bone nut; re-stamp original serial number; refinish guitar with nitro-cellulose lacquer and give it a light distressing.

LaFleur says an indication of their attention to detail comes with his claim that they have got closer to the original inlays than anyone else, including Gibson. "We have the original nitrate inlays manufactured by the original Italian company, cut for the Historics. That's something that no one has done in 50 years."

The Makeovers won't fool anybody into thinking they're the real thing, says LaFleur. "But we wanted to get those appointments right and get the guitar back to be just about as cool as you probably can get on an affordable budget – although it's not a cheap process."[12] At the time of writing, Historic Makeovers had shipped 27 completed guitars, with a further 20 awaiting work, in three levels priced from $1,530 to $2,550. That's on top of the $5,000-plus for the reissue, of course. And all this will of course depend on how good your reissue guitar was to begin with.

Another question that often pops up, with the modern reissues now so good and accurate, is that an unscrupulous person might attempt to pass one of these instruments off as the real (old) thing. Experienced guitar people will say they can easily tell them apart, but what about the novice? Or, for that matter, the experienced player not conversant with the constructional minutiae of late-50s solidbody electric guitar production in Kalamazoo, Michigan. Gibson has considered this.

Edwin Wilson at the Historic Program told me about some of the checks they now build into the instruments. The most important is a tiny chip that goes into a very small hole drilled into the neck tenon of every Custom Shop reissue guitar.

The chip stores a number – not the serial number – which corresponds to a database kept at Gibson. "It has a couple of purposes," says Wilson. "The first is to help us track the guitar through production. The second is that if someone buys a guitar or is about to purchase a guitar and they have a question about it, they can send it in, if they think it's one of our guitars. We can scan it and say yes, it's one of our guitars that someone might be passing off as a fake. Or we can say that it's not."

There is also a die-stamped inked number that should be seen in the control pocket of all modern Les Paul reissues. There on the lower ledge of the pocket is stamped R9 for the 1959 reissue, R8 for the 1958, and R0 for the 1960. There are further R-style numbers for the Goldtop reissues, too.

Wilson's bigger concern in this area is the matter of replicas made by other parties, without these security checks, that are more likely to be sold as originals. Fakes, in other words. "Gibson frowns on that, as I do also. It's not good for anybody. But I would say to these people: if you're going to do it and you think you're that good, then put your name on the headstock, not our name, and see if you can get the money for it."[13]

Take a real original Burst or a good Gibson reissue: the fact remains that you are not guaranteed a great guitar. But that's hardly a peculiarity of this model. All guitars vary, one from the next, whatever the period of production – whether it was during those glorious months of 1959, whether it was last week, or anywhere in between the two.

Guitar-makers and the guitars that they produce have almost certainly become more consistent in terms of build quality over the years. But even now, if wood is the primary material and there is human involvement in the construction, the instruments they turn out will vary.

One (anonymous) dealer put it like this: "I've had a million Les Paul reissues through my hands. You have to kiss a lot of frogs there. Some of them are OK. But, you know, you don't have to kiss nearly as many real 58 to 60 Bursts to find a good one."

David Wilson of *The ToneQuest Report* magazine examined a good number of Historic reissues as part of an investigation into the sound of Bursts in general and PAF and patent-number humbuckers in particular. He didn't say if this involved intimacy with amphibians.

"On some level, I think Gibson is making some of the best guitars they've ever made," Wilson contends. "When you get a good reissue – and that's *when you get a good one* – they're phenomenal.

"But you can't blame Gibson for the proportion of them that are good. It's always going to be an arbitrary thing, when you're throwing wood together from different trees and different parts of trees. Some of them work, and some don't work as well. I find that it's still fascinating to get out there right now and try to find great guitars. They're out there: new guitars that are also great guitars."

Wilson's precise requirement was to find a few specific Historic Les Pauls that were consistent, no matter which of the test pickups he put in them.

"I finally found them, but it took me six months of going over to a store and just picking up what they had. The number I played was in the dozens, and I bought six between July 2007 and March 08, of which I kept two."[14]

That works out at something like one great guitar for every 15 made. Not an entirely scientific test, for sure, but an indication of the kind of odds you might be up against.

At the time of writing, Gibson was offering three reissue Burst models – 1958, 59, or 60 – which since 2006 have been named as part of the Custom Shop's Vintage Original Spec series. They are list-priced between about $5,200 and $8,000.

And Gibson of course makes a whole range of regular production Les Paul models in its main factory, as it has done for years. Currently they amount to about eight models that link, to a greater or lesser extent, back to the Burst – from the Studio, listing at $1,650, to the Standard Premium Plus, at $4,300.

You might argue that the Standard in sunburst finish is today's version of the Burst. It would be quite a convincing argument, too. It's certainly the everyday production version of the Les Paul – just as the original was back in its day. In the modern line-up of all these Les Paul variants, the reissues, on the other hand, are aimed squarely at collectors. So, to put it simply: the Standard is today's player's instrument; the reissues are for those who want something more like the old guitars.

Gibson has moved from its early position as something of an outsider in a foreign land to its vantage point today, where it now speaks almost fluently the language of the Burst fanatic. In its publicity material for reissues, Gibson today constantly emphasises many of the tiny details that their customers demand.

There's the long tenon on the neck joint at the body, the rounded neck profile, the vintage-profile fretwire, the vintage-style carve to the belly, the properly-sized rear control pocket, the correct distance between the pickups, the weight-limited solid mahogany back, the period binding style in the cutaway, the nitro-cellulose lacquer finish … and so it goes on.

Despite all that attention to detail and the expensive and sometimes alluring results that these Burst reissues offer, it's worth bearing in mind a simple warning from Tom Murphy.

"I have said many times to people: this is not a 1959 Les Paul. It's a 2000-and-something Les Paul or whatever," explains Murphy. "That's not to misunderstand what it's supposed to refer to and what they want it to be. But it's not a 59."[15]

10. FLAME

Collectors find beauty in the Burst

Why do collectors make such a fuss about the Gibson Les Paul sunburst-finish guitars made between 1958 and 1960? They can be great instruments, of course. But there are other great instruments – and they do not generate anything like such an extraordinary level of enthusiasm. No solidbody guitar shakes up the peace quite so much.

There are a few rarer items – an original Gibson Flying V or Explorer, for example – and they can fetch higher prices. But they do not have quite the same aura and mystery around them. They do not excite the same passion. Why such fervour?

Collecting can be like a disease. When it does take hold of you, it can be difficult to control. And sometimes you don't even know you've got it until it's too late. In that way, collecting sunburst Les Pauls is no different to collecting anything else. Some record collectors do actually listen to their carefully found vinyl; others simply need to tick off a particular catalogue number and file it away. Similarly, classic cars are not often acquired for driving, whatever the owner might insist.

"I think you get affected," says Peter Svensson, a Swedish musician and guitar collector. He owned six Bursts when we spoke recently. "You get attracted by what is considered the best, basically. You want to get there too. I have become more and more attracted by the myth and everything else that comes with collecting these high-end guitars."[1]

"I like all guitars," says Bill, who lives in the Southeastern US (and prefers a degree of anonymity). "People assume that because I've got a Burst or two, I don't care about this guitar or that guitar. But I like 'em all. I used to describe my work as my wife but guitar as my mistress. And the mistress is always luring you away from the wife."

Mike Slubowski is a healthcare executive based near Detroit. "I have a pretty stressful job," he explains, "going a mile a minute. A way for me to move into a different world is either playing the guitar or reading about and scouting for nice guitars and talking to people about them."[2]

Scot Arch, a collector who lives in Pennsylvania and is also known as John Lennon in the tribute band Beatlemania, echoes that feeling. "There's always been one thing that I've been able to do to get away from it all, no matter how stressful my life, no matter what might be going wrong in it. When I have a guitar on and I'm playing music at a show, my mind is free for that time. I'm in there for the music and there isn't anything in life that's bothering me."[3]

So what is it about these lovely Bursts? Bill says it's all to do with them being an important piece of the past. "They are a kind of link to all the great music that was ever made on them," he explains, calling to mind the historic players we pinpointed earlier in the book who put them to such brilliant use and placed them so prominently on the six-string map: Clapton, Page, Green, Bloomfield, Beck, Allman, and the rest.

Joe Ganzler, who's based in California and runs a business authenticating original Bursts, says for him it was specifically Jimmy Page. "The first time I heard *Led Zeppelin II* it was like oh, so that's what a guitar is supposed to sound like. I was all done! But then you look at Chuck Berry. Why didn't a Gibson thinline like his become the guitar everybody wanted? Maybe it gets down into Freudian territory, too. The shape of the damn thing: maybe it's because it's shaped like a woman? I don't know."[4]

Bill talks about the playability of his four Bursts and how that too draws him to these instruments. "It's the way it makes me feel when I play my favourite. When I really bond with that guitar, I'll be playing … and the guitar disappears. There's no weight on my shoulder. It's almost like I'm not even holding a guitar. Everything just works. That's the way it is. It's 49 years old, and I can do anything with it, from practically acoustic strumming to wailing blues-rock."

Vic DaPra, a collector and dealer based near Pittsburgh, also finds something of a transcendental quality in his Bursts. "There's always this underlying thing, mentally," he says. "Sometimes you can almost 'go back' with these guitars, pretend you're back in the 70s or whatever. You get that vibe every once in a while but then reality hits. They are … quite expensive."[5]

But, given the expense, are they really that good? Are they really above and beyond anything you'll ever play? Bill is completely sure that his favourite one is. Friends who have gigged and been in bands for decades feel similarly when they pick it up. But isn't there the danger that because you know the history and you know the story – and the value – that looms so dominantly behind the instrument, that this makes you feel differently about it? Even before you pick it up? "It does," he admits. "But that's part of the human psyche."

Perhaps it's also part of what some people call the hype or the myth surrounding this guitar. It's as if you're the boy looking at the emperor's bare behind. "It's almost impossible to look at the Burst in an even and balanced way," says collector Clay Harrell, who lives near Detroit. "You're going to be tainted by the fact that you know it's old, that Jimmy Page played one – all that stuff weighs in your mind and you can't empty it from your brain. You can't press a button and flush that stuff out and take a completely unbiased view of this guitar."[6]

Peter Svensson thinks the hysteria surrounding the Burst is based upon the myth, which is bolstered by the classic images of those great players with their Bursts. "But it's impossible to deny that these guitars are fantastic," he says. "Once you've played one, well … most guitar players never will, and maybe that's for the best. Because once you've played one, I think you realise that they are superior. They really are. I wish it was different."

Svensson says that for him it's the feel of the entire instrument. He compares it to a good car. "It's maybe not the fastest or the most outrageous or the heaviest or the biggest, but it's the most perfect or complete piece, somehow. It's like driving a really nice car where everything is really good – the speed and the engine and your position in the car. It's exhilarating."[7]

Suppose you're at a fine restaurant and about to eat a very expensive meal, suggests Bill. You assume that it's going to be better than, say, something you might have had next door at McDonalds. "I think even blindfolded, I would know my favourite Burst when I played it. It feels that different and it plays that different. For one thing, the guitar is like a tuning fork in your hands: it sustains and shakes as you play it."

There are fabulous guitars being made now, including some ridiculously good sunburst Les Pauls. Why not just get one or more of those instead and cash in your chips? "There are good and bad guitars of all eras," says Bill. "There are 2008s that are incredible and then there are 2008s that sound like wet cardboard."

There are Les Pauls from 1959 that don't sound that great, too, surely? "Well, at the Dallas guitar show this year, one of the booths had a 58 and a 60, and a bunch of friends of mine would sit in the booth and play both guitars back to back, handing them around, trying different amps," Bill recalls. "And they pretty much decided that the 1960 was really, really good and the 58 was … not horrible, really, but shall we say generic?"[8]

Timm Kummer, a dealer who runs Kummer's Vintage Instruments in California, says he's played a few that were duds. "But very few. Almost all of them are pretty special guitars. At one time I guess we had about 40 of them in inventory when I was at Guitar Trader in the 80s, and we weighed them, measured the output of the pickups, and did a blind tone-test on them. We tried to determine if the lightest ones with the hottest pickups were better, or the heavier ones, or whatever – and it just really turned out to be the middle of the road as far as our ears went."[9]

Putting the playability aside for a moment, the most celebrated visual aspect of the Bursts is undoubtedly the appearance of the maple top. It's the flame, the curl, the grain, the figure, whatever you want to call it, combined with how well the colour of the sunburst has survived or how pleasantly it's aged. This guitar is a tantalising mix of art and science.

Vic DaPra is unstinting in his desire to find Bursts with the greatest tops. He was in possession of eight when we spoke. "There are so many variables that people want to see in these guitars, but for me it's strictly the top," he explains. "I'll take a guitar with issues, but it's got to have the top."

DaPra defines the attraction quite simply: no two are the same. "If you buy a Les Paul Custom, it's black with three pickups. But with a Burst, every one is different and each one has its own little nuances: the fade, the colour, the top. That's another reason why I think this guitar is so collectable, because every one is different."[10]

There is almost always some level of disappointment when you finally own something you have longed for. I've seen it described as anticipointment. For many collectors, the real fun is in the chase. Ownership comes a poor second to that kind of excitement. Shopping can be like that.

How many times have you bought something in a store and felt wonderful, and then when you got home found that you were somehow deflated?

It's another explanation of why Bursts are so avidly collected. It's this desire for the slightly better one, the next best thing, that drives a lot of Burst collectors to own more than one example. And that next one might just be the ultimate one: the Burst with the most spectacular figure, with the finest colour, with the greatest tone. You'll only know for sure when you possess it. And go round and round and round in the circle game.

Philipp Blom, in a recent study of collecting and collectors, wrote: "The most important object of a collection is the next one. While the hands still grasp one thing, and while the mind still determines its place in the order of our chattels, the hungry eyes are already far ahead."[11]

For Burst collectors, the desire to acquire more examples is all part of the search to own the perfect one. "And," Bill points out, "perfect for you is different from perfect for me. A guy asked me what I'm looking for. I said there's two guitars I'm looking for. One is the one I don't have, which is in near-mint condition, untouched from the factory, lots of colour, and hopefully some flame. The other is the really great sounding guitar at the bargain price."

It might also explain why a 1957 or 58 Goldtop, which with its humbuckers is the same guitar but with a gold finish, sells for considerably less than a Burst. "Every time you open the case on a Goldtop – it's gold," explains Joe Ganzler. "Let's say you have a nice sunburst 335. There really wouldn't be a tremendous incentive for you to be continually looking for a nicer 335.

"But if you have a Burst, after about six months you forget how damn lucky you are to have one, and you start thinking well, boy, I sure would like a little bit better one. I think that's what makes people keep coming back to these guitars. Everybody that I know that has one of these guitars, in their heart of hearts they want to find one that's just a little better. Once you've fulfilled that desire to own one, well, then the desire becomes to upgrade. All of that tends to drive the frenetic nature of the market for these guitars."[12]

Bill says he may be responsible for coming up with the term 'vaporburst'. He says it means a Les Paul you've heard about but have never quite managed to get to see. "The person who told you about it says, 'Oh yeah, it's out there, I know where it is. This guy owns it and I've seen it. It's really cool.' But until he shows me something a little more concrete than a story, I don't believe it's real."

Bill talks about a vaporburst about two hours away from his house. It's a mint, unplayed, all-original, early-60 Burst with all 59 features. "And I've tried my darnedest to get to it. But the man who owns it now is a wealthy doctor. He just thinks it's cute, knows what it's worth, and has no desire to cash in on it. He has no interest in selling it. So I'm stuck."

And while we're with Bill, he underlines an interesting point about the individuality of every single Burst. "One beautiful thing is that they all have faces. You can look at the grain pattern of a particular guitar and say hold on, I know that guitar. That's not a 59, or whatever the guy is saying, it's a 60 and I know the serial number, it's zero-such-and-such."[13] Timm Kummer backs him up: "They're kind of like snowflakes. Every one of them is different aesthetically."

Restoration specialist Clive Brown finds this all rather worrying. "When you hand someone a sunburst Les Paul, nobody ever goes: Hey, that's a nice neck. Or: Wow, this plays good. Or: Don't these pickups sound good? They always go: Oooh, look at the flame on that! Oh god. Quick nurse, the screens! You know?"[14]

When I spoke to dealer and repairman Steve Soest some years ago, he told me about a particular Les Paul a friend of his had come into contact with. "Apparently when Guitar Trader in New Jersey were having Gibson make those early re-issues for them," says Soest, "they sent an original out to Gibson, and so Gibson took off the neck and everything to check this thing out and make some measurements. Guitar Trader got the body back with no hardware.

"So, my friend found out they were selling it. He bought this pretty flamey body, but it had faded to that almost green-ish gold colour. It was terribly pitted and checked, and had nothing else on it. So he put the parts on it, had a neck made for it, and sold it to one of the big collectors for more money than you could imagine – re-necked, terrible finish, just because it was flamey. Amazing.

"And then he finds one, with tags, for another collector. It was a 60, which some think is pretty undesirable anyway, had hardly any flame but a nice birdseye kind of burl if you hold it just right. It didn't have the killer top, though, so he couldn't sell it at any of the shows. So he unloaded it – it went sideways – and he didn't make any money, just to get rid of it.

"And what amazes me is that this one was a great guitar," laughs Soest. "I plugged it in, played it – it hadn't even been set up, had a big old back-bow in the neck when they'd shipped it – but it was fantastic. Nobody had played that guitar, I'm sure, and it was a great one; those collectors had just looked at it and said nah, no top, not interested."[15]

Joe Ganzler has seen a similar thing in action. "The individuals shopping for flame and condition say playability is more important, but when you show them a guitar that's flamey from tip to tip, they say I'll take it. I don't really blame them for that, because I've only ever played one in all these years that was a real turd. It's like being one of the Miss America judges: you or I would go home with the worst or ugliest Miss America contestant ever.

"I think that particular one was a tone turd because it had sat in the case for 20 years and the guy never changed the strings. It was in dire need of a truss-rod adjustment, pickup-height adjustment, that kind of thing. A lot of the negative stuff you hear about these guitars is because many of them sit in bank vaults or safes."[16]

Collectors have built up an extensive vocabulary to describe the different flame and colour that a Burst might have. As with any specialist area, this jargon can seem impenetrable, even meaningless, to outsiders. And as with any jargon, that can be part of the intention. It can also be used as a badge of membership. If you speak the language, you must be one of us. If not, go and play with your Stratocasters.

Amberburst, darkburst, faded, honeyburst, lemon-drop, tangerine, teaburst, tobaccoburst, and unburst are some of the descriptions used for colour, while birdseye, blister, curly, flame, pinstripe, ribbon-curl, and tigerstripe are some of the names used to describe types of figure.

"Mineral streaks are desirable too," says Mike Slubowski. "They are the dark streaks that usually run vertically, looking at the guitar in the playing position. People will talk about guitars that have a dark, almost cherry colour," he says, "and they still sometimes say it's like the Brockburst. That was a famous Burst named for its owner, and it had a real dark colour. So people will say a guitar is sort of a Brockburst colour."[17]

Bill has already told us that individual instruments have recognisable faces, so perhaps naming them is simply an extension of that idea. Veteran collector Tom Wittrock in Missouri reckons maybe more than half of the Bursts in private hands have been given names. It's a trend that has been going for some time.

"Some of the names are descriptive, like the Brockburst, which describes a previous owner – the collector and dealer Brian Brock," explains Wittrock. "I can tell you the names of some of mine, if you like. The first one that I bought I named Curly – which seems a little bit too generic, in retrospect. The second I got was another late-60 with an unusual burled maple or marbled-looking top: I called it Burly. So my first two were Curly and Burly." Another of Wittrock's is named Sandy. The story here is a touch more complicated. "That went through the hands of a dealer called Bruce Sandler," he explains, "and for a short while was called the Sandlerburst. Then one of the collectors who owned it thought that wasn't a nice enough name, so he gave it more of a feminine name. He changed it from Sandlerburst to Sandy."

It can be a convenience, too. Wittrock: "When people talk about, say, the particular guitar Gary Moore is playing in a specific picture – because he had more than one – they'll say oh, that's his favourite, that's Stripe. Stripe is the name I gave that guitar, the 59 he still has with the open covers. I don't know if Gary has ever heard that name or considered using it, but because I used it years ago, and because in more recent times on the internet there are broad discussions on these things, I brought the name back out."

But let's get back to the flame. Wittrock too is a confirmed fan of the figure. "My eyes just notice it," he shrugs. "This is the way my mind picks these things up, and I guess it's largely subconscious. I like the type that's often called ribbon curl, because it's big and thick, often as wide as your fingers, in wavy stripes. It can be irregular, but it still looks like stripes across the face of the guitar.

"I also like some of the guitars that have extremely irregular patterns, which are almost impossible to describe, except that there is lots of figure going on. You couldn't put into words what it looks like." I press him. He has a go. "It's like an explosion of maple wood grain going crazy."

Wittrock says the type of wood that Gibson used in the 50s was of a fairly consistent style, in terms of the kind of figure that would turn up. In the last 20 years or so, however, guitar makers have used wider-ranging and more blatantly figured maple than the sort that Gibson used back in the day.

"Looking at that highly figured maple you get on guitars today," he says, "it doesn't move me in the same way. Quilted maple, for example, doesn't move me in the same way. I will see pieces that I find absolutely stunning and beautiful. I will see guitars that are made with all kinds of figured maple. But if it doesn't have the quality of maple like from the 50s Les Pauls, then I just look at it and say yes, that's one more beautiful piece of wood. Admire it for what it is, and move on."

Figure is often the determining factor for some collectors in the decision to buy or not to buy a particular Burst. Take a look at some of the fine archtop guitars that are about, suggests Wittrock, the kind that often have beautiful figured backs and sides. It's a very attractive part of the guitar, but while it might be seen as a bonus, in itself it rarely dictates whether someone will buy the guitar.

Old Fenders may be finished in a custom colour, and these too have their fanatical followers. But for those guitars it is straightforward paint alone, collected for a particular colour and its originality, that drives desirability. The underlying wood is completely hidden away and of no consequence.

"But the wood varies on every single instrument with the Bursts," says Wittrock, repeating the mantra. "It's not like there's only a hundred in green and that makes them rare. No: every one of these is different. Each one of them is unique."

But doesn't that mean you would have to keep every one that you got hold of? Aside from the financial implications, Wittrock is at a loss. "People say, well, why did you keep this one and sell that one? And I'd say that I can't give you an answer in words. It's emotional. Sometimes we part with guitars and we're happy to see where they go. Maybe I have three, a friend has none, and I want him to have one, or something like that.

"It always has made a certain amount of difference to me where the guitar went and who got it. Being a businessman, however, I could not let that dictate business," says Wittrock, who has long run his Third Eye Music store. "But it still has made a difference. There have been times when I have let go of guitars that were phenomenal, and people say hey, why didn't you offer that to me? And I tell them I can only offer it to one person. I decided who to offer it to."[18]

Sometimes the beauty of the Burst is not immediately evident. In fact, it can be hidden away. Roger Giffin told me about a wonderful example that came into Gibson's West Coast workshop that he ran in the early 90s. Someone walked in with a Les Paul that he'd bought in South Africa a good few years earlier and had played regularly since then. It was black.

"We poked around," says Giffin, "and there was a chip of paint off at the bottom corner. I could see what looked like red down there. So I asked if we could take off a few bits. We pulled the pickups out, and sure enough it was red inside the holes. So I thought well, obviously this was a sunburst at some point in its life. Then we thought about it a bit more, looking at the way it had been finished, and I said I really think it might be worth stripping this thing off."

Instead of the normal trick of getting out the paint stripper, Giffin simply used a block of sandpaper and rubbed the back of the headstock for a few minutes. "The black went through and there was red underneath, and the first thing that came up was an 8," he laughs, recalling the revelation of the serial number that confirmed this was a 1958 Burst. "I thought, yes, we've got a winner here! Over the course of about year I just dry-sanded the whole guitar, a little bit at a time, top to bottom. All the original finish was there underneath the black, and it was the most beautiful flame-top you ever saw. Not faded; real deep colour; incredible three-dimensional maple. And it was a great guitar."[19]

Figure is rarely captured completely in photographs of Bursts. A shot may present one aspect of the flame, but you only have to see a few of these guitars in real life to know that the best of them have a fascinating three-dimensional quality. There is a look to the figure that changes as you turn the guitar slowly before your eyes.

"Once you hold anything in your hands made out of figured maple or figured wood and you see for yourself how it changes by barely moving it, you realise that photographs only give you a brief moment of what that thing can look like," explains Wittrock. "Sometimes in photographs, guitars can look absolutely stunning, and then in your hands they are a letdown in some ways. But then sometimes the photograph doesn't capture what it has, and when you have it in your hands you are amazed."[20]

Joe Ganzler agrees. The almost holographic character of the flame can be breathtaking. "But the irony is that sometimes the photograph is better," he smiles. "It's one of the characteristics that makes these guitars fascinating."

It's a quality that can baffle the observer trying to match a picture of an instrument, or even the real thing, with a photograph of a player on stage or elsewhere with a particular Burst. Are these really the same instrument? They have a habit of never looking quite the same, even when you know they are. More mystery.

Every time you open the case on one of these things and gaze at the flame, says Ganzler, you see something different or something you didn't see the last time you looked. "They are works of art, from that standpoint. Any work of art, in order to stand the test of time, has to have a continual fascination to the viewer. That's critical. I hate to use the example of the Mona Lisa, but if you look at that picture you do see subtleties in the shading, in the characteristics, and in … well, it just has a certain, as the French would say, I don't know what."[21]

Quite a few of the collectors I talked to mentioned this parallel of Bursts to art. Art hangs on a wall or it stands in a room or wherever. It is made to be looked at, considered, reflected upon. It does not usually exist to do something, in the way that a tool like a guitar does.

Perhaps you saw Yasmina Reza's play *Art?* It's about how Serge buys for a very large sum of money a five-foot-by-four-foot painting by a fashionable artist. It is completely white. We find out how it affects Serge's friendship with two of his good mates, Marc and Yvan.

Should they pretend they 'appreciate' it too or should they tell him he's wasted his money? Should they do what Marc in fact does and tell Serge that the new acquisition he adores and that he wants everyone else to like is in fact "white shit"?

Serge fancies himself as a connoisseur and explains that price depends on how fashionable the painter is. "I don't blame you for not responding to this painting," he says. "You haven't had the training."

It sums up the way that the modern art world can leave some of us thinking that it's simply a huge çon trick, while others are dazzled by the presence, real or imagined, of culture and money and celebs. Museums and art galleries bolster the art world's view of its own importance. That doesn't exist for collectable guitars: there are no institutional buyers to add valuable elements of prestige and trust to the market.

Clive Brown reckons there are parallels. "An original sunburst Les Paul is a holy grail that's untouchable to the majority of people, unless you happen to be an industrialist or a multi-millionaire rock star. It is a bit like getting a Salvador Dali or something, actually. You have to rave about it, but other people can't see what you're raving about. I think these Les Pauls have in one respect turned into a bit of an art form. If you go around art galleries, you find people raving about certain pictures – and you're looking at it thinking well, it looks like scribble to me."[22]

Peter Svensson sees the connection bertween guitars and art more positively. "The appeal of the Burst is based on myths, certainly," he says, "but that's what it's like with art and anything that people strive to get and pay a lot of money for. It feeds itself, somehow. But if it was all crap, it wouldn't have worked. There is something there!"[23]

I've held and strummed dozens of these instruments, and yes, they are all different, and some are unquestionably beautiful. But then so is my friend's dining-room table with its magnificent figured maple top. I've come across a very funny but unquestionably derogatory term for Bursts and other gorgeous-looking instruments: a furniture guitar. I mentioned it to Mark Knopfler when I was asking him about his love of Gibsons, as opposed to his better-known passion for Strat-like guitars.

"Yes, I've heard that," he laughed, and mentioned a guitar he'd once owned that came into that category. "It was all about fancy-looking tops, you know? But I think a lot of English players actually prefer the plain top, which I do. My 58 Les Paul is kind of a yellowish top, and I really like that: a pale burst. I'm not a big fan of all this over-glossy tigerstripe thing."[24]

As we have learned in our search for a million-dollar Les Paul, for many collectors it is the flamey look that is the primary appeal. The beauty of the Burst is what drives many to acquire one, then another, then another, and on and on, presumably until the money runs out. There is an element of art there, for sure, in a way that most other electric guitars do not possess.

But another function of a collection is that it can represent a more ordered and controllable world than the one we usually inhabit. It can take us away from the worries and everyday realities of our lives. And life was simpler when we were younger. Or at least it might seem to us now, on reflection, to have been simpler back then.

For men of a certain age – and nearly all the collectors I spoke to were, like me, men in their fifties – guitars can come to represent that youth, that sense of freedom, that hazily recalled yearning. For others, motorcycles offer a similar haven. And often, the type of guitars or bikes we wanted then that were out of reach can now be had. Collecting can create an idealised past, a better version of our youth.

For some, that sense of youth and all that it represented can be summoned up by spending (a great deal of) money on a guitar from the period in which we grew up. But of course it can't be as simple as that. Even the simple act of buying that guitar will have a most definite impact on our lives now, as adults, here in the early 21st century.

"More than anything," says DaPra, "I think it's my age. Believe me, mentally, no matter how old you are, you probably always think you're 18 years old," he laughs.[25]

I laugh with him, but point out that we are reminded on a regular basis that this is not the case.

The French writer Marcel Proust spent large parts of his now famous multi-volume novel *In Search Of Lost Time* trying to pin down and evoke the power of memory and the associations that objects from our pasts can throw in our way.

"The smell and taste of things remain poised a long time," he wrote, "like souls, ready to remind us, waiting and hoping for their moment, amid the ruins of all the rest; and bear unfaltering, in the tiny and almost impalpable drop of their essence, the vast structure of recollecting."[26]

11. UNREAL

Was it made 50 years ago or 50 days ago?

When is a Burst not a Burst? Answer: When it's a fake. The accompanying joke goes like this: Gibson made 1,500 or so sunburst Les Pauls between 1958 and 1960. Now only 2,000 survive. Fakes have always been with us, ever since the first cave-woman said yes, darling, that was fantastic. The art world is full of them (fakes, not cave-women). The antique market too is crowded with fakes. Any business with large sums of money involved is bound to attract the attention of forgers. Jeans, handbags, perfume; everything seems to be a target these days. Vintage guitars in general and the Burst in particular are no exceptions.

"It's amazing," one collector told me, "that in a business that's involved with so much money now, it can all still be so vague and seemingly underhand. Very expensive guitars are sold in parking lots. People pay with travellers cheques. Other stuff I can't even tell you about. It's all very weird."

Kerry Keane at Christie's puts it bluntly. "Fakers poison the well of knowledge that specialists and collectors rely upon. I learned in the violin trade that the moment there is an opportunity to profit through deceit, they are there. They're there in a moment, without batting an eye. Fakers are absolutely convinced that they are smarter than everyone else. And their pride rests in being able to pull the wool over someone's eyes."[1]

Let's get our terminology quite straight before we swim out into these evidently murky waters. There are fakes, there are replicas, there are conversions, and there are restorations. Each one is a slightly different take on the same general idea, but, much more importantly, some are entirely legitimate and a few quite definitely not.

A fake can be many things, including a guitar built entirely from scratch to pass off as a genuine old Burst, or a guitar that has some original parts and some newer parts but that is offered as entirely original.

A replica may be legitimate – although Gibson and many of the rest of us wouldn't view it that way if the guitar had 'Gibson' on the head but had not been made in their Kalamazoo or Nashville factories. A replica is precisely what the name implies: a guitar that is made to have the precise look and playability of an original Burst. Sold as a replica rather than the real thing, it has legitimacy. Sold as the real thing, it is a fake.

A conversion is another legitimate offering, and we've already come across the idea earlier in the book. It's a Les Paul 'converted' from one specific (genuine) model to look and play like another, most commonly a mid-50s Goldtop to a Burst lookalike. The level of work varies depending on precisely which period the Goldtop is, but the idea is the same: you get very close to a real Burst at a lower cost.

A restoration is a real guitar that has been through the wars and is repaired and cleaned up and generally taken back to get as close to its original look and feel as the skill of the person doing the job allows. In essence, entirely legitimate.

These three categories – replica, conversion, restoration – can all 'become' a fake. They should all begin life as legitimate instruments.

Perhaps different levels of legitimacy, depending on who's doing the work and what their intention is, but the potential, at least, is for these to start as honourable workarounds. And they often do. The danger comes when they move on to a second, third, or later owner. Especially if that owner is inclined toward deception or, to be more charitable, simply isn't sure of exactly what he has.

When I asked around about replicas, one name kept coming back: Max. This is Peter 'Max' Baranet, whom I spoke to at his home in California. In the late 70s he found himself working at Image Guitars in Los Angeles, a small shop in a good position that got regular high-level customers. "We had a lot of celebrities coming through that tiny place," says Baranet.

He did a good deal of custom work, building mostly Strat, Tele, and Les Paul-style guitars to customers' requirements. Those requirements mostly being: make them look and play like old ones. Nothing unusual in that: it's what a lot of guitar-makers do. "I could build a Les Paul with a whole set of original parts for I think under $2,000. Having the repair shop in the same place, I had access to a lot of original parts," he says, "because people would bring guitars in and pull the original stuff out. Everybody wanted DiMarzio Super Distortion pickups back then, for example."

He enjoyed doing this work and is proud of the guitars he made when he was active between about 1974 and 1996, after which he was mostly working on conversions. "But I have to tell you, I think people have the idea I was mass-producing replicas all my life. They're actually very scarce. I can tell you there are less than a hundred. Way less than a hundred – and that includes Flying Vs, Explorers, Strats, and Teles as well as Les Pauls. The reputation that I've got is out of proportion."

What sort of reputation? Among the unprintable descriptions I heard was the suggestion that "this guy is the biggest scammer in the world" and, positively polite this time, "he's a scoundrel". Well, are you, Max?

"I did a lot of vintage repairs and restoration," he laughs, "but people are probably not going to want to hear that. They'd rather think I just did replicas. But I did a lot of restoration work – and the point is that nobody really wants you showing that work around. No one wants to admit that they have had restoration work done, so that pretty much stayed low-key – and replicas got all the attention. I kind of let it go like that, because it kept the restoration under cover."

The replicas that he did make, he argues, were unmistakably brand new guitars. "Twenty-some years later, I've seen a few come back, looked at them, and thought oh my god. It was all the right materials, and they have aged the same as the older ones. It was like wow, yes, that thing looks real."

There are no intentional marks on his guitars to identify them as being made-by-Max. "But if you're in the business of buying $500,000 guitars and you can't tell that one of mine is not the real thing, you're in the wrong business," he insists. "They were great guitars, but they were never built to pass as real."

His website has a simple message saying: "I will verify the authenticity of guitars I have built." He can do that by serial number and his collection of pictures. "Otherwise I wouldn't have had a website at all. I don't get any business that way and, as it says, I don't build guitars. I'm not looking for any replica business. I figured I had to stick that up there: number one, so they don't get lost in the shuffle, because they are nice guitars, and secondly, so they didn't get passed as real."

Baranet's next project, he tells me, is some kind of journey, at present unspecified. "I've shut everything down and I'm selling my house," he says. "It's a personal thing. I'm looking for some new challenge."[2]

Conversions come in different categories, based on the idea of Goldtop into Burst. The earlier the Goldtop used as the source, the more work there is to do. The earliest will require pickup routs to be recut, humbuckers fitted, and the neck reset, for example; the later ones only need 'bursting'. But as Baranet points out, with prices for Goldtops too taking a hike (and, at the time of writing, something of a plunge in the other direction), the equation is not quite so clear. Plus you never know exactly how good the top is lurking under the gold paint until you strip it.

"I was never a conversion guy," collector Vic DaPra tells me.[3] And that's quite understandable: collectors who've been into Bursts for some time, like DaPra, and who have a number of examples of the real thing, have little evident need of a conversion. Conversions also have to compete now with the generally well regarded reissues that Gibson has been producing for some years.

Restored guitars come next on our list, and our guide here is British restoration specialist Clive Brown, whose work is widely praised. "I don't like mint vintage guitars," he tells me, "because you might as well buy a new one. I think a worn vintage guitar has an element of history. There is something there that a lot of people like about it." And that gives you your business? "All of my business, yes: recreating it for folks."

He restores all kinds of guitars, recreating a finish here, patching up previous poor repairs and making good there, generally bringing the guitar to a state that it may not have enjoyed since a time much closer to its creation. He's worked on a number of Bursts in recent years. "Normally that means complete restoration," Brown explains, "in other words back to the correct type of finish, and then I age it up so it looks like it never lost its original finish.

"I had one where a guy had decided he'd convert a real 59 to left-handed, by drilling five eighth-inch holes through the front as guide holes for where the new pots and switch was going to be. Then he stopped and change his mind." He laughs heartily at the memory and proceeds to give me a blow-by-blow account of how he brought it back to life.

Is it still a 100 per cent Les Paul Burst if it's had restoration done to it? "It's still a Les Paul: it just has a different coat of paint on it. What are you going to do? Throw it away? If you get an old vintage car, you restore that and nobody would say a thing. You don't go down the road on original tyres, do you? Or with original brakes.

"There has got to be a variation in price, but in the car industry the price would go the opposite way. If it was unrestored and rusty, with holes in it, it would be worth less. The restored version would be worth a lot more." In the peculiar world of the vintage guitar, however, everyone seems to want an instrument that is exactly as it was when it left the factory. Brown points out the absurdity of that idea.

"Say the volume pot doesn't work in your vintage guitar and you put a new one in it. Well, you've just devalued it. Devalued it from what? It wouldn't work! So is it worth less now, when it works? If you want it just to look at, fair enough. But for playing?

"It's an unrealistic expectation to want an old guitar to be factory-fresh," adds Brown. "Unless it's never been played, of course, in which case it probably wasn't a good one in the first place. Yes, there are guitars that have escaped the rigours of normal guitar life. But that's more by luck than anything else."

The question mark against restoration is that, further on in the guitar's life, say a few owners from now, somebody might not know that the restoration was done. And, as people who have sold things have done since the dawn of time, they might well exploit that to their advantage.

Brown says he normally stamps his guitars to identify them. "I've had to start doing that, especially on Fenders, because you take them apart. But if anybody thinks they've got a restored guitar and they think I might have done it, I'll tell them. I won't lie for anybody."[4]

That's all very well, but the craftsman is not usually the source of the problem. As we've said, it's the second or third or however many owners down the line. And if you collect vintage guitars, there's nothing much you can do to protect yourself, other than to learn as much as you can about what makes an original guitar original.

I asked a number of insiders to tell me how they would look over this Burst I have just put in front of them to determine if it is indeed what I say it is. I regret to say this is an imaginary exercise.

Kerry Keane at Christie's was sent some beautiful pictures of a 1960 flame-top two years ago and then had the guitar shipped to him for closer investigation. "I pulled the pickups off and we had one PAF decal on there, which looks a little dodgy, and the other one without a PAF decal. OK, that might happen in 1960. Pull the back cover off and I see a lot of resoldering. Your antennae go up. Something about the guitar wasn't right."

And there we have the recurring phrase among those who know. "Something isn't right." You get to have a feel for this once you've seen a few and looked them over closely and taken them apart. The other common phrase is: "It doesn't smell right." That's not a joke: they do have a smell. It might be the guitar's case as much as the instrument itself, actually, but a good nose is still a valuable asset for any guitar hound.

Dealer Phil Winfield, an Englishman now living in the US, tells me: "You rely on your gut feeling. You get that by handling a lot of guitars. You get to know. You smell it. It's a sixth sense, and that only develops over time."

Keane's "60 Burst" turned out to have probably started life as a Goldtop. A conversion, no less. "It was stripped to reveal the nice flame underneath, rerouted, fit out with humbuckers, and one bad decal put on a PAF. Deception has to be subtle," he smiles. "And the neck was thin, as you'd expect on a 60, but the angle's a little funny. It's an SG neck that had been married up to it! So there it is. And when the guitar is worth several hundred thousand dollars, that's all worth doing."

There is some technical assistance available that doesn't rely on gut instinct and "just knowing". This is the black light, an ultra-violet lamp long used in the antiques trade and now a common piece of equipment for the vintage-guitar expert.

Winfield explains the simple process. "The first thing you would do is to pass it over the guitar, and you can see if it's been refinished or if there are any otherwise invisible repairs. It shows up almost like an X-ray. When you shine a black light over a repaired area, you can see glue lines, fractures, internal strains and stresses, and where there's overspray of a finish. It shows up as a ripple, a dark line." Overspray is paint or lacquer sprayed where it's not intended to go, such as in routs.

If somebody has done a very good job of, for example, putting on another fingerboard, they still can't hide that from a black light. "Nothing they can do can beat that test," says Winfield. He thinks about that, and then adds: "Although someone is probably working on it right now as we speak."

The black light is useful too to check over the guitar's plastic parts and the logos, or decals. Kim LaFleur of Vintage Checkout habitually uses a black light on the parts that he sells, in order to confirm their authenticity. "They just glow. When you find one that doesn't, or it glows a different colour, you know something's wrong."[5]

Kerry Keane at Christie's urges some caution, however, suggesting that black light is not an instant and foolproof method in all cases. "I would first of all be sure to completely look over the guitar in daylight, and I'd want to look especially at the texture of the lacquer. Then I would use black light, although that can be deceptive. It's expertise through forensics."

The next thing that everyone said they would do to check if my mythical Burst is real is to start pulling it apart, at least as far as is possible. The back pocket where the wiring harness lives and the rout for the neck pickup are the primary targets.

In the controls pocket, my guides show me how to check the originality of the components, including the wiring itself. They also try to date the pots, although the solder may prevent you reading the codes. No matter: how is the solder itself? Is there evidence of resoldering? Has anyone been messing around in there? If they have, why? Ideally, collectors want to see that nothing has been touched, at all, ever.

"It's a matter of putting all the different pieces together," says Keane. "And sometimes you just open up the case and it's perfect. You don't have to pull anything apart. You *know*. It smells right."[6] You need a score of 100 out of 100? Yes, he says; 90 is not good enough any more.

Phil Winfield talks me through some close examination of the internal routs, the dimensions and construction of those routs, the fingerboard and inlays, and the tenon joint. That's the neck-to-body joint, visible in the neck-pickup rout, which is achieved in a very specific way on an original Burst.

"The Brazilian rosewood of the fingerboard can't be replicated, and the inlays have a particular look," he explains. "But someone could have bought a cheaper Goldtop, when they were cheap, and pulled off the fingerboard, so the board and the inlays will be right. However, you can't hide that: there will be a line."[7]

Artificially ageing an object, or relic'ing as it's generally known in the guitar world, is something else that's been around for a long time in the antiques trade. That'll be the bare-chested chap out the back whacking that table-top with a rather intimidating set of chains. Guitar restorers use more restrained techniques, but the intention is much the same. So the trick is to be able to tell if this guitar in front of us has genuine 50-year-old ageing, or 50-day-old ageing meant to look as if it's 50 years old.

So, we've held the guitar and looked it all over closely, we've plugged in the black light and checked it out, and it all feels good. We've opened it up and looked for all the little constructional nuances and original bits and pieces, and they too seem fine. Where to next?

"For me, the place to go next is someone whose opinion I trust, to ask them to take a look at it," says the experienced collector and dealer Tom Wittrock. "Sometimes, a second pair of knowledgeable eyes will find things we miss – even though when it's pointed out to us we may say gosh, why on earth didn't I notice that?"[8]

Joe Ganzler is one of the people who will, for a fee, check out a Burst and give his opinion on its authenticity. "I think he's the go-to guy," says Wittrock, "although there are others – Uncle Lou Gatanas, Perry Margouleff, Terry Mueller. If any of those were around, I'd say hey, what do you think of this? I might even ask the opinion of some of my friends who are Burst collectors but not known for detecting fakes, because again it's the value of that second set of eyes. But for vetting and authentication, Joe wants that business and he's good at it."

I heard some complaints that Ganzler hadn't been doing this stuff long enough to really know it inside out. "Three years ago, this guy didn't even own a Burst," goes a typical moan.

Ganzler smiles when I bring this to his attention. I have a feeling he's heard it all before. "I have an eye for detail," he says. "I've had a couple of good mentors that brought me up to speed. And I have a passion and desire to keep looking at these guitars a different way than some other collectors look at them. A lot of collectors look at them and it's, wow, look at that top! They never really get into the nitpicking of looking at every anal detail of these things in the way I have."

He tells me he's been involved with vintage guitars since the mid 90s and has had probably between 50 and 75 Bursts in his hands. He's been involved with the sale of maybe a dozen so far. So, his job is authenticating guitars?

"I'd say that was my primary job," he replies, "but a lot of guys that buy these guitars don't have time to go across country and stay there, possibly for several days, while the transaction is completed. Occasionally a collector will go with me, but as many times they won't. They will trust my eyes and my camera and my evaluation. I'll take a laptop and hi-res camera, shoot the guitar and send them the pictures, and they can look at it and ask what I think it's really worth."

So how difficult can a job like that get, I wonder? Ganzler tells me about a call he got as a result of a piece in the *Los Angeles Times* that mentioned his work and that was syndicated across the country. The caller was in Nebraska, the daughter of someone who was the original owner of a 59 Burst and had just died. She sent pictures first, including some shots of her pa playing it in the 60s. It looked promising – mildly flamed, strong colour – although it did have a extra '2' near the serial number, which is how Gibson would mark factory seconds.

"I get up there and I was fully confident, based on the story, that when I opened the case this guitar would not be at all difficult to authenticate. I thought it would be a replay of my trip to Ohio where I popped a case on a one-owner guitar and I was all done in 15 seconds."

This time he popped the lid … and swore quietly to himself. Ganzler's first reaction was that this guitar could not be real. "The colour was like nothing I've seen Gibson paint. It was almost a deep magenta around the edges, and I'd never seen a gradation of the sunburst like this. It was literally a tri-colour sunburst. It looked like they'd said to the guy who swept the floor for Gibson, 'Hey, the guy who shoots these is sick today. I know you painted that 42 Buick back in 53. Can you do this one for me?' But then I'm thinking, OK, this guitar has a '2'. A second. Exactly."

But it got more worrying. The flame did not look like any bookmatched figured top he had ever seen on a period Les Paul. "It was what we call barbecue-grill flame: straight across with a slight chevron. No, I thought, this can't be right. It can't be."

Among the kit that Ganzler carries with him is a series of templates that he matches up to the guitar in various ways. "They tell me with about 90 per cent certainty that a guitar is a real 50s Les Paul. To be honest, the guys that make fakes just can't get it quite right. And then I move on from there. Well, it was definitely a real 50s Les Paul: it passed that test. So I thought OK, let's go forward and consider if it's a re-top." This means a guitar where someone has put on a new maple top, often with illicit intention.

Next, Ganzler looks at the serial number again. It's in the 9 1300 series. Which is a shock if you know your Les Pauls. "There have not been any 59s in the 1300 series yet," explains our guide. "In fact, there has been conjecture that Gibson took the month off and built something else during that period."

Our man in Nebraska is by now a very uncomfortable guitar authenticator. Here's one that's the wrong colour, the wrong type of flame, and with a serial number that surely can't be right. "And this one was going to be easy," laughs Ganzler.

There's more in store. He flips the guitar on its side and takes a look at the neck binding on the wound-string side. There are no position dots like there should be. "I summarily excused myself to go void my bowels, which I did. A guitar that I planned to look at for about an hour and a half, finish the financial transaction, and then wait around at this cornfield airfield for a few hours, took me four and a half hours to look at."

He tells himself that this must be a fake. And then he looks at the '2' again. "I allowed myself some healthy scepticism. Then I said well, Joe, what if it is real? Then the woman brings out this sheaf of photographs of the guy playing the thing in the early 60s. I looked at one that was taken over his left shoulder and you could just see enough of the fretboard and binding to one place where there should have been a dot. There was no dot."

So now he's back to saying yes, this thing has got to be real. But that means he has to make the financial transaction and take it back to the collector who's buying it. "And he will pop the case and say *what on earth were you thinking?*"

He calls the collector. He tells him it's real. He tells him that he will take one look and say it's not, but it is. It is real. Then he has to tell the daughter that her dad's guitar has … how to put it politely? Some anomalies.

"I tell her I believe these to be factory anomalies. The '2' means it's a factory second. You would think that would make the guitar rarer: yes it does. You would think as a result of that, that would make it worth more money. Here's your problem. There's probably three guys in a hundred that call themselves Les Paul aficionados that would look at this and say yeah, Ganzler was right on this one. The other 97 are going to say that guy is a bloody idiot; he has no clue; he has bought a retopped, refin'd, renecked I-don't-know-what-it-is. I said to her, as a result, the marketplace for this guitar is very small, which does reduce the value, because till the end of time there will be people who say I've made a mistake on this one."

So Ganzler negotiates a lower price on the guitar. The woman is happy with this. The wire transfer takes place; he packs up the guitar, races to the airport, and watches the corn blow around for a while. "We originally agreed on a price somewhere north of $300,000, and the actual delivered price after my fees was about $250,000. For my troubles I made 20 grand on that."

And surely the point of this story is that no one can ever be 100 per cent sure that this or that guitar is right. "I'm glad you said that," Ganzler tells me. "I was involved in a court case recently as an expert witness where the authenticity of some guitars was in dispute. The case went to deposition, not trial, as it turned out. But one of the things I was prepared to say in court – and when you think about it, this is true and kind of scary – is that there's no real way to be 100 per cent sure about this.

"How can you or I or anyone else say that this guitar was built in 1959 and it was shipped from Gibson? If it got to court, then it would have been one opinion against another. It's circumstantial at best. And part of that is why I can exist in business! I have to tell everybody who will listen that I've been wrong before and, by golly, I'll be wrong again. I'm proud of it: if you don't learn to admit you're wrong, well … I'm not going to mention any names, but some of the people you'll talk to have never been wrong in their lives. And, of course, they have."

I don't envy Ganzler and the other individuals like him who offer similar services. If they make a mistake, they have a customer bearing down on them with a raging six-figure-sized temper in tow. "My life has been threatened more than once, I can assure you – and it will probably be threatened again," says Ganzler.

"And sometimes I say to myself, now what in the name of suffering Jesus Christ am I doing this for? There's only going to be worse and more of it. There's going to be more fakes out there, as the prices go up, and more grief. Here it comes."[9]

12. VISIBILITY

An interview with Dan Hawkins about bringing the Burst into the light

Dan Hawkins is the guitarist in Stone Gods, but you might know him better from The Darkness. They broke up in 2006 after a remarkable run that saw their album *Permission To Land* reach Number 1 in their native Britain and go gold in the US, while the maddeningly infectious single 'I Believe In A Thing Called Love' made Number 2 in the UK and 23 in America.

Some wondered if the band was entirely serious, if it wasn't all some kind of tongue-in-cheek faux-pomp joke from a distant planet where Queen regularly met and did peculiar things with Aerosmith. But there was no denying Hawkins's presence with a very in-your-face sunburst Les Paul slung around his neck. At a time in Britain when the Fender Telecaster was the fashionable axe du jour, The Darkness made Les Pauls visible again.

"Highly visible," laughs Hawkins when I catch up with him just before some Stone Gods rehearsals. "In my head," he says, "I've always identified the image of a guitar with a Les Paul, ever since my dad had a copy when I was a kid. That was always knocking around when we were growing up.

I thought, when I'm a serious guitarist, I'll get a Les Paul. And I did. I still like Teles, they're my other favourite guitars, but there's something very direct about a Les Paul."

Jimmy Page, an inevitable presence, loomed there in the background as Hawkins grew up and found his own place with a Les Paul. "But then Jimmy seems to have a knack of making a Les Paul not even sound like one. I've got one of his signature sunburst models – the recent one – and it sounds nothing like a Les Paul a lot of the time. I think it's just how the pickup works, and the out-of-phase section – there's a push-pull knob that throws the pickups out of phase.

"It just screams at you, basically, it sounds really gnarly. You listen to it and think, well, that sounds horrible – but there really is something about it once the band's playing that just sounds ace. I also have a black Les Paul Custom that the Gibson Custom Shop built for Jimmy Page but was too heavy for him."

Hawkins admits that he had to fight to get one of the signature-model Page Bursts in 2004. I tell him people are paying a fortune already for the original run of 25 hand-signed ones; a dealer told me that he'd sold an early-serial example for $125,000. "I got it for the second Darkness album," he insists, a little offended as I suggest he might have got the guitar as an investment.

"I wanted something with a bit more character and a bit more diversity. It was all over the album and I use it live a lot. Most of my lead stuff on the new Stone Gods album is done with it."

He tells me that he'll happily throw his Jimmy Page signature Les Paul about the place, without a thought of the many thousands he paid for it. "But I'm almost scared to take my £500 one out on the road any more." That's a late-90s Standard, and it remains his absolute favourite Les Paul. "Nothing collectable: a honeyburst Standard," he explains. "I've tried to find Les Paul Standards to match it and I just haven't been able to."

Has he tried an original Burst, perhaps? He sounds almost the perfect candidate to be playing a proper 50s one. "I had some guy come over to a gig in northern England when we were playing there a few years ago," he tells me, looking back to the second Darkness arena tour of the UK. "He was a friend of Tim from Ash. Tim was trying out some vintage equipment. I really wanted an original 59-era Standard, and I wanted to play it live. You just don't find them any more – because the collectors have got them all. Which I think is a real shame."

Why is that a shame? Because collectors keep them away from players, he reckons. "I wanted to buy it to put it straight on the road. At the end of the day, you can insure anything for whatever it's worth. If it breaks it breaks. It's a guitar. It's supposed to be played.

"The trouble with these collectors hoarding all these amazing guitars, it sends prices rocketing, and people like me don't get to play them any more. Oh, woe is me," he laughs. "But anyway, it was too expensive." What was it like? He says it was all right, without much enthusiasm. It was also a great deal of money. But more importantly, to Hawkins it did not feel and play as well as his customary, comfortable 90s Standard.

Well, why should it? Some guitars are good and some are not so good, whether they were made last week or 50 years ago. "And until you take it apart, which I suppose you'd never want to do," says Hawkins, "you don't know if you're even playing what you're supposed to be playing."

It wasn't just that he couldn't afford the asking price of several hundred thousand. He would make a *point* of not affording it. "I'm not going to buy a guitar for that sort of money. Not in my lifetime." He pauses for thought. "Well, OK, I suppose you should never say never. If I picked one up and it felt like coming home, and I had half a million sitting around, maybe then. But unless I wanted to take it on the road and it would work in a live set, I wouldn't buy it. I don't want to be one of those bloody collectors. I would just add to the issue."

We talk about the idea that a guitar needs to be played to sound better. Hawkins agrees, but by way of amusing sidetrack mentions a back-up Les Paul he had in his early days that suffered when too much beer had managed to get inside. Don't ask. His guitar tech showed him the damage this had caused, shorting out electronics and generally causing internal havoc. It looked disgusting in there, apparently.

But back to overpriced and out-of-reach Bursts. "When we were making one of the Darkness albums we hired in a couple of £250-a-day original 50s Les Pauls, and they just sat on the back burner. Maybe they just don't suit my style of playing. I'm not sure."

There's all this witchcraft or mojo or whatever you want to call it that lurks around a vintage guitar. And there's a whole set of often unreasonable expectations. "It's like picking up a Brian May guitar and thinking that it's going to sound exactly like Brian May," says Hawkins. This is a ridiculous idea, but so many people still seem to imagine that it can happen. It's what fires much of the signature-model guitar market. "It takes years to perfect a vibrato like Brian's," he says.

When it comes down to it, you have to trust your ears, he tells me. And the differences that people talk about that exist between this guitar and that guitar – no matter if they're old, new, or somewhere in between – can get to be extraordinarily subtle. "They can get very anal about it," he laughs. "I suppose in a studio you notice it a lot more, those differences between guitars. I see that now, as a producer and as an engineer. I see how important it is to have a lot of instruments at your disposal when you're tracking guitars."

Hawkins, now 32 years old, tells me about another Les Paul he has. Before The Darkness, he used to scout for session work, playing around and trying to make a name for himself. One of those projects was for a singer called Liz Horsman. He was pleased to be asked to play on some album tracks.

But there was one large problem. No guitar. He'd sold his Fender Telecaster to cover a dangerously overdue bar bill. The keyboard player on the date was best mates with Neal X from Sigue Sigue Sputnik, a briefly notorious British mid-80s glam-punk outfit. Hawkins borrowed Neal's Les Paul. "I just loved it. It was a Standard, and the first proper Les Paul I ever played. I was surprised how much of a nose it had, as I call it. I thought Les Pauls would sound really fat and meaty, but wow! This had a nastiness about it, it had a real bark about it."

Years later, Hawkins managed to buy the Les Paul from Mr X, and he reports that it still sounds great. "It's battered like you wouldn't believe. I don't know when it was made, and I don't care. It rocks, and it has a lot of history to it. It's led a very punk rock life. And it continues to.

"I'm not too bothered about low-end and the richness of tone," adds Hawkins, "I just want it to bark at me. I like Les Paul Standards. Customs tend to sound a bit nicer, I find. They do have that richness. But sometimes they just don't misbehave enough."[1]

13. COLLECTABILITY

Just what is it like to live with a fistful of Bursts?

How do you know when you've become a collector? Is there a point you cross? First things first: to qualify as a collector, you ought to have more than one of that thing you're aiming to collect. A collection by its nature has to be a quantity of items, a gathering together of multiple objects. So, do you have more than one guitar? Well, by definition, you're a collector.

Collecting is a long-established human trait. It was evident in 17th century Europe through the fashion among wealthy folk for the cabinet of curiosities. Some of these cabinets grew into museums and became imbued with all the academic baggage of classification and scientific study. But the owners of the cabinets of curiosities were content to show off to their friends the riches within, impressing with this or that trinket from overseas: shells, coins, gems, indeed anything blatantly exotic and with that all-important extra notch or two of one-upmanship.

Not quite so long ago, but rather early for guitar collecting, dealer George Gruhn was writing about one-upmanship in the six-string world. In a 1976 piece about collectable guitars, Gruhn said: "We may question whether snob appeal is a psychologically healthy reason for buying a musical instrument, but let's face it, the right instrument will do more to impress friends and fellow musicians in some circles than a new Rolls Royce. It will also get plenty of attention at festivals and concerts – free tickets, backstage passes. Some people who don't even play carry around a [Martin] D-45 or a [Gibson] Flying V for just that reason.

"Owning a superlative instrument is sometimes a compensation for inferior musicianship," Gruhn added. "Of course, this is not true of most collectors and musicians. But it is a fact that certain pieces do have enormous resale value. In the counterculture, owning expensive instruments is one of the few forms of prestige one can indulge in without being accused of having sold out to the establishment."[1]

Collecting great guitars can seem like an admission ticket to rock'n'roll culture for people who aren't good enough to be in a successful rock band. But very few collectors have gone quite so far as William Randolph Hearst, the newspaper tycoon of the early 20th century. He comes to mind as the epitome of the worst excesses of the collector gone mad, far beyond simply wanting to impress anyone or to be the member of a particularly exclusive club. Hearst, a control freak with little evident self-control, amassed vast castles full of plundered riches, monuments to the old cliché about having more money than sense. Inevitably it all came tumbling down around him.

Collectors may not go to the extremes of a Hearst, but they still share with him at least that need to accumulate, to amass things. They want to get as many of this or that thing to help explain them, to classify them, to compare and contrast, to understand. It's the same desire that leads to albums full of stamps, for a cabinet packed with coins, for drawers full of comics, for a garage bulging with Bugattis. It's a boy thing. I couldn't find one woman who collected sunburst Les Pauls during my search for the world's most valuable guitar.

Eric Clapton has been a guitar man amongst guitar men. To some, in his time, a god. He used the magic c word quite early on, in a 1968 interview. "I collect them now," he said when asked about his Les Pauls. "I've got two in sunburst, one gold, one black, and one standard finish."[2] But professional guitarists collect guitars in a different way to the cabinet-of-curiosities approach that some individual collectors like to take.

A pro player needs a guitar for a purpose – at least at first, although they too can get infected and lead a parallel life as a collector. But a pro will usually act a little more like a workman collecting tools.

He may love the tools he collects for the way they're made, for their ergonomic sense and efficient design, for their beauty. At least at first, it is their use to him that attracts the workman to his specific tools. It is their ability to get a particular job done well that inspires the acquisition. Maybe he only uses them once or twice and finds that they do not quite do what they were supposed to do. Maybe they go into storage with the rest of the also-rans; perhaps they get sold. But some are with him every day: the special ones. The ones he cannot put down. The ones that call out to him. Some collectors recognise the moment they become a collector because the habit that they thought was under control suddenly seems to run away on its own.

I first met Scot Arch back in the 90s when we photographed some of the instruments in his enviable guitar collection for an earlier book. His I-am-a-collector moment came during 1992, when he was regularly playing a 70s Flying V. He felt he had enough discretionary savings that he could collect some vintage guitars. His plan was to buy four: an example of each of the three classic styles of the Fender Stratocaster, and a sunburst Gibson Les Paul. "And really," Arch smiles, "it was supposed to stop there." Ah, now you've guessed: it didn't.

One of the dealers he connected up with was Gil Southworth. "I bought two Les Pauls from Gil," says Arch, "and I wasn't even supposed to be buying one of these guitars. But there they were for sale." Friends who had been keeping an eye on the market told him he was crazy to even consider them. They told him in very clear language that they were overpriced.

"I paid $40,000 for the pair," says Arch. "One was the sunburst that you photographed, a 59, near mint, with tags, at 25,000. The other was a 58 Goldtop, also very near mint, at 15,000. I did pretty good if you look at it from our perspective right now. At the time, I think they were both strongly priced. I was a new mark for Gil at that point," he laughs. Today they are worth many, many times those figures. We'll be looking more deeply into today's values a little later.

A note on terminology there, too: a guitar that's said to be 'with tags' comes with all the sales tags and little booklets that the guitar would have had when it was originally sold. Even the cleaning cloth. Ideally unused. Another term that is used by collectors for these increasingly hard-to-find odds and ends is 'case candy'.

"I try not to feel like a kid in a candy store, that feeling when I'll hear about something or see it and I've got to buy it," explains Arch. "I try to give myself some time to think about it. But you can't always. There are times when you have to jump on it, for whatever reason: call it instinct, or you just decide 'I want it'."[3]

Our friend Bill in the Southeastern USA discovered that he too had the beginnings of the collecting disease, what he aptly calls "the fever", during freshman year in college. He found that his best friend in the dormitory played and owned banjos. At first, this meant that Bill got a taste for acoustic-based music – The Eagles, America, folk-rock – but then he moved on to all-electric bands. Soon he decided to buy his first solidbody guitar, which was a used 73 Stratocaster.

"I began to realise that all guitars have different voices and personalities," says Bill. "So rather than the Rory Gallagher school of have one guitar, play it your whole life, and beat the heck out of it, I decided that a Strat was one voice, a Les Paul was another voice, an ES-335 yet another. I decided that no one guitar can do it all."

This was Bill's moment of I-am-a-collector. Actually, he says, more like I-am-a-mechanic. "I describe people as being either mechanics or talent. I'm a mechanic. I play OK, but I know people who, sound asleep, if you put their hand on a fingerboard, they'll play the most amazing music without even being conscious. That's talent. I jam with friends, I play guitar with all sorts of friends and stuff, but mostly for my own enjoyment."

Before he was out of college, Bill found himself with four or five guitars in tow. "And then the sickness proceeded from that," he laughs. "If you have two or three of the same guitar, you are collecting at that point. A different guitar for its different voice is one thing. If you want to play, oh ... let's say like Danny Gatton, then you've got to get yourself a Telecaster. But if you've got four Telecasters, that's another thing altogether."

Bill's own entry into Burstland came relatively recently, in 2003. "The one that I bought was from a wonderful dealer. He'd just found one literally under the bed, which came with photos of the original owner playing it back in the 60s. That became the dealer's new baby, and so the one he had owned for several years became expendable. The price was 80 grand, which was maybe eight times more than any other guitar I'd ever owned."

That must have been something of a shock. Anyway, Bill acquired the guitar and took it home. "I spent that evening with guitar-loving friends," he recalls, "and my new guitar was locked up in the back of my car. I took my own car to the restaurant so I knew where the car was, but I never even showed it to my friends. It was like I had found drugs or something else that I couldn't admit to anybody.

"I couldn't believe I'd spent that much," says Bill, "and my friends are very analytical. I suppose there was an element of thinking: what if they say this sucks? It turned out later that they'd known about this guitar longer than I had, they'd photographed it, they knew it inside and out, and they loved this guitar. I need not have worried about it."[4]

We met Mike Slubowski earlier, the collector and health-care executive based near Detroit. He describes himself as health-care exec by day and weekend warrior the rest of the time. He plays guitar in a band that does charity events during the summer, and he considers himself a latecomer to guitar collecting.

"I always had in my mind a memory of the guy in my high school rock band who had a 57 Goldtop. Number one," says Slubowski, "he was an awesome player, and number two, as I think back on the history, he was the classic Les Paul-with-humbuckers-and-Marshall guy. So then when I started playing again in earnest, in the mid 90s, that memory still intrigued me. I had to have a Les Paul. And from there I went crazy," he laughs, aware of the fact he's already admitted to me that he now owns three Bursts among his 12 vintage Les Pauls.

I ask if there's a line between having an instrument to play and being a collector. "I don't keep anything that I don't enjoy playing," Slubowski replies. "I've collected some vintage instruments that I just couldn't get on with, so I've sold those right away. I definitely am a much better collector than I am a player. I collect them because I enjoy the music and theinstruments themselves, the tone of these guitars, the feel of these guitars.

"It's hard to describe to people who say well, what could the difference be between that and one of Gibson's Historic reissues? I say you just have to sit down with an original and strum one chord in front of a nice amp. You will know the difference."[5]

Peter Svensson in Sweden has been collecting for about 15 years. He has the advantage of being in a successful band, The Cardigans. He is also, at 33, just about the youngest guitar collector I came across in my travels. He admits to being one of those people who simply has to collect.

"When I was a kid, it was vinyl, and then different things at different times. I was just attracted to stuff. Some boys are. I like art and fashion and cars. I don't collect all of those things, but as I'm a guitar player, I think if I go back to wondering why I play the instrument, it was a fascination for these guys having that thing hanging around their neck. It appealed to me: the whole look and the whole idea."

Svensson recalls going to the local music store after school and gazing at the guitars on show, dreaming of having one. Or perhaps all of them. "And when we suddenly had success with the band and made some money, even if we didn't make a lot of money from day one, when I got my first pay cheque I bought a guitar. And that's what I have been doing ever since. I didn't buy anything else, really."

He agrees with the general view that collecting is a form of disease, although he says that's only really a problem if you don't have the money to feed the habit. "I have many friends that collect and are worse than I am," he says, "in that they can't control it. I think I'm pretty controlled. I don't just go and buy *anything* out there. I'm quite selective. I have a couple of really close friends who I can tell collect more than they should."[6]

Tom Wittrock in Missouri says he too has collected a number of things at various times. He and his brother have been through coins, stamps, and the other common collectables. "There's a lot of the collector in me," he admits, "and in a lot of people of my generation in the United States. In some sense I already knew what being a collector was when I got hooked by the guitar bug generally and the Les Paul specifically. It wasn't the first thing and the only thing I ever collected. But these days, guitars are pretty much the only thing where I have an active collection going."[7]

A collector who caused a big shake-up in the guitar world was Scott Chinery. In the late 80s, as a 20-something multi-millionaire from New Jersey with lots of money to spend and a passion for guitars, Chinery started to collect. With a vengeance. He decided he wanted to construct a big collection of the most significant guitars, and he was especially worried because he thought too many were leaving American shores for Japan and elsewhere. Some collectors felt that in the process of accumulating hundreds of instruments, Chinery paid too much and skewed the market.

I worked with him in the 90s on a book about his collection, and naturally we talked at length about all this. "When I entered the market," he told me, "I was very interested in these instruments, and that's when the Japanese were purchasing at the peak. There was literally an exodus of guitars. They were just being siphoned out.

"I really needed to make myself visible," said Chinery, "and my agenda was that I wanted to do my part in preserving this art form, here in the USA. I jumped into it in a very visible way, and made a concerted effort to make all the important purchases as quickly as I could. Whenever you do anything like that, it's bound to rub a few people the wrong way. I have no qualms about that."

We included a touch over 300 of his instruments in the book, and I was proud of the result. It seemed to make him happy, too, but I was never sure. I liked Chinery, and I enjoyed watching the effect he could have on other people, but I found him a sad character too. His wealth didn't seem to help him find his place in life, aside from the benefits of all the material stuff he now owned.

Oddly, the availability of large piles of cash seemed to make collecting less of a treat for Chinery. He could pretty easily have any guitar he wanted – and that took away the fun of the chase, the saving up, the trading. It appeared to take away most of the things that more down-to-earth collectors enjoy about their passion.

Chinery expressed a feeling common among his fellow collectors. "I'm the caretaker of these instruments at this point in time," he told me. "I feel privileged that I'm in the position where I can take care of them, that they are preserved for future generations. But really I'm just a caretaker now." He did not have long to take care of them. He died suddenly in October 2000 at the age of just 40.

Collector Scot Arch witnessed the gloomy aftermath. "I happened to be at Scott Chinery's house when all the guitars were being purchased and moved. There was a tractor-trailer sitting in front of his house and it was literally full of guitars. I stood on the back of the trailer and, looking forward, it was top to bottom and front to back just completely full of guitars. An unbelievable sight, and very sad too."

Chinery had three 1960 Bursts among the collection, which was indeed sold after his death. He'd acquired the trio to illustrate some of the visual variety that the tops of these models can have. "As far as electric guitars go," Chinery told me, "those are my favourite instruments." The key to their importance, he said, was that they just can't seem to be duplicated.

"There's a soul to these guitars that the new ones, although they're very nice guitars, don't seem to have. Nobody really understands it, because they're just metal and plastic and wires and wood. But there really is some quality about these guitars that just transcends modern instruments. I never could figure it out."[8]

Can the soul of an old Burst really be captured in Gibson's Historic reissues of recent years? Kunio Kishida is a professional guitarist and a collector, and he runs the Nancy vintage guitar stores in Tokyo and Nagoya, Japan. Despite his vintage habit – he has two 59 Bursts, one of which is ex-Dickie Betts of The Allman Brothers Band – he also likes the reissues.

"In fact," he says, "many vintage Les Paul lovers have started to buy these new items. But new is new. Vintage is vintage. Even if the new instruments are getting close to the originals, vintage-guitar freaks still chase vintage guitars. That really hasn't changed since the vintage guitar boom started around 1970."

Kishida thinks current Gibson efforts have greatly improved since the idea of a reissue of the Burst began properly in the early 80s, and he owns and enjoys playing a Historic Duane Allman signature model. "I've discussed the original Les Pauls with Gibson people many times. The Historics are certainly getting better. I believe it's close to 95 per cent of an original now, but I hope they will get even closer. I believe these are the instruments for the new Les Paul lover of the future."[9]

Bill from the Southeast United States remembers a quote by a friend on an internet guitar forum. "Asking how a Burst sounds is like asking if a Ming vase is microwaveable." Do new guitars exist now that do the job as an instrument just as well as an original Burst, he asks aloud? Sure they do. Are there new basses, too, that do just as well? Sure there are. "But a Ming vase will always be a Ming vase," laughs Bill, "and an original Burst will always be an original Burst. To put it simply: they aren't making them any more."

He owned a Heritage Standard 80, a Guitar Trader Les Paul, and several others of what he calls 'Burst wannabes', long before he ever played a Burst, let alone owned one. "I remember the first time I ever saw one. It was the summer of either 80 or 81 and I was in Houston, Texas, and went to Rocking Robin Music. *Guitar World* magazine had published their first issue that had the centrefold with the Brockburst. I walked in the store and talked Bursts like I almost knew what I was talking about.

"Then the guy said, hey, wanna see one? And I'm like, oh, er, sure. They took me up to a loft, opened a brown case in front of me, and it was the first one I'd ever seen. I was afraid to touch it or even get too close to it. It was like …" and here Bill makes what can only be described as a noise of greatly unsettled confusion. "It was a holy grail moment. I've talked to the owner of that store since, and I've told him exactly what he did back then. He corrupted me for life."[10]

As a store owner, Tom Wittrock sees a great deal of used instruments every single day. As a guitar collector, he loves his Bursts. What would he say to someone who's perfectly happy with a 2008 sunburst Les Paul? "I'd say don't lose that happiness. Don't let somebody else's words make you unhappy. As long as you're happy with your guitar, it makes no difference what the brand name is on it or what day it was made."

Good advice. Think about it: it's exactly what you would have wanted to say to any of the early adopters of Les Pauls back in the 60s and 70s. Only you can know when a particular guitar is right for you. Wittrock's store experience underlines his general view that hallowed brand names do not necessarily translate into the greatest guitars.

"I must have had tens of thousands of different instruments go through my hands in 30-plus years," he says. "And I'm quite often amazed how many guitars played really wonderfully that had brand names that normally ought to say: this should be a piece of junk. And on the contrary, I've seen major brand names where the guitars were poor and where there wasn't a simple way to make them better. I suppose in the long run, if we've got enough opportunities to try enough guitars, we'll find that perfect instrument."

Wittrock says he has never been what some people call a vintage snob. The kind of guy who will find it hard to be in the same room as a guitar made before 1965, let alone lower himself to actually soil his hands by playing such a thing. "I'm happy to play guitars of other generations, or guitars with other modifications," he says. "The guitar that I play regularly – and have done for 28 years now – is a 56 Goldtop cut with humbuckers. And the humbuckers are not PAFs, they're Seymour Duncans.

"The people who hold my guitar, for example here at the shop, say wow, this neck feels fantastic. It's the neck the guitar came with, and it's as good as any Burst I've ever had. It sure doesn't look like it. In fact it's quite ugly," he laughs. "And I think that's part of the appeal, too."[11]

Kerry Keane, the instrument specialist at Christie's auction house in New York City, sees many clients and customers wondering about old and new guitars (and violins) and their pros and cons. "There are great guitar-makers out there now and they're making magnificent instruments," says Keane. "Whether it's mystique, voodoo, or mojo, I haven't met anyone who says, you know, this modern reproduction plays just as well as my 59 Gibson Burst. Not so with other manufacturers. I remember Stephen Stills telling me one time: 'I'm not going to play my Gretsch White Falcon on stage, because the new ones are just as good.' That's telling. Why have them if the new ones are just as good?"[12]

For a musician like Scot Arch, who has been John in Beatlemania since the early 80s, there are clear practical considerations in the old-versus-new debate. "I travel on airplanes often, for instance, and I normally take three or four guitars with me," he explains, "packed in various ways so that I can get them on as baggage. And I don't want to take vintage guitars, that's for sure. They get broken, they get banged around, and they get lost. All these things are very realistic dangers and all of them have happened to me.

"You almost can't think of taking them out. Of the guitars that I use when I work, most of them are reissues and new guitars. And I can get them all to sound great. Do they feel as good as the older ones that I collect and do they play as well? No. The necks feel different, some are a bit heavier, lighter, not shaped perfectly. But especially with today's amps and today's pedals, you can usually tweak them and get them to sound just how you want."

Arch tells me a story about a guitarist he saw who had two guitars on stage he'd use for different songs: one was an original Burst, the other a model by a modern and respected high-end maker. "And you know what? He didn't sound anywhere near as good on the new one as he did on his vintage guitar. Same guy standing there, different guitars. That said to me that he just didn't feel as good about the new one."

The old guitar did something psychologically for that guitarist when he picked it up, beyond its playability and ergonomics. "To me," says Arch, "if a guitar feels good in your hand and it just has that mojo, as some people call it, you play better. You just do."[13]

Collectors in search of the mojo might wake up one day to find themselves with one Burst, or perhaps a few of them, or maybe even multiple Bursts. But as David Byrne once put it so well, you may ask yourself, well, how did I get here? Joe Ganzler is of course very busy with his authentication business, but he knows that at the end of a hard day's checking for original solder on 50s pots he can come home to a warm welcome from Gladys.

He introduces me. "Yes, this is Gladys. She's easy on the eye, ain't she? As my dad told me, it's just as easy to fall in love with a beautiful woman as an ugly one. I guess the thing about Gladys is the first time I saw her, I knew she was my guitar. I took possession in November 2002."

Gladys is, as you've probably guessed, a 1959 sunburst Les Paul. And what a stunner. "I had seen the guitar a year before when it came up on George Gruhn's website. I saw it and I said man, now that is what I'm talking about." But the guitar went to someone else. A good friend of Ganzler's – and a keen Les Paul aficionado – said it was one of the best he'd ever heard. This made things worse. Next time Ganzler caught sight of Gladys was at the Arlington guitar show.

"It's like when you see your future wife in a crowded room and all the others just go out of focus, you know? Yours stands out like a diamond in a goat's ass. I went over and picked it up, and I said to the owner: this is my guitar. Course, he smiled." Over the coming weeks, Ganzler indulged in the ritual offering of stupid money. It worked. Eventually.

"I got my equity line," says Ganzler. "I flew down there and I brought the guitar back. Never been the same since! I had myself figured to pay off the guitar in two years – I talked my wife into it – and I paid it off in four months. So it's living proof that where there's a will there's a way. Happy ending."[14]

Kunio Kishida in Japan tells me about his two original Bursts. "I bought my 59 in 1989, and I called it Nancy after the store I'd opened a year earlier, when I'd sold my tigerstripe 59 to a customer. I went to Los Angeles in 89, to an old friend who'd got together a few Bursts for me in his house, and I chose Nancy.

"She has a great sound," laughs Kishida, "as well as two double-white PAFs and changed Grover tuners, and is very lightweight. I took it to Muscle Shoals to record my second album, Alabama Boy. I still play it on stage. I've sold many great original Bursts since the early 70s, but Nancy is special to me. She still grabs my heart."

Kishida's other 59 belonged to Dickey Betts of The Allman Brothers Band. He's very proud of it. "It's one of the most famous Les Pauls in the world," Kishida declares. "Dickey recorded 'Jessica', 'Ramblin' Man', and many songs on this guitar before he played his Goldtop. It was refinished before he got it in November 1971."

Kishida acquired it during the sessions for his first solo album, in 2002. He soon understood why Betts had sold it. "It was buzzy, the tuning was unstable, and it was really hard to play. Our repairman, Moe, fixed it up after I got it back to Japan. He did a refret, changed the pegs and the nut, fixed a head crack, and quite a few other jobs. It took almost two years. It plays beautifully now. Its sound is so different from other original Les Pauls. If you know the album *Brothers And Sisters* you'll know it has a special sound. I've played over a hundred original Bursts, but I've never known a sound like this."[15]

Mike Slubowski says it was pretty scary when he finally took the plunge and decided he'd like to acquire a Burst of his own. "You don't know what you don't know," he says, simply and honestly. There are many potential concerns facing the virgin Burst buyer: authentication, buying from someone with a good reputation, knowing how to balance the appearance of the guitar with its functionality, and a lot more besides. Slubowski at first locked in on a 58 that seemed to be the one for him.

"But I just had these nagging feelings about it, and I asked the dealer to send me a few more photos. I didn't get to see it in person. It had more wear on the back, and it kind of spooked me. I backed away from the transaction. In fact I would come back and buy that one at a later time. But he had a 59, which was considerably more expensive. I fell in love with it the moment I saw the first photo. That ended up being my first Burst."

This one is not, he reports, an exceptionally flamey guitar, but it has a good rich colour, unfaded. And it plays like a dream, says Slubowski with a twinkle in his eye. "It's bright and crisp," he explains, "and you can dig in."

As it turned out, he purchased all three of his Bursts from the same dealer. "I came to trust him over the years, and he has a great reputation. He is very anally retentive, if you will. I bought that 59 in the late 90s and I paid about $90,000. Looking at it today, it was a fair price."[16]

Peter Svensson of The Cardigans has found quite a few instruments that have a solid history within his own country. "I'm happy that I've been able to find Bursts that were originally sold here in Sweden," he says. "It's a part of my collecting that's driven by the history of the guitars. I like to track down the old guys who once owned the guitar."

He's not limited by that approach – he also owns, for example, a good 1958 Burst that has been owned by Mick Ralphs (Bad Company) and Micky Moody (Whitesnake). With his first Burst, however, which was a 59, Svensson was able to get in contact with pretty much all the people in Sweden who had owned it through the years. "It was great to call an old guy, tell him my name, and then say well, this might sound strange, but I have a guitar I think you owned. And they would tell me all these stories. I think I almost killed one guy when I told him how much they were worth now. He got all silent on me."

Svensson acquired it from someone out in the country in southern Sweden who had a small collection and a music shop. Sweden is relatively small and its guitar community even smaller – so as soon as the instrument came on the market, the dealers knew about it. "I guess they'd all been there trying to buy it," says Svensson. "This guy knew I was collecting – he knew of my band – and got hold of me through a mutual friend, asking if I was interested. He wanted to sell it to someone who would keep it and not just make some money on it."

Svensson bought it and, after some detective work, managed to trace it right back to the original owner who had got it around 1961. He heard about a character nicknamed The Flower who supplied the band with their gear. "He would come to their rehearsal space with stuff that he bought from what he called the major city where the Hagstrom shop was. The Flower turned up with this guitar, and the guy liked it. I guess it had been hanging in that store for a year or two, because this was in 1960 or 61, and it was a 59 Burst."

Hagstrom was a guitar brand and also the prime instrument distributor in Sweden, with a chain of stores in all the big cities. "So they imported and sold most of the Bursts here," says Svensson. I mention to him that in Britain at that time, we were just coming out of a long post-war ban on imports of American guitars.

"You're probably aware that Sweden was neutral in the war, and always has been," says Svensson. "So we didn't have any of that. And that's why you can find guitars like that in Sweden. I have many guitars that I have bought from original owners, including another Burst that was also sold in Sweden, a 59 that I believe was sold in 1960 in Stockholm.

"Hagstrom imported these guitars from Gibson in the USA, and in the 50s when countries like Britain and Germany and France were rebuilding after wars, we were playing rock'n'roll and drinking Coca-Cola and driving American cars. When I tell collectors or dealers in England, say, that last year

I bought a 56 Goldtop and two 56 Customs from two guys in northern Sweden who were original owners, they don't believe me. In England that can't happen, apparently."[17]

One of the recurring dreams for all collectors, whatever the object of desire, involves buying a rare undiscovered gem from someone who has no idea what they have. The forgotten Bugatti under a pile of garbage in the cobwebbed garage. The unseen Picasso bought at the swap meet for a few pennies. The Ming vase that great-aunt Maud leaves you as a reward for all that selfless errand-running. It really happens, and, of course, it really should happen to you.

In the guitar-collector version of the dream, a little old lady calls the collector out of the blue. She says she knows he's a nice boy and would probably like to have this old guitar she's had under the bed that her dear husband never got to play because he died young. To cut a long dream short: collector goes to see her; has some nice tea; buys mint 59 Burst for $3,000 cash; lives happily ever after.

Versions of this have been known to occur in real life. Back in the 80s, collector Clay Harrell used to put ads in Penny Savers, the local free newspapers across America that were mostly full of ads for local businesses. Harrell's ad would read: "Guitar Collector will pay $400 to $10,000 for old guitars, Gibson, Martin, Fender." Plus his toll-free 800 number. He was living in upstate New York at the time and ran the ads in maybe half a dozen newspapers, giving him up to an hour's driving radius from home to seek out original vintage guitars. He was after some of those guitars that really are out there somewhere.

He'd get all kinds of calls, as you can imagine. Mostly, says Harrell, his respondents were hillbillies, out in rural communities, and the best of a very mixed bunch would turn up the occasional Goldtop or Stratocaster. He did get a 1960 Burst, but the guy knew what it was and Harrell paid a pretty high price. Then he moved to Michigan in the late 80s and started the process again from scratch.

A music store owner saw one of the ads, gave him a call, said he had two brothers, customers, who'd been left a sunburst Les Paul by their daddy. "These guys were hillbillies too," reports Harrell. "The store guy tells me they're kind of fighting over this Gibson. And what they really want is two guitars: one each."

He goes down to Ann Arbor and meets the brothers at the store. They're fighting about everything, not just the guitar. "They didn't really know how much they wanted for it. So I said look, you guys can pick out any two guitars you want in the whole music store. I'll take the sunburst and you get any two guitars you want. They thought this was really great. The store owner was thrilled too.

"So the one guy picked out a Lucille, this new Gibson ES-355, and the other guy picked out a Strat Plus. I handed the guy my credit card and I think the two guitars came to, what, less than $2,500 for the pair? And I walked out with a 59 sunburst." It wasn't a perfect example. Someone had put a Bigsby on at some point and the head was cracked. But it was still at the time probably a $5,000 guitar. Good deal.

Let's bump forward to the summer of 2007, and by now for Harrell it's goodbye Penny Savers and hello web page. With the same 'I buy guitars' message – but more potential viewers. And many, many more useless time-wasting calls. However.

"I get this call from a guy in Florida. He says I run a music store and this old black lady has come in with an old Les Paul. It was her brother's. He died, and they were cleaning out his house – they'd pulled a dumpster onto his driveway and were busy throwing everything away. They came across this guitar. She didn't even remember him having it. It was in the closet. So, the store guy says, would I be interested in buying it?"

This was more like it. Or might be. The store owner said he'd done some research and believed it to be a 1959 Les Paul sunburst. Another benefit of our brave new world is that he could instantly send pictures. "And oh man! It was beautiful. Really flamey," says Harrell, "nice colour. Didn't have any issues I could see. Did have an original Bigsby on it, but other than that it was pretty much the dream Les Paul."

Eyes wide open and most definitely not dreaming, Harrell threw out a number. Store owner says well, OK, let him run that by the family and see what they say. Heard nothing for a month. "Then I get an email. The family have thought about it and they want to accept your offer. I was like, right, OK – and now I've got to buy this thing."

He asked the store guy how he wants to do this deal. Store guy says the family doesn't really want it all in cash: they want half the money to go into their bank account. So Harrell opens an account at their bank's branch in his own town, puts in an amount ready to transfer so there would be no holdup, and gets the other half in cash so he can take it along. Arranges to fly down to Florida and rent a car and meet them at the bank's office.

"It was kind of odd," reports Harrell, "because I had 100 grand cash on me. It's definitely weird going through airport security with that much cash on you." He arrives with his cash intact. The bank manager is shaking his head. The family walks in. It's the sister of the original owner who died plus her two nephews.

"I give them the cash," says Harrell, "and they take out $20,000 and hand it to the guy who owned the music store. He got a ten per cent cut. So he walks out with twenty grand cash. They give $500 to the bank people and say, 'Buy lunch for everybody!' So before I even get the guitar, they've already thrown around part of the money.

"They're saying to me, come on! We can all go to lunch! Let's go to a barbecue! But I now have a $200,000 guitar. I think it would be best if I just went to the airport. They're driving this Chevy Caprice that has the muffler off and no hubcaps. The people at the bank must have thought it was a drug thing, but the guitar showed up. It was just the oddest thing in the world."

And the guitar? It was a remarkable find. It was also covered in grime, a mucky haze that had long settled over much of the instrument. "Which was good," explains Harrell, "because it meant no one had messed with it. The frets were rusted, the strings were all black. You could tell nobody had touched this guitar in a long time. Plus it was from Florida, which is a real humid environment, so I'm sure that contributed too."

This 59 Burst cleaned up beautifully. Harrell had his repairman remove the Bigsby and carefully hide the vibrato's original fittings. "Oh yes, I still have that guitar," he smiles. "I keep most everything."[18]

14. WORTH

Coming to terms with the price of everything and the value of nothing

How much is an original sunburst Les Paul worth? Now there's a piece of string. The answer isn't easy, I'm afraid. It all depends. It depends on the condition and originality of the guitar; it depends on how much a particular buyer really wants to own it (or, better still if you're the seller, several buyers); it depends on what the seller needs from the sale; it depends … well, as you can see already, it depends on a lot of things. So let's take a look at all this in more detail.

First, however, it's worth pointing out that, with almost no exceptions, the collectors I talked to emphasised that they didn't get interested in Bursts for their value or as investments.

Scot Arch and Vic DaPra sum up the overall view. First, Arch: "I've seldom ever purchased a guitar with appreciation being the primary reason. I have done that over the last couple of years with just a handful, less than five guitars probably, in my whole career of purchasing guitars.

"I buy them because I love them. They evoke all these feelings of the past, and I just love them. If I'm in my house, I'll be sitting around with a guitar in my lap almost all the time. If I'm watching TV, I have a guitar in my lap – whatever I'm doing. I love guitars."[1]

And DaPra: "This sounds totally crazy, but I never got into this for the value of the guitar. I just bought the guitars. If the guitars were worth $2,000 tomorrow, to me, I don't care. I just love the guitars. I mean sure, you'd look at yourself and say you idiot, you should have sold them," he laughs. "But I just love the guitars."[2]

For something to be valuable, people must want to possess it. The old cliché is true: an object is worth what someone is willing to pay for it. Collectors might not like the idea, but collectability and value are a little like a house of cards: very delicately balanced, and likely to tumble down at the merest draft of doubt or scepticism. But like-minded collectors and all the associated dealers and other supporting characters don't think like that, of course. They all band together and they bolster one another's notions of value and of prestige.

You don't have to be a collector for too long to realise that just because something is rare, that doesn't necessarily mean it's valuable. Quite a few guitars, especially handmade ones, are one-offs. They are unique, which is as rare as it gets. Despite that supreme rarity, they can be almost impossible to sell. If no one wants this unique object – maybe because it's just too quirky a one-off – then it will not be valuable, no matter how rare.

The 1958–60 sunburst Les Paul is quite a rare guitar. It's also, as we know, very desirable. Rare enough, you might say. But how rare?

An especially intriguing part of the mystery of this model is that the specific record log, the one that would show us in detail exactly how many Gibson produced, is missing. Gibson's archive includes books that log the serial numbers and shipping dates of virtually every instrument that left the factory. However, the one that would cover the Burst in most detail is missing from the archive.

Walter Carter, who is now at Gruhn Guitars in Nashville, Tennessee, was formerly the historian at Gibson, and I talked to him when he was there in the 90s about the strange case of the missing book.

Essentially, Gibson's archive has two primary sets of records. The first set is the serial logs, and in these were recorded serial numbers of guitars as they were produced, in number order. The second set is the day-books, in which was recorded models and their serial numbers, in date order. There is also a third set, the shipping totals, where annual figures were reckoned up for each model.

"It's the day-books that are missing for the Les Pauls and, in fact, all the solidbody models of that period," says Carter. "The other main set of books, the serial logs, do go all the way through – but unfortunately they are for the 'A' numbers only, the hollowbody serials, and not for the solidbody 'ink-stamped' numbers.

"So what we have is: day-books up to June 30 1958; A-series hollowbody numbers complete; and the new 'impressed' numbers, for all models, in numerical order, beginning in 1961 and complete for the first few years. And there's no shipping log for the 60s."

Carter's guess is that the missing day-book, the one that would show exactly which Bursts were made when, is simply lost. "I don't think someone would have taken it as a souvenir not knowing what they had. And I think if the culprit knew what they had, then he couldn't have gone all these years without leaking out a little info, such as whether there is a Moderne in there, or when the first Explorer shipped, or exactly how many of them there were. Frustrating, ain't it?"[3]

It certainly is. The existing day-book that ends on June 30 1958 includes the entries for a couple of early sunburst Les Pauls, possibly samples, shipped from the factory on May 28. Before that, there are also a handful of experimental sunburst-like Les Pauls, but these two in May are probably the first proper sunburst models as we know them. Bursts, in fact. We can assume that production of the new sunburst look, which replaced (but may have overlapped slightly) the previous Goldtop, started around July or August. However, in the absence of the missing day-book, that is all it can be: an assumption.

For production numbers, we have to rely on the factory's shipping totals for the relevant years of what Gibson called "Les Paul & Bigsby" – in other words the Les Paul Model, in gold or sunburst finish, with or (usually) without Bigsby vibrato unit. These show 434 for 1958, 643 for 1959, and 635 for 1960. The figures for 1958 and 59 are typewritten on the sheet; the number for 1960 is handwritten.

We can use five-twelfths of that 1958 figure as a crude way of removing the production from the earlier seven months or so of the year when this category of model was still the Goldtop. So, adding together 181, 643, and 635 provides us with a rough total of 1,459 sunburst Les Pauls. And that's about the best anyone can do.

Let's keep on the statistics for a moment, while we have the logs and a calculator handy. Gibson produced 17,772 Les Pauls – Customs, Goldtops, Bursts, Specials, Juniors, TVs – in those three years from 1958 to 60. Which makes the sunbursts a little over eight per cent of all the Les Pauls made during that relatively short period.

Let's mess with the calculator some more and concentrate on 1959. Gibson shipped a grand total of 34,123 guitars of all types and models that year – at least according to the annual reckonings logged on the sheets by the factory managers. All Les Paul models made that year totalled 7,828 – including a mighty 4,364 Juniors, the biggest single production run that year, and 1,821 Specials – making them 23 per cent of total Gibson production. Gibson made 643 Bursts that year: again about eight per cent of that Les Paul total, and a little short of two per cent of overall guitar production.

The point is that while Les Pauls figured prominently in Gibson's sales effort, mostly due to those cheaper Special and Junior models, the Burst hardly mattered at all in the greater scheme of things. As ex-Gibson man Tim Shaw puts it: "What we now consider as the flagship product was a small percentage of production. And based on that fact, Gibson's people would have made it as well as they could, as cleanly as they could, as fast as they could. But if LG-0s were carrying the factory, they would get a lot more floor space than the Les Pauls did."[4]

And so back to value. Anyone outside the circle of Burst collectors will usually look at the prices that these instruments can go for today with incredulity. Jaws around their ankles, they might ask how a guitar can be worth so much money. Thinking about it some more, they wonder aloud if it isn't just a little obscene. Perhaps they might be the owner of a modern Les Paul. How can an original guitar be that much better than my new one, they ask, and worth so much more, just by being old and rare?

Kerry Keane is Christie's International Specialist and Department Head for Musical Instruments, based in New York City. As an auction professional, he wrestles with such questions on a daily basis. Keane plays guitar – he has an especially nice 1954 Martin 00-18 – and started in this world working with guitar makers and repairers. He knows his stuff.

Has the internet hit auction sales? "The net has been this great platform and this great equaliser," says Keane. "Mrs Winterbottom from Frickston, Massachusetts, can turn to her 16-year-old nephew and say: I want to sell this. He goes on the internet, walks her through it, and she'll be able to broadcast that instrument to a very wide audience."

Has eBay eaten into the auction market just as it has the dealer market? Keane says it has certainly removed a number of instruments that might normally have come to them, but more so at the lower end of the scale. "Still – and this is something that's growing – when people have something that's really wonderful, and they learn that it is, they will turn either to who they think is the most trusted private dealer or they'll turn to auction. They like auction because of the transparency. You know what it sells for."

And the drama of an auction sale can be intoxicating. As you'd expect, Keane suggests there are many reasons why an auction works. "But certainly one is that auction is theatre. And the best way to create theatre in the room is to offer great property and have a crackerjack auctioneer."

Why is a "great property" such as a Burst worth so much money? "This is the rarest Les Paul model," says Keane, "but it's also linked to the fact that they are the most desirable among players. I think that's something we have to come back to all the time. It's the perfect tool for a guitarist of a certain style, and that's why they're desirable."

Does that mean that Keane's wrestling takes place mostly around the line between intrinsic value and perceived value? "Intrinsic value is what a new one's worth," he says. "What it costs to buy a new one to do the job. A high-quality product coming out of the Gibson factory."

And the perceived value is your world? "Amongst those 1,400 guitars, or however many it is, the value varies. Of course for condition, of course for originality. But if you erased all of that, it's been my experience that if you line up a group of mass-produced guitars from 1959, and you have good players come in and try them, then by and large they are all going to gravitate toward the few that, for lack of a better word, are players. They play like a mother.

"That's what drives it," he says. "That's what puts a premium on value, that's what drives desirability. And that's putting aside provenance and celebrity association, which is a whole other world."[5]

Ah yes, celebrity guitars. Which means an instrument owned at one time or another by a famous player. And which in its strongest form can bring to mind the curious phenomenon that is religious relics – the bits of saints and the like, or things they owned, saved over long periods and now revered by churches and other centres of faith. "Yes," laughs one of the Burst collectors when I mention this parallel, "sometimes it can be a little like worshipping false gods."

Philipp Blom, in a recent book that looks into collecting and collectors, writes: "To the mind of the believer, relics are imbued with talismanic qualities. … Relics are both dead and alive – parts of dead bodies or inanimate objects, but alive with the aura, the spirit of something greater, and more holy, than we are."[6]

The famous saint-like players who originally played Bursts and brought them to the attention of the rest of us together form another driver of this guitar's collectability. As we learned earlier in the book, those heroes of earlier times – Eric Clapton, Jimmy Page, Michael Bloomfield, Duane Allman, and others – made this guitar what it is and, indirectly, made this guitar as collectable as it is.

So the guitars that they and other great players owned can take on a special relic-like significance. It was Christie's that hosted the best-known auction of celeb instruments of recent times with its two sales of Eric Clapton's guitars in 1999 and 2004. Some point to those sales as triggers of the most recent boom in collecting and, consequently, prices. Before you get too excited, neither sale included Bursts from Clapton's classic 60s period – because he didn't have any left. If you were paying attention earlier, you'll know that the Les Pauls he used back then disappeared at the time.

Keane says: "I think that, across the board, the quality on the vintage front on condition and purity was higher in the second sale than the first." Clapton himself was aware of the difference. "These are the instruments that I kept back from the last sale because I just couldn't bear to part with them," he said. "This is the A-team, the guitars that helped me shape my vision and taught me to play."[7] As with the previous sale, the beneficiary was his admirable rehab project, the Crossroads Centre in Antigua.

The second sale included his 1964 Gibson ES-335 and his 'Blackie' Fender Stratocaster from the classic periods, and these were the instruments that attracted most attention, selling for a remarkable and record-breaking $847,500 and $959,500 respectively.

"In the first sale," says Keane, "the majority of the vintage collectors I knew turned their nose up: I'm not interested in a guitar simply because Eric Clapton played it; I want it because the instrument is right and pure. In the second sale, because much of the property was right and was pure, we were able to dig deeply into another well."

Is the celebrity area where auctions really score? "I look at an instrument and there are six determinants of value," Keane explains. "First is attribution – who made it? Then it's quality – out of that body of work, which instruments are more coveted than others? And with musical instruments, part of that quality is always about playability. Next it's condition, and with guitars it's condition and originality together."

Fourth on the list comes freshness to the market, he says. "If I pull a 59 flame-top out from under the bed of Mrs. Peachtree in Providence, Rhode Island, and the strings are still rusty, well, that's going to cause excitement when it comes to market. That freshness is going to instil a sense of discovery among collectors and they'll compete for it."

Only then in Keane's checklist does 'provenance' appear, the category in which celebrity association would fit. The implication being that for the Burst, where playability is the key, and with its particular kind of buyer, celebrity is not a terribly important aspect.

"Lastly, it's fashion – and we certainly see guitars come in and out of fashion," says Keane. "During the early 90s, if you look just at Les Paul sunbursts, 58s were selling for more than a 59. At that time the perception was: this is earlier, so this is better. Earlier made it more valuable among collectors, until these guitars started to get into the hands of collectors and they began to assess playability.

"Now," says Keane, "everyone agrees that the 59s are the best: the necks are nicer, for instance, faster. Now it's the 59s that sell for more. And if you just looked at rarity and numbers, that doesn't make sense. Which, for me, again underlines the importance of the quality aspect when it comes to selling original Les Paul sunbursts."[8]

What does a 59 sell for today? It depends. OK, I know I already said that. But it really does. Tom Wittrock has been collecting Bursts since the 70s and has a broader view than most on the subject. "The majority of us collectors try to look at previous prices to get a starting point, whether it's known sales, or discussions of prices, or what somebody else asks. But still, with a guitar like a Burst that is individual from one to the next, it comes down to the same question: how do you decide which one is worth what compared to the other?"

Wittrock lays out a hypothetical scene for us. Look, here are ten original Bursts right in front of you. I know, I know. Try not to get too excited. Each is virtually perfect and in exceptional condition. How on earth do we decide which one is more valuable than another? The answer is that it always comes down to how an individual reacts to the guitars.

"How do we decide the final worth?" says Wittrock, still in hypothetical mode. "The schoolteacher says when it's sold, that's the answer: that's the value. So how do we reach that point? Well, we have to reach inside ourselves and ask what it's worth to us. I don't know an easy way to answer that."

Oh go on. You're teasing us. "Well, when there's something you can't just go to the corner store and buy any time you want, even if it's expensive, like a brand new Rolls Royce, when it's something that you cannot just buy every day, we all have different thoughts about what its value is to us. When it becomes something that is a very strong passion, something we desire greatly, obviously we will put more into it – whether it's money, the effort to find it, whatever."

Wittrock says that when he comes to sell a Burst – he owns seven at present and estimates he's had more than 50 pass through his hands over the years – there is no fixed process that takes place. "I can tell you from experience that, many times, I have reached too far and asked too much for something, and other times I know I have offered one at too low a price, based on the reaction of the first buyer.

"But I look at what else has gone on in the field of selling. I judge those prices and the feelings of other people when I present pictures and talk about a certain guitar. And if there's a strong overall reaction, I would generally and naturally value it higher."[9]

A crude interpretation of all that might be that you should get as much as you can get, but that no one's going to help you decide just how much. No one else is responsible for the dizzying, spiralling prices of Bursts other than collectors and dealers themselves. And often they are one and the same.

Many collectors are also dealers, because at some point they may sell a guitar or three. Many dealers are collectors, in that for a while they will put aside for themselves particularly nice guitars. Collectors often have a fantasy about being dealers, and vice versa.

Timm Kummer seems unusual in that he's strictly a dealer. "I own one guitar that I would never sell, because it was a gift. Other than that, everything's for sale," he says. Some dealers aren't like that, however, and the line can seem blurred between collector and dealer.

"It makes it very confusing," Kummer agrees, "because they all seem to put their collections on their sales lists, to fatten them up. And then when someone calls, this particular guitar is either on hold, or sold, or it's so much money as to make no sense at all. But that's fine: I've been dealing with it for 35 years. It's the way the world works in my business."[10]

An aside: the 'on hold' status for a guitar is a much-loved ploy. Many people told me how, if they were having trouble selling a guitar at one of the big shows, slipping an 'on hold' card into the strings was a sure-fire way of attracting more attention. Someone else wants this guitar? It must be a good one; let me take a look.

The guitar business has a habit of making some collectors feel that prices are changing too fast around them – even if they are partly responsible for those changes. Scot Arch voices a popular sentiment. "The guitar market today is almost not fun any more, because everything is so expensive. Unless you have tons of cash sitting around doing nothing, or unless you have some guitars that you wouldn't mind selling to move up, it's just no fun.

"And even if you have the cash, it's so expensive," says Arch. "It makes it hard to accumulate new stuff. You can see something attractive and think wow, I really want that – but I don't want to pay that kind of money. It's not that I don't have the money, but I just think it's ridiculous, crazy."

It is also expensive just to stand still – no matter if you own a single Burst or a lot of them. Storage, insurance, and security start to loom from the moment you get the thing home.

"Every time the insurance bill comes I almost fall over," reports Arch. "And every time I think hmm, I've got to cut down, I must sell some guitars. And then I play a few, I look around them, and I think no, I don't want to sell any of these! So I shake my head and pay the bill – on time, but I wait until the last minute. I move on and forget about it until the next bill comes."[11]

Tom Wittrock agrees that if you properly insure your guitars it can be expensive. He reckons on paying about $7,500 a year – far more than he pays on house insurance. "That financial burden just to continue to own the guitars can work at a person," he says. "I am not fabulously wealthy, and a sum like that every year, when the guitars themselves would mean the same to me if they were worth less money, is a burden I have to take on."

Wittrock says he's more concerned about the safety of a guitar than the insurance. It's next to impossible for him to take them out and feel safe. "The kind of music I do is in small clubs that don't have much in the way of a stage and nothing between you and the audience. The people aren't likely to damage a guitar, but things are just more likely to happen in a situation like that."

So he's less inclined these days to take out his special guitars where he plays. Which surely is their point. "It takes away some of the enjoyment of the instrument when they're worth so much money. Some people think oh, who cares: if I had one I wouldn't care about all that. But once you've owned one for a while, those things will weigh on your mind."

Maybe it's what financial people tell us are 'market forces' that have brought about a change in values? At the time of writing we were in the middle of what is politely called a 'correction' in vintage guitar prices. Less politely, a crash. It's the economy, stupid. The same thing was happening to house prices. And as with houses, those at the top end seem, for now at any rate, less affected. So it is with Bursts, apparently. To try to understand that, we need to look at the way prices for Bursts have generally risen since they first became collectables, back around 1970.

Our primary guide though this is Tom Wittrock, again, for his experience and his ability to look at it from the point of view of both a passionate collector and an objective businessman. First, let's spread out here on the table exactly what we know about the way that Burst prices have moved since the earliest days.

Details from the 60s are pretty spotty. We know that guitarists in London were paying up to about £200 around the middle of the decade ($500 or so at the time). They were rare and in demand. Prices from later in the 60s in the US were anything from around $80 up to about $500. A decent price for a decent used guitar.

Wittrock says: "I started dreaming about these guitars and considering them seriously around 1973. They were advertised then at about $1,500 to

$2,000." Word was getting around, demand was building, prices going up. In 1973, the Nashville dealer George Gruhn put up a 59 for $1,200 and a 60 for $1,300, and the following year offered an "excellent" 59 at $1,800.

"I bought my first Burst in 1975, for $2,000, by which time I knew they were going for $2,500," says Wittrock. "It was a clean late-1960, which I still have." By 1977, Gruhn was advertising a 60 in 'near mint' condition at $2,750, even though it came with a Bigsby, which today would decrease value. A year later, Wittrock acquired his second Burst, a 60 with condition issues, in a trade that pegged its valued at about $2,000.

"In early 1981, I started buying and trading Bursts mostly in the $5,000 range," says Wittrock. "Throughout the early 80s they were selling between $5,000 and $6,000, although something really special, with notable flame and great condition, would bring more." The New Jersey dealer Guitar Trader offered a couple of 'very good' 59s in 1982 at $7,500 and $9,000, and their first $10,000 Burst, an 'excellent' 59, appeared on their lists in December 83.

Wittrock summarises his own experiences in the 80s, emphasising the way look and condition was now having an increasing effect on the range of prices. "I first sold one for over $10,000 in 1987, actually for $11,000. But in that same year, I sold them as low as $4,500, $5,000, $5,250, $6,000, $6,500, $7,000, and $7,500. So you can see that prices varied radically, largely due to flame, but also condition – as they still do. None of these were broken or seriously messed with.

"By 1989, for example," says Wittrock, "I sold one for $6,000 and bought-and-traded another at the equivalent of $21,000. I was regularly buying and selling them for well over $10,000 and mostly around $15,000."

Into the early 90s, and the rate spiked again, moving solidly into the $20,000 range and upward. Wittrock sold two in 91 for over $30,000 each. *Vintage Guitar* magazine started to publish price guides in 1989 that attempted to summarise the market, at first in tables published in the monthly magazine and soon in a separate bi-annual and then annual book.

Vintage Guitar showed ranges of $10,000 to $40,000 for 1991, $18,000 to $42,000 in their 1993 *Price Guide*, $22,000 to $55,000 for 95, and $30,000 to $55,000 for 98, and those prices are by and large borne out by other sources we've seen.

Those rates remained fairly stable into the very start of the 2000s, but by 2002 there was a jump that sent *VG* 's top rate, for a "highly flamed, good colour" 59, to $125,000.

The following years saw a tremendous series of leaps in prices, with *VG's Price Guide* showing $45,000 to $210,000 for the 2004 edition, $190,000 to $250,000 for 06, and $240,000 to $420,000 for 08. "But please remember," says Wittrock, "the huge price ranges are based on the quality of flame and colour. No other guitars vary so much, per instrument, than Bursts."[12]

Despite those last sets of figures, virtually everyone I spoke to told me there had been a slowdown in prices during 2007 and that it was continuing into 2008. (Bear in mind that the *VG* summaries are made in advance of the date on their guides.) Estimates of the size and importance of this 'correction' varied, but it affected more or less all vintage guitars.

Archtop guitars have certainly lost value. "It's because they're not the kind of guitars that today's players use," says Scot Arch. There's been a bit of a slowdown, I suggest, wanting to soften the blow for my suitably-named friend who has quite a few of these instruments. "Well that's incorrect: it's been a whole lot more than a bit! There really has been a huge dip. They were hot for a minute and everybody wanted them; now they're not. But I still love them.

"Guys walk around the guitar shows saying oh, is it time to sell? My feeling," says Arch, "is that if you have Strats, Les Pauls, Teles, 335s, then definitely don't sell them. Because those are the ones that people play."[13]

It's impossible not to notice the way that prices for vintage Fenders in particular have softened. One collector told me, with an especially vivid phrase, that prices for old Strats and Teles have "tanked". Stories are rife, whether or not they're true. Like the guy attempting to sell an original Telecaster – the black-guard model as it's known – for $30,000 at a recent show, where the previous year he would have tried for 80 grand.

"The more mass-produced guitars like the late-50s and early-60s Strats and Teles have taken a big hit," says Kerry Keane at Christie's. "I think there's a readjustment there that's more realistic. A 1960 sunburst Les Paul that I would have sold last year for $300,000 is not going to do that in this market today, and it will be a while before it gets to that level again.

"The collectors that I've met," he continues, "they appreciate the property, they educate themselves about the items, they're players that love to play this stuff. And I think what's driven a very large segment of the solidbody electric guitar market in the last three years is a vast amount of capital being pumped into this market from people who are using them not as musical instruments but as investments. And we're paying the price now. The market is overheated."[14]

Some see the Burst – along with some of the better vintage flat-top acoustic guitars, including the classic Martins – as having weathered the 'correction' with a little more resilience. But no one seemed to dispute at the time of writing that there were very few Bursts for sale. Overtly for sale, that is.

Joe Ganzler, who has a business authenticating Bursts, has seen lower demand since 2007 and, at least on the face of it, less supply too. "The really flamey ones have virtually dried up," he says. "They're gone. I don't know now – with the exception of a few collectors with huge, ridiculous piles of money – where you would get to choose between, let's say, four or five really flamey Bursts that would not be for sale. Not for sale, but … they could be bought."

How can something be not for sale but for sale at the same time? In this world, quite easily, apparently. "I have two clients now who have a selection of flamey Les Pauls that are not for sale," explains Ganzler, "but if you want to pay close to 200 per cent retail, you can buy one of them. And I'm advising anyone that has the wherewithal to go ahead and do that." Which would mean? "Nine hundred thousand, a million dollars. And I don't think that would be a foolish thing to do right now."

Bursts, says Ganzler, are passing into the hands of people who can afford to not sell them. "The demand's been a little off, but the prices haven't come down. And they haven't come down because 98 per cent of the individuals who own these guitars don't need to sell them today, tomorrow, or next week."[15]

I should bring in Clive Brown at this point, an Englishman (or, to be more precise, a Yorkshireman) who is an expert not only in guitar restoration but also in lightening the load of weighty discussions. In an unguarded moment, I ask him why he thinks Bursts are still worth so much money. "Because of the stupidity of rich people!" he laughs. "People who listen with their eyes instead of their ears, or can't play. It's a status symbol: 'I have a Burst.' Actually, I hate the term Burst. A burst what, exactly? A burst appendix? A burst pipe? 'I've got a Burst!' Well, don't worry, it'll soon be better."[16]

Tim Shaw too says he just doesn't get the multiple-hundreds-of-thousands of dollars thing at all when it comes to old Bursts. "That's just trading in commodities," he shrugs. It is a difficult one to get your head around, I suggest. "Well, with a straight face it is," says Shaw, with an admirably straight face.[17]

Another kind of story I heard quite a lot, in slightly different versions, was about a (possibly mythical) Burst, usually a 1960, with a very nice-looking top, that failed to sell at a recent guitar show for $250,000, or thereabouts, and which would normally have been snapped up. Again, I can't vouch for the truth of this, but I heard it often enough to conclude that it at least expresses what a lot of people are feeling: that even Burst prices have gone down a little, but that they've been spared the kind of unsettling drops which other vintage instruments have suffered.

"This isn't the first time that the Burst has softened," insists dealer Timm Kummer. "Everyone would like to think that it's gone in a straight-arrow line from zero to 500,000. It hasn't. In the late 80s they got very soft too."[18] The Strat was king then – but suddenly along came Slash and Joe Perry playing Les Pauls and everyone cheered up again.

I ask collector Vic DaPra if the Burst market is growing. "I don't think it's growing that much," he says. "I think there's more interest in it, but because of the values it's not growing. I think the spike already happened, and I think things are stabilising a little bit."[19]

Tom Wittrock says the climb before the stall came between 2003 and 2006. "The vintage guitar market drastically increased in dollar value through those years, and Bursts were at the forefront of that in some people's minds, and right along with it for others. In late 2006, that whole market came to a grinding halt. Since then, it has proved very hard for it to recover and very hard for all of us to figure out where it's at."[20]

The highest recent Burst price that I've had confirmed was a very flamey one-owner 1959 in excellent condition that sold in 2007 for $525,000. No trades, no side deals: a straightforward cash sale.

Naturally, I heard many, many rumours about other guitars that had sold and were selling for this, that, and the other price. It's always a friend or someone just out of the frame.

For example: "This friend of mine told me a year ago that he knows point blank of two Bursts that each sold for a million and one that sold for a million plus several very special 50s guitars." That was certainly the story, exactly as it was told to me. But … no evidence. Just another rumour. If I had a dollar for every one of these rumours I've heard over the years, well, I might be able to afford a Burst tone knob.

The million-dollar Les Paul – the one I set out to search for when I started this book, and the one that is looking ever more elusive as I reach the end – featured heavily in the rumours. Everyone had a story or two, but no one could point for sure and offer me firm evidence.

As usual, Tom Wittrock offers good sense and as unbiased a view as it is possible for him to give. "I would say there have been guitars that have sold probably well in excess of half a million dollars in the last five years," he says, "but I don't have details on them."

So those too – even if not quite up in the lofty regions we're looking for – are in the merely-a-rumour category? "They are. But depending on how deep you are into this world, and I'm pretty deep into it, when you hear the rumour from certain people you have a tendency to give it a lot more credibility. Even though it is not made public. And on the other hand, there are certainly still Bursts that are good guitars that will probably sell at $200,000 or less."[21]

Joe Ganzler echoes this notion of deals going on behind closed doors. The type of doors that have no windows. In rooms that have the curtains closed. And the phone switched off.

"Yes, the details on these transactions remain pretty dark and murky," he says, "because a lot of times there is a significant amount of cash involved. The guys that buy these guitars, they really do want to stay off the grid when it comes to any details about what they paid, mainly because when they go to buy one, they don't want anyone to know what they paid for the last one. It does jack the price up."

I mention to Ganzler that almost everyone talks about the 600-grand-plus Bursts but suddenly go quiet when I ask for hard evidence. "Well," he says, with a glance over the shoulder, "I know of a guitar that traded hands, probably two years ago, and the cash value that I would assign to it would probably be close to three quarters of a million."

He emphasises that the deal included two "really great" Les Pauls as part of the trade, plus an undisclosed amount of cash that he can only guess at. "But in my opinion the whole deal was probably worth $750,000. You're talking about an open market in that kind of stratosphere where there's probably only a dozen buyers in the world," adds Ganzler.

"The reason that the guy that owns that guitar now doesn't really think it is worth 750 grand is because he paid considerably less for the other guitars he traded as part of the deal."

And so it is that we nudge just a little bit closer to that elusive million-dollar Les Paul we're looking for. But not without the ever-present haze of rumour and innuendo – as well as good old lies. "Yes," smiles Ganzler, "it all makes it very difficult to say for sure that a certain guitar sold for a certain amount."[22]

15. LEGACY

An interview with Joe Bonamassa, the guitarist with Les Paul history in mind and a fine future ahead of him

Joe Bonamassa is the new king of blues-rock guitar. He's 31 years old, he loves Les Pauls, B.B. King has called him "one of a kind", and he plays almost as if he's been reincarnated from the 60s. With a very 21st century edge and feel, of course.

Bloodlines, the band he'd been in, broke up around the turn of the millennium. He had something of a change of heart. "It was right around that time I really dedicated myself to the English blues," he says. "And I felt that I was on a one-man crusade. Everybody wanted to do Stevie Ray Vaughan type stuff. Kenny Wayne Shepherd was hot, Jonny Lang was hot – they were all doing the American straight-up Texas thing."

He had a different idea in mind, a different set of CDs in his tour bag. "I liked The Jeff Beck Group better. I liked John Mayall better. In America then, that was complete sacrilege. I was plugging away on my Les Paul and Marshalls, going out and playing gigs, trying to get a following. Then I met a guy named Tom Dowd." Dowd was the legendary engineer and producer who'd worked with an astonishing list of great artists, from John Coltrane to

Aretha Franklin, from The Allman Brothers to Otis Redding. Most notably for Bonamassa, Dowd had engineered the classic Cream records and produced a good number of Eric Clapton's later albums.

"He said to me, yes, we can do something like that – but you have to find out who *you* are, too. You have to embrace different kinds of music, and it will all come out of the way you interpret it."

He made a few albums with the great studio man before Dowd died aged 77 years in 2002. With each subsequent release and with almost incessant touring, Bonamassa has really begun to make his mark. When I talked to him in Columbus, Ohio, on a day off during his latest round of concerts, we watched the tour bus go off for a well-deserved wash and then settled down for a coffee and a Les Paul pow-wow.

He's always been a Les Paul guy, he says, although he was known as a Strat guy for a while because photographers would snap away whenever he occasionally took out a particularly photogenic gold Fender.

"Everybody has a sound in their head that they want to hear and they want to be perceived by the audience. And with the Les Paul, for me, I can always achieve this sound in my head. It hits the amp input hard, and I like the guitar to kind of wrap around your head and not punish you with treble and that very strident kind of sound. I like it really warm and dark, and that's always been my reason for going for the Les Paul. I can instantly fall into it and it does what you want."

A lot of his favourite players – Peter Green, Paul Kossoff, early Eric Clapton, Jeff Beck – played Les Pauls too and got that kind of sound. "To me it was so inviting, and it didn't hurt my ears to listen to it."

If he had to choose one of those? "It would be Paul Kossoff, for the simplicity. It was so devastating. If you had to boil down what a 59 Les Paul should sound like, it's pretty much Paul Kossoff on 'Fire And Water' or 'Mr Big' or something like that. Big, but clean and clear. Really rocking. He and

Free were a lesson in space in the music. Simon Kirke and Andy Fraser worked so well together and Kossoff would fill the holes. They really were such a brilliant band."

You pick up a Les Paul, he says, and it's hard not to be aware of that legacy behind you. Impossible, in fact. He's found that some younger guitarists – the kind he meets at festivals on mixed bills with local bands – might have an Epiphone Les Paul or something similar and not even realise what the name means. He tells them the next time they're in New York City on a Monday night to treat themselves.

"I say go see Les while, god bless him, he's still kicking at 93. They say Les who? I go: the guy on your guitar! They don't even realise he's a person, let alone what I call a hillbilly-jazz guitarist. You have to go see The Man if you play his guitar!"

Now Bonamassa finds himself part of the ongoing history of the Gibson Les Paul. Not only by playing his own Les Pauls on stage and on record, but with a Gibson special-edition guitar that, when we met in Columbus, was just hours from release.

It's Gibson's Custom Shop Les Paul Inspired By Joe Bonamassa model, in a limited run of 100 guitars. Most of the specs are based on the Historic Bursts that he plays, but it has a gold finish. That was the result of Gibson suggesting a Goldtop rather than yet another sunburst.

He drew inspiration from a wrecked and otherwise unwanted 54 Goldtop that his dad had picked up at a guitar show for $1,000 back in the early 90s: black plasticware, a black-painted back to hide repairs, a crazed and dinged finish.

"In fact, a complete basket case," he laughs. "But it was one of the best playing and sounding guitars. It was such a lesson in the collectable guitar market. The ones that are museum pieces are normally the ones that are shit. No one's ever wanted them. The one's that were beat up and completely trashed are the ones everyone plays, because they were and are the best. I want the Joe Bonamassa Les Paul to be a played Les Paul."

His first proper Les Paul was a Heritage 80, bought used for him by his dad in 1988, when Bonamassa was 11 and raring to get moving with a decent guitar. It was a good start, he says, but not quite right. He certainly had a decent teacher.

"I met a guy named Danny Gatton that same year and he became my guitar teacher. I was playing gigs, jamming with Danny, switching back and forth between a 68 Telecaster and this Les Paul. I actually found it easier to get Danny's tone with the Les Paul than the Tele, though I never told him that. But then, he had a 53 and I had a 68. There's a difference."

He traded the Heritage for a 90s 59 reissue with a nice top. His dad – quickly becoming a star of this story – had bought a fire-and-flood-damaged Gibson that provided a set of real PAF humbuckers for the new acquisition. There's a difference.

"Then I got another Les Paul, a 72, a very rare sunburst model. I think it was one of the Gibson factory guys trying to make something that looked like a 59. It had a chunkier neck for a 70s Les Paul and it was light. So I thought, right, now we have a candidate."

He put most of the old fire-damaged guitar electronics as well as the PAFs into the 'new' guitar. "And this thing just soared," he says, smiling at the memory of a great discovery. "When you get a magic Les Paul there is no better sound. Anything you would do, it would respond to your slightest whims and desires. It was inviting to play."

People sometimes ask how he knows when he has a good one. "I say that when you listen to the frequency range, it really shouldn't change too radically from the wound strings to the unwound strings. The G-string should still have some bottom to it and be thick, you know? It's easy to get bottom end from the wound strings and it's easy to get bottom from two-note power chords. But the single notes, like the Kossoff bends on the third string, even the stuff Peter Green and Clapton would do, it's very difficult to keep the bottom end. When you have it, you've got a special one."

It was at this time of guitar that he met Tom Dowd, that he signed to Epic Records and started gigging and making records as a solo artist. Dowd gave him some more good advice. "He wasn't a guitar player, but he'd been around so much and he'd been around so many great players. And he told me it was completely about touch, not how much volume comes out of the speakers. If you want the guitar sounds to come forward, you back off. You let the guitar do the work.

"And that was pretty much the day, ten years ago, that the Strat went away. I realised by backing off on a Strat, it just got thinner. But backing off on the attack of the Les Paul – by that time I had a couple of Historics, which I still have on the road today – by backing off on those, it just sounded bigger.

"I thought, well, *this is how they did it.* The volume wasn't always on 10, they weren't always playing as hard as they had to. They had plenty of headroom and they had these guitars that were very cooperative. It was a real watershed moment. Before, I would just leave the guitar on 10 and use a boost pedal. Now, the guitar is rarely on 10, and mostly, if I want a little more gain, I just eke up the volume a little and it drives the amp harder. And that's it."

Bonamassa carried on using his 72 until the frets wore out and then he retired it to storage. That's when he got the first of his Historic reissue Bursts, around 2002. The friend who sold it to him kindly left a pair of early-60s humbuckers in there. These days that remains a favourite. He also takes out a prototype Joe Bonamassa and a couple more Historics, a 59 and an aged 58.

Has he played an original Burst? Well, he and his dad owned a real 58 for about three months around 1995. "We paid $26,000 for it, sold it for $28,000.

That's all it was worth then. To have that much tied up in one guitar was outrageous at the time. We always bought it to resell, as an investment. I can't even ... it hurts me to even say that out loud."

He's played maybe five or six real Bursts in more recent years. He knows some of the dealers, goes to their shops, and they say he really ought to try this or that original. At which point he usually asks how much. "And they're going, well, this one is $275,000. I say come on, I'm not buying a house."

Bonamassa says the pressure just of owning such a thing would be outrageous. You could easily put a $10,000 scratch in it. He's had offers of short loans of real ones, to use on a record. "But I really beat the hell out of guitars when I play. I want to feel that I can move it around and really dig into it, and a lot of those original ones that go for that kind of money have no frets left. I'm like, OK – if you want to refret it and put Grovers on it so it stays in tune. Obviously, no takers."

He used to take vintage instruments out on the road – a 1959 Tele, a 1962 ES-335, a 1956 Goldtop – but often people would come around backstage and congratulate him on owning such a great piece of aged work from the custom shop. He realised that to people in row GG, or even a lot closer, it made no difference. And to him? "The only reason that I would know the difference is because I would never get any sleep that night in fear of someone who might come and take my valuable guitar."

That, he says, is a terrible situation for musicians. "The 56 Goldtop that I bought for 3,800 bucks back in the day is now literally worth 75 or 80,000 dollars. Crazy. So I play it in the studio – because it's beat up and I don't care. But it's terrible because a lot of musicians will never be able to play a real authentic guitar. Those instruments are out of their price range."

He sees that changing. Perhaps in the next ten years – maybe less, maybe more – prices will take a turn, he reckons, as all the baby boomers who own these things at the moment start to cash in their chips. "They're collecting those guitars because they remember them from the 60s and they want a piece of their childhood back.

"They're also buying for investment. When they realise, or when the wife realises, that they want that holiday home or whatever, what's the first thing to go? Not the jewellery. It will be the scratched-up gold thing in the closet. That's when I really think it's going to come back down to earth, hardcore."

Even the Burst? "I don't think so. I think a Stradivarius will always be worth that money. Supply and demand: the demand will always be there. I think it's the rank and file vintage guitars that will come down.

"The cool thing with Stradivarius violins is that millionaire investors and philanthropists buy them and loan them out to players like Josh Bell, so that they're being played. Nobody has offered to loan me out a Les Paul in a philanthropy deal."

Maybe that's the way it will have to go. Bonamassa says he would never own one, so a loan like this might become a solution, along the lines of an organisation such as Japan's Nippon Music Foundation, one of the most famous of the funds that lend great violins to great musicians.

"I bought a 5,200-square-foot house in Athens, Georgia, for $600,000, a beautiful brand-new house, five bedrooms, way bigger than my girlfriend and I require, but there's a music room and, you know, it's a lot of fun. The thought of carrying that house in a guitar case is a daunting one. I can't get my head around it. Especially in the States. Because as you know, we all get along here so well and nobody ever robs anyone. I would have to hire a guy for 50,000 a year just to handcuff it to himself so nobody gets robbed at gunpoint – and it still wouldn't prevent that. It would have to be a very special scenario."

The 59 Les Paul itself came from a very special place and time, he says, when America was manufacturing what he delicately describes as mofos. "If it was made in America, that was a quality thing. We had our act together.

All those factories that were cranking out, oh, pickguards, they could have been cranking out bullets. We were used to having things made to a high tolerance and quality. You could get a good piece of mahogany that was light. There was a readiness of availability of good things."

And, he explains, it was a time when, for guitarists, louder and cleaner was the key. "Now, it's like I have to go through eight million gain stages to have it still sound like a vacuum cleaner. That's the new priority. But back then, it was loud and clean. Everything was on the edge of its tolerance, especially the amp. I think all that adds up after a while."

He's just 31. Why is he so taken with the players and with a sound that started way before he was even born? "I don't feel like I'm the only guy in my age group that appreciates that kind of guitar. There will always be an interest in them, because there will always be an interest in Led Zeppelin, those great Les Paul players, the Jeff Becks, the Claptons.

"Every kid loves Led Zeppelin. Unless there's something wrong with them. 'Whole Lotta Love' still resonates. You look at some of the real good footage of that band, and Jimmy Page with his Les Paul is just so front and centre. It has such a cool factor. I don't think it will ever be not cool to want a Les Paul and a Marshall and to want to play like Jimmy Page.

"That's the legacy," says Bonamassa. "I'm just hoping to carry the torch with a degree of dignity and to not tinker too much with it all."[1]

16. FUTURE

In the years to come, will every Burst be equal?

If we're going to understand more about the place of the Burst in the world of investments and big money – and that's certainly the world our beloved guitar is beginning to inhabit – then we really ought to talk to someone who knows the ins and outs of high-rolling cash.

Please let me introduce Andy Rappaport, a financial professional who is a partner at August Capital, a venture capital firm based in California's Silicon Valley that invests in hi-tech companies. Rappaport is an amateur guitarist and collector with numerous vintage axes to his name, so he brings to the table a welcome combination: sound financial know-how as well as a passion for guitars.

He says that his love for guitars stems from their utility and from the emotional connection he makes with them because of their craftsmanship and beauty. Value starts to muddy that relationship. "I'm troubled that I have a few guitars that are so valuable I won't take them out of the house," says Rappaport. "I don't like that. It bothers me that I'm forced to consider the price people will pay for them in addition to their function as instruments."

Based on all the data we had before us, Rappaport put together a useful illustration that aims to show what you would have had in January 2008 if you'd invested $1 in December 1992 in each of four areas: the Dow Jones average (the US stock exchange's industrial performance index), some Microsoft stock, some Cisco stock, and an original Les Paul Burst.

Why 1992 as the start point? "Because Microsoft and Cisco are exemplars of very successful stock investments of this period," Rappaport explains, "and had been public companies for long enough that they had gone past their initial rise. They were somewhat less speculative by 1992 than they were earlier. Microsoft went public in 86 and Cisco in 90. The second reason is that this goes back before the internet stock bubble by about the same number of years as we are past that."

So, his illustration indicates that if we bought a Burst for the same amount of money as we bought Microsoft stock in 1992, we'd have ended up in about the same place. We would have taken a different path to get there, thanks to that bubble, but we'd be more or less at the same point: about $20 or so up on our $1 investment. We'd be slightly worse off with the Burst than if we had bought the Cisco stock, which has performed a little better, but not dramatically.

"The average annual return on the Dow Jones between 1973 and now was 8 per cent," says Rappaport. "The average annual return on a Burst between 1973 and now is 18 per cent, so it's comfortably outperformed the Dow over that period.

"Over the period of my illustration, from 92 to 08, the average annual return on the Dow was 9.7 per cent; the average annual return on the Burst was 19.3. So it outperformed by about the same margin. Very consistent. The average annual return on Microsoft was 20 per cent, so about the same as the Burst, and Cisco was 23.8, so a little bit higher. What that says is that the Burst had about the same performance as the two bellwether tech stocks."

After what Rappaport calls the internet stock bubble and most others call the dotcom crash, the market very rapidly 'corrected', a piece of financial jargon that means values took a tumble. "So an average line drawn through our four $1 investment curves would make them all look much the same. Which means that, over the long term, they have represented reasonable investment."

Looking more closely at all our Burst data, Rappaport first states the obvious, which is no bad thing: these guitars have increased in value pretty steadily since the early 70s. "They've been very good investments relative to the Dow Jones through that period, but over the last several years they've taken a pretty spectacular jump. So we look at the data point now and we say OK, a Burst is worth maybe $250,000 to $400,000.

"What is the likelihood," Rappaport asks himself out loud, "that, two or three or four years out, it's going to be 500k to a million?" Meanwhile, I'm busy studying a handsome Collings guitar in the corner of his office. "A couple of years out, maybe that might be so, but it wouldn't take very many of them coming on the market before you could also envision their prices falling back to $100,000."

I'm attentive now. OK, this leads to the obvious question: if that is a possibility, then when, exactly, might enough of them come onto the market to unbalance supply-and-demand – enough to give a sharp decline in value of the kind that surely comes at the end of any speculative trading?

"My own view is that the rate of increase in value is not going to continue at anything like what it's been," replies Rappaport, "because at some point – and I don't know whether it's next year or the following year or five years after that – at some point people who have collected guitars are by and large older and getting older and are going to start to sell them."

Rappaport does not see museums lining up to buy these guitars. He does not see another generation of buyers prepared to put this kind of money into them. And he does not even see himself, a confirmed vintage-guitar junkie, buying them. He's more or less stopped, he says.

With his financial hat on and his guitar-nut cap tucked away, Rappaport's view is that any collectable guitar he might buy today will be available to him in a few years at a much lower price. He might as well wait. "The adage in my business that's been proved time and again is: if you're not a buyer, then you're a seller. In other words, if you're not willing to buy more of something, you should probably sell what you already own.

"It's causing me great consternation," he smiles, "because in my head I know that's true, and I know that I could sell a few guitars today, probably recovering the value of my entire collection in the process, and then just plan on three or four or five years from now buying back the same guitars. But unfortunately that's treating them as assets and not as guitars. And I'm not able to do that."

Ah, the Collings had me again for a moment there, but now I see that Rappaport's guitar-nut cap has reappeared. And to me it looks just as worn as his financial hat. "If there are an increasing number of people like me who look at these prices and say, well, I think I'll wait till they fall," he says, "that becomes a self-fulfilling phenomenon. This is what happened to vintage Ferraris in the late 80s. The prices would collapse fairly quickly."

You buy a new guitar, a modern one, for utility. It's just like your car: you don't generally expect to be able to sell it for more than you paid, and indeed it's usually quite the opposite. Collectable guitars, however, are what economists call a positional good, explains Rappaport. "That's something whose value is created essentially by its demand and scarcity. Its value has far exceeded its utility or intrinsic value. Its value is created precisely by the fact that people put value on it, where the value of ownership is the ownership itself."[1] This is what people mean when they say that the Burst has accrued its phenomenal value because of the myth surrounding it. They are trying to express the evident fact that there's nothing intrinsically there amid the wood and plastic and metal that provides this value.

Roger Giffin put it quite well some years ago: "These prices are bloody stupid! As a guitar builder, I look at them and think, OK, there's 25 bucks worth of wood there, perhaps, and maybe 10 or 15 dollars worth of plastic and metal. So why? It's just perceived value. I mean, sure, they're great guitars – but even then, not all of them."[2]

When a guitar itself becomes so valuable, so too do the parts that you might need to complete an instrument that doesn't quite have all its original appointments. We met Kim LaFleur earlier in the book as the boss of Historic Makeovers, telling us about his Historic reissue upgrades. He also runs a parts business, Vintage Checkout, one of the dealers who will happily sell you anything from a truss-rod cover to a humbucker. All original, ready to wear, and at a fair old price.

"It's like going to a junkyard and saying yes, I could build a car around this," LaFleur smiles. "Maybe about six or seven years ago we started doing the guitar shows, and it's turned into a legitimate business."

He tells me the scarcest Burst parts are the plastic pickup rings (or surrounds), the poker chip (the Rhythm/Treble pickup-switch plate), and the pickguard. "The plastics are the hardest parts to find," he confirms. "You have to remember that the plastic on that guitar was made only for that model. The jackplates were on lap steels, the pots were in several different 50s guitars – exactly the same in an ES-225 as they are in a Burst. The knobs were on everything."

He gives some examples of his mid-2008 prices, starting off with strap buttons and truss-rod covers at maybe $200 and a jack-plate for nearer $300, up through a set of tuners, with the original unshrunken tips, at $1,500, a complete wiring harness for around $2,500, a pair of PAF humbuckers ("with covers that have never been off") for maybe $6,500, and a pair of pickup rings or a pickguard for close on $10,000.

And a deal, as it's Thursday, for a complete set of Burst parts, plus a case? "Maybe 60 to 70 grand," says LaFleur.[3]

One more important point from Rappaport before we move on.

Collectable guitars should not be thought of in the same way as stocks or bonds or real estate or even art. He did another calculation for us that placed the market cap of Bursts at $500,000,000. That means market capitalisation: the total value to investors. That's based on the assumptions that an average value for a Burst is $325,000 and that 1,500 exist.

"The reason that's important," says Rappaport, "is that you can't move very much money into something that, even though it sounds like a lot of money to you and me, is only worth $500m on a global scale. That doesn't account for a measurably large amount of capital. The value of Google today is north of fifty thousand million dollars – a hundred times higher. The value of the Dow Jones is comfortably in the million millions."

It's a tiny investment class, he explains, and while that means it will probably continue to behave irrationally, it also means it will almost certainly not attract the interest of professional investors. "So my feeling is that it's an unwise place for people to invest, outside of their desire to own the instruments. And it can't increase to the point where it would interest professional investors and so become a kind of stable asset class that is defined by a relatively efficient market."[4]

Rappaport looks quite relieved at that conclusion at the end of all this analysis. Time for him to go home and plug in his 58 Custom, I think, for a little string-bending therapy. Time also for us to get back to the search for that million-dollar Les Paul. The first contender for the title I can't tell you much about. The story involves a famous player's Burst with a large price attached – and with so much legal action surrounding it that I can only allude to it in the vaguest of terms.

I know for sure that this guitar was sold quite recently and I have indeed spoken to some of those involved in the sale of the instrument. I know exactly what it is supposed to have sold for, and if that figure is true it was, disappointingly for our purposes, quite a chunk less than a million dollars.

There we have to leave that instrument. One of those involved explained: "This guitar came to represent for me the good, the bad, and the ugly of high-dollar vintage guitar dealing. The guitar itself is legitimate, the seller's legitimate, I'm legitimate, we paid our money – and here we are screaming at each other. The guitar itself rose above all the litigation and all the human stupidities involved. The guitar's a lot bigger than that."

And the second contender … guess what? I can't tell you much about that one, either. Mainly because I don't want to mess with the present owner's chances of selling it. This is another very high-profile guitar with a number of top-league names associated with it. A sale almost took place as I was putting together the final bits and pieces for this book, and the price tag would have been a few hundred thousand dollars over a million. By the time you read this it may have sold.

So that's a story we might well take up another day and in another book. It's a story that would link back to the early days of Burst history, or at least the Burst's popularity as a viable instrument. And that in itself highlights a concern for many of the Burst fanatics who play and collect and discuss and idolise these guitars today. Where is the brand new generation of players and collectors who will ensure the continuity of that popularity?

It's not an entirely selfless question. It's to do with nothing less than the future of guitar collecting, and feeds into another worry that collectors must address at some point. What happens to my collection when I am no longer here?

Dealer Timm Kummer says: "I always have these arguments with younger guys about vintage guitars. They're telling me about their 74 Strat and how it's a vintage guitar because it's 30-plus years old. I say look, a hundred-year-old bottle of ripple is still belly-bosh. It doesn't get better in the bottle. The best materials were not in the 70s. The best craftsmen, the best designers, were doing it in the 50s and 60s, and that's what makes vintage. Everything else is just sort of trying to catch up."[5]

I spoke to two guitarists, Ben Wells and Chris Robertson of Black Stone Cherry. They're both in their early 20s. They both play and love Les Pauls. They were recording their second album when we met and they had a good diary of gigs to work their way through. Exactly what you would call an up-and-coming band. And, I think, exactly the guys to tell us more about the future of Burst collectability.

Wells reckons it was Aerosmith – Joe Perry and Brad Whitford – who turned him on to what this guitar can do. "That was probably the first band that made me go mad to have a Les Paul," he says. "We did a show in Hyde Park, London, with them last year, and oh man, I was just shaking up all the time. Aerosmith has always been a lifelong influence with me and the whole band. Pretty awesome."

His bandmate Robertson says it loud and clear. "The Les Paul is the ultimate piece of rock'n'roll equipment. Don't get me wrong: every guitar that's made has its place in music history. But we must be honest. Without a Les Paul, rock'n'roll wouldn't be what it is."

OK, we certainly have Les Paul fans here. Wells plays a 2000 Les Paul Classic sunburst and a 2000 Les Paul Standard in gold. Robertson has a 1988 Standard in what he describes as brown tobacco burst and an 87 black Les Paul Custom.

Have they ever been tempted to try or even own a really old one? They tell me their drummer's dad and uncle are both in the Southern rock group The Kentucky Headhunters. Greg Martin, the Headhunters' guitarist, has an original 58 Burst.

"He takes it out on the road with him," says Wells, "and I yell at him all the time, 'Why do you even take this out of your house!' You know? If I had one of those guitars I would probably keep it in a fire safe or something."

He's played it, of course. "There's nothing like those guitars, and this one felt so good. It has this beautiful orange burst on it, the pickups are original 58s, and it just sounds great, man." Robertson too has had his turn. "It's like the sky opens up and there's this big white light that hits you when you play it. It's one of those guitars you can hit one note on and it sounds better than Yngwie playing 46,000 notes. It's got stuff, man."

Could they imagine owning such a thing? Wells says that he loves the Les Pauls he has now, especially his Classic. "I don't think I could ever get rid of that. Plus I've played it so much that I've worn the paint off of it and the neck down. It pretty much just fits me."

Robertson reckons, simply enough, that a great guitar player is a great guitar player, no matter what he's playing. "Who wouldn't like to have a 50s Les Paul? But we ain't making no money – we're just playing music and just having fun. The average guy like myself doesn't have that kind of money. My Standard and Custom, plus a 69 SG Junior I just got, fit me where I am now. I don't consider myself a great guitar player: I consider myself learning."

He says that it would be hard to imagine owning a Burst, because for him a guitar is there to use and play on the road. "That wouldn't be a smart move with a guitar like that. And I don't see the point of $250,000 or whatever for something that you sit and look at on the wall. If you've found your calling with a guitar that you can go buy for $2,500 and you've gotten as far as you can with that, then a $250,000 guitar is hardly going to get you any further."

Wells doesn't know anyone of his own age who collects guitars beyond what they need to play. "I think the older guys that collect grew up at a certain time, and I guess they have a little more knowledge on how to manage it and the history behind those guitars."

Are you tempted to collect guitars, I ask Robertson? "It might be a hobby I get into when I'm older," he smiles. "But for now, if I can't take it on the road and play it live, and it's something I don't have to worry about every day, I don't need it, man."[6]

Anyway, it's time for them to get back into the studio with their Les Pauls. Wells bids me farewell with but a parting thought. He reckons that some collectors are only that: collectors. "A lot of them don't even play guitar. You have to have a passion for the instrument alone, not how much money it's worth. You don't see that in someone who just collects guitars, because they don't know what kind of love a player might have for that instrument."[7]

Now there's another prickly subject. The argument goes like this: guitars tucked away in collections and accumulating in value are being kept away from the people who ought to have them: real players. They are out of circulation, and speculative price increases mean that these real players simply can't afford them.

Writer Philipp Blom has an interesting take on the way a collection transforms the objects within. His view is that the act of collecting usually removes them from their regular functions, placing them in an artificial environment. "No collector of stamps will plunder his collection for correspondence," says Blom, "even if some of his stamps might still be valid. No collector of teacups scours markets and antique shops simply for cups from which to drink his tea. Even the occasional use of objects in a collection – musical instruments, books, or vintage cars – is incidental, and not what the collection is about."[8]

Albert Lee tells me: "There are people buying old Les Pauls that aren't going to play them. They're people who are just collectors. I hate to see that. It's happening with old Fenders too."[9]

As you'd expect, the collectors themselves do not see it like this. "Does the person who owns a Ming vase keep it away from somebody who is somehow more deserving of it?" asks Bill, our partly anonymous collector from the Southeastern US. I throw him another question to answer.

If the Burst was somehow magically priced at $10,000 again, and was therefore available to more professional musicians, would it be only professional musicians who would own them? "Of course not," he replies. "If they were $10,000, a whole lot of other people, maybe more or less deserving, would be able to afford them also."[10]

His point is well made: you can't restrict use of any object to a particular class of people. If you put a 'musicians only' sign on the instrument you're selling, who's to say the buyer will really be one? You can't police these transactions, even if you wanted to.

"I don't see any guitar players that are wanting for a great guitar because I own so many or anybody else owns so many," says Tom Wittrock. "There are always more great guitars available than people who need them. And there are people who flat out cannot afford a great guitar at all, even a $500 or a $300 guitar. And that is not going to be affected at all by collectors."[11]

He says that collecting will, obviously, take a particular guitar out of circulation for a while, but the collector also helps to preserve and take care of a good guitar. And if collector X doesn't buy it and remove it from the potential for others to use it, then guitarist Y coming along and owning it would have exactly the same effect.

Who knows what tomorrow may bring? There may be trouble ahead. I can see clearly now the rain has gone. I should stop quoting songs and ask some collectors what might become of their beloved guitars in the years and decades to come. None of us will be here forever. So what will happen to all these collections after their curators have gone to the great gig in the sky? Or even before they check out, but have a roof to fix or a kid to put through college or any of the other real-world expenses that plague our daily lives?

Bill's view is not exactly cheering. "I have people ask me if they should buy a vintage guitar, and I tell them two things. First of all, discretionary income only. Second, you must realise that one nut-job setting off a nuke anywhere in the world will probably ruin the world economy for quite some time to come.

"So, if you're thinking of buying such-and-such a guitar for 100 grand today and selling it for 150 five years from now, bear in mind that one terrorist incident, one horrible event like that, could change the whole thing. I can't predict the future."[12]

Joe Ganzler squints into the sun and sees some of us before too long heading off to the nursing home. But he doesn't see too many guitars in there. "So maybe there'll suddenly be 50 or more of these things for sale. It has happened in other collectables. The Model T Ford had a big run back in the 80s, and then all of a sudden nobody wanted the damn things. Now you can buy them for $2.98."

Same thing with jukeboxes, he says. "Big run in the 80s and 90s – now nobody wants them. It's like having an extra refrigerator in your house. And you can buy an iPod that holds however-many-thousand songs. So why do you want something that has 24 plays?"

Ganzler reckons if his own treasured Burst crashed down to be worth $25,000, it wouldn't trouble him. "But it would be a concern for the guys that are coming into the hobby now. It's musical chairs, and they don't want to be the last guy without a seat when the music stops. At the prices now, the biggest thing that everybody asks me is if they're paying too much. My old answer used to be you can't pay too much, you can only buy too soon. Are you paying too much now? I don't know."[13]

Finally, Kunio Kishida lines up an ideal future. "I wish the prices for Bursts could split into two different directions," he says. "One way is the beautiful-condition and high-price Les Paul, for the collector. The other way is the Les Paul in playing condition and at a good price, for the player."[14]

Nice idea. But I wouldn't put money on it.

17. LESTER

To the very end with a genuine Les Paul

I didn't quite find the million-dollar Les Paul Burst, or at least not one for which anybody was prepared to provide definite proof. In some ways I didn't really want to. To be honest, I would rather they were $265 again, just as they were when they came out in 1958.

That's not going to happen, of course. These guitars are hugely valuable and they will probably remain so, to a greater or lesser extent. We now know some of the reasons for their value, we know a lot about why they are great and who made them great, and we know something of the modern offshoots and reissues – and fakes – that they have spawned.

We've seen the extreme responses players and collectors have to them. "Just what is it about these guitars that makes them capable of reducing grown, hirsute men to jelly?" guitarist Elliot Easton of The Cars once asked himself. "Yes, there is the fabulous curly maple top, the PAF humbuckers, the fast-action mahogany neck. Yes, there is the guitar's superior tenability and tremendous sustaining power.

"All these attributes are beyond wonderful," Easton said. "But the best explanation for the beauty and desirability of the late-50s sunburst Les Paul cannot be adequately expressed on paper. A chemical reaction transpires when this guitar is plugged into an appropriate amplifier – say a vintage Marshall or a blackface Fender Twin Reverb. Magic."[1]

Some let their enthusiasm for the Les Paul carry them away, convinced they have found the ultimate guitar. Others are a little more sceptical. Guitar restoration specialist Clive Brown: "The vintage guitar industry has turned Les Paul sunbursts into something they aren't. Some people associate a sound with a guitar. But it's the guy who plays it who makes the sound.

"Jimi Hendrix proved that," says Brown. "He played an SG, a Les Paul, a Flying V, as well as a Stratocaster, but he always sounded like Hendrix. He didn't suddenly sound like Jimmy Page because he played a Les Paul. That's where everybody's perception seems to go wrong. It's the playing, and not necessarily the guitar."[2]

The truth lies somewhere in the middle. A great guitar matched with a great player can equal great music. And surely no one knows that better than the man whose name is on each of those 1,500 or so Bursts made between 1958 and 1960. The real Les Paul. Not *a* real Les Paul. *The* real Les Paul.

Les has been sidelined since we first met him near the start of this book, mainly because the collectors we've met along the way aren't quite so concerned with his contributions. Their microscopes are focussed on the workbenches and machines of the Gibson factory of 1959.

But Les represents a timely reminder that musical instruments exist to be played by musicians. Aged 93 years at the time of writing, he famously still plays every Monday night at a club in New York City. I asked him what he thought about people paying so much money for old Les Paul guitars these days.

"Well, it may be because the person they admired played one," says Les. "It may be because of a myth that this guitar is better than that guitar. I believe that the guitar that they're making today is far superior to the guitar that we had back then. Not that there was anything wrong with the guitar we had then. We've just learned over a period of years how to make them even better."

Every guitarist has a sound in his head that he's trying to reproduce, says Les. No two people are looking for the same sound or will play the same way. "So this may mean that when he plays his thing, it sounds better on this particular guitar. And so the price goes up. And others follow the leader. I think if they admired some guy and he came out with a washboard, we'd be paying $50,000 for one of those."

I tell him that there are people who will pay more for a particularly fine pattern in the maple on top of the guitar. I'm not telling Les Paul anything he doesn't know, of course. But does that seem crazy to him as a musician? He laughs out loud.

"The whole world looks crazy," says Les, still laughing. "I'm having a tough time trying to figure it out. I've never seen times like this. Whether it's music or whether it's war, whether it's politics, whether it's the price of gasoline, it doesn't matter: everything is in a change. The type of music is changing, and it's far from the original rock. When they say rock, oh my goodness – well, it's far from rock as I remember it in the beginning."

He's always meeting people who seem surprised to match up his name with the name of a guitar they know. "Whether it's in a dentist's office or it's a fella that owns the biggest grocery store in the world, I talk to him and I say my name is Les Paul, and he says oh my god, do you know how many guitars I have of yours?"

It amazes him, he says, because it seems now that everybody plays these guitars. "And I guess there's a few out there that love to listen to them, that don't play. But so many of them say oh, my son is playing that guitar, or I play it.

"When I grew up, there was only one guitar in my whole town. They didn't even have a music store. It was just the beginning of it, like Indians and covered wagons. And it's moved into something completely amazing now."[3]

ENDNOTES

An entry with surname only refers to a title listed in full in Books on page 288

1. INTRODUCTION (pp18–19)

1 Author's interview April 24 2008
2 Author's interview March 1 2008

1. BIRTH (pp20-39)

1 Author's interview April 25 2008
2 Author's interview March 1 1989
3 Author's interview March 1 1989
4 Author's interview March 1 1989
5 Author's interview March 1 1989
6 *Time* October 29 1951
7 Author's interview October 27 1992
8 *The Music Trades* February 1952
9 Author's interview October 27 1992
10 Author's interview March 1 1989
11 Author's interview October 27 1992
12 Author's interview March 16 1993
13 Author's interview October 27 1992
14 *The Music Trades* August 1952
15 *Melody Maker* September 13 1952
16 Author's interview March 16 1993
17 Author's interview March 16 1993
18 *Gibson Gazette* December 1958

2. ORIGINALITY (pp40-47)

1 Author's interview June 4 2008

3. BLUESBREAKER (pp48-75)

1 *Melody Maker* November 28 1959
2 Author's interview April 23 2008
3 *Zigzag* February 1972
4 *Guitar Player* June 1969
5 *Melody Maker* March 13 1965
6 *Music Maker* May 1967
7 *Beat Instrumental* February 1968
8 *Guitar Player* April 1985
9 *Beat Instrumental* April 1966
10 Clapton
11 *Trouser Press* October 1977
12 Author's interview May 13 2008
13 *Record Mirror* September 1999
14 *Guitarist* September 1999
15 *Beat Instrumental* June 1966
16 *Beat Instrumental* September 1966
17 *Beat Instrumental* August 1967
18 *Beat Instrumental* September 1967
19 webchatguitar.com May 21 2000
20 Summers
21 *Beat Instrumental* August 1967
22 Wolkin/Keenom
23 www.mikebloomfieldamericanmusic.com
24 *Record Mirror* October 29 1966
25 *Union News* October 28 1966
26 Author's interview April 23 2008
27 Author's interview April 22 2008
28 Author's interview May 19 2008
29 Author's interview April 22 2008
30 Author's interview May 29 2008
31 Author's interview May 29 2008
32 *The Beatles Monthly Book* November 1968
33 *Melody Maker* March 26 1966

4. PEARLY (pp76-84)

1 Author's interview April 10 2008

5. HEARTBREAKER (pp85-106)

1 *Guitarist* September 1999
2 *Guitarist* September 1999
3 Author's interview April 5 2002
4 Author's interview May 13 2008
5 Author's interview May 13 2008
6 *Beat Instrumental* January 1967
7 *Beat Instrumental* March 1967
8 Author's interview May 13 2008
9 Author's interviews January 25 1984, February 12 1993, April 27 2005
10 *Guitar World* June 1991
11 *Guitar Player* July 2004
12 Dave Lewis & Simon Pallett *Led Zeppelin: The Concert File* (Omnibus 2005)
13 *Guitar World* January 1998
14 *Guitar Player* July 2004
15 *Guitar Player* July 1997 and www.modernguitars.com/archives/003340.html
16 *Guitar Player* July 1997 and www.modernguitars.com/archives/003340.html
17 *Guitar Player* July 2004
18 *Guitar Player* July 2004
19 *Trouser Press* October 1977
20 Author's interview May 18 1993
21 Author's interview January 20 1993
22 *Trouser Press* October 1977

23 *Guitarist* December 2003
24 Author's interview June 11 2008
25 Author's interview April 20 2008
26 *Guitar Player* July 1976

6. VINTAGE (pp107-120)
1 Author's interview December 10 1992
2 Author's interview January 29 1993
3 Author's interview December 10 1992
4 Author's interview January 29 1993
5 Author's interview May 8 2008
6 Author's interview April 4 2008
7 Author's interview March 31 2008

7. RESTRUCTURE (pp121-136)
1 *Guitar Player* June 1974
2 Author's interview May 8 2008
3 *Guitar Player* December 1976
4 *Guitar Player* October 1975
5 *Guitar Player* December 1973
6 *Guitar Player* April 1974
7 *Guitar Player* January 1975
8 Author's interview March 8 2008
9 Author's interview April 24 2008
10 Author's interview October 29 1992
11 Author's interview April 24 2008
12 Author's interview October 28 1992
13 Author's interview March 15 1993
14 *Guitar Player* November 1989
15 *Guitar Player* April 1988
16 *Vintage Guitar* November 2005

8. WORKMANSHIP (pp137-162)
1 Author's interview April 27 2005
2 Author's interview May 8 2008
3 Author's interview May 8 2008
4 Author's interview May 15 2008
5 Author's interview April 24 2008
6 Author's interview April 2 2008
7 Author's interview April 24 2008
8 Author's interview October 27 1992
9 Author's interview May 8 2008
10 Author's interview April 2 2008
11 Author's interview May 2 2008
12 Author's interview April 2 2008
13 Author's interview May 2 2008
14 Author's interview April 2 2008
15 Author's interview October 30 1992
16 Author's interview June 6 2008
17 Author's interview May 8 2008
18 Author's interview April 2 2008
19 Author's interview May 8 2008
20 Author's interview May 15 2008
21 Author's interview April 10 2008
22 Author's interview May 15 2008

9. REISSUE (pp163-184)
1 Author's interview December 12 2001
2 Author's interview March 4 1993
3 Author's interview October 29 1992
4 Author's interview February 11 1993
5 Author's interview December 12 2001
6 Author's interview December 12 2001
7 J.K. Rowling *Harry Potter And The Deadly Hallows* (Bloomsbury 2007)
8 Author's interview April 24 2008
9 Author's interview March 26 2008
10 Author's interview April 7 2008
11 Author's interview March 31 2008
12 Author's interview April 24 2008
13 Author's interview April 24 2008
14 Author's interview May 8 2008
15 Author's interview December 12 2001

10. FLAME (pp185-200)
1 Author's interview May 10 2008
2 Author's interview March 26 2008
3 Author's interview April 22 2008
4 Author's interview April 7 2008
5 Author's interview April 9 2008
6 Author's interview May 2 2008
7 Author's interview May 10 2008
8 Author's interview May 1 2008
9 Author's interview April 24 2008
10 Author's interview April 9 2008
11 Philipp Blom *To Have And To Hold: An Intimate History Of Collectors And Collecting* (Allen Lane 2002)
12 Author's interview April 7 2008
13 Author's interview May 1 2008
14 Author's interview April 2 2008
15 Author's interview November 2 1992
16 Author's interview April 7 2008
17 Author's interview March 26 2008
18 Author's interview March 31 2008
19 Author's interview October 29 1992

20 Author's interview March 31 2008
21 Author's interview April 7 2008
22 Author's interview April 2 2008
23 Author's interview May 10 2008
24 Author's interview April 5 2002
25 Author's interview April 9 2008
26 Marcel Proust *In Search Of Lost Time: Swann's Way* (Vintage 1996)

11. UNREAL (pp201-214)
1 Author's interview March 14 2008
2 Author's interview May 8 2008
3 Author's interview April 9 2008
4 Author's interview April 2 2008
5 Author's interview April 24 2008
6 Author's interview March 14 2008
7 Author's interview April 8 2008
8 Author's interview March 31 2008
9 Author's interview April 7 2008

12. VISIBILITY (pp215-219)
1 Author's interview April 23 2008

13. COLLECTABILITY (pp220-239)
1 *Guitar Player* May 1976
2 *Beat Instrumental* February 1968
3 Author's interview April 22 2008
4 Author's interview May 1 2008
5 Author's interview March 26 2008
6 Author's interview May 10 2008
7 Author's interview March 31 2008
8 Author's interview January 25 1996
9 Author's interview May 15 2008
10 Author's interview May 1 2008
11 Author's interview March 31 2008
12 Author's interview March 14 2008
13 Author's interview April 22 2008
14 Author's interview April 7 2008
15 Author's interview May 15 2008
16 Author's interview March 26 2008
17 Author's interview May 10 2008
18 Author's interview May 2 2008

14. WORTH (pp240-258)
1 Author's interview April 22 2008
2 Author's interview April 9 2008
3 Author's interview April 5 1995
4 Author's interview May 15 2008
5 Author's interview March 14 2008
6 Philipp Blom *To Have And To Hold: An Intimate History Of Collectors And Collecting* (Allen Lane 2002)
7 Christie's *Crossroads Guitar Auction* catalogue, June 24 2004
8 Author's interview March 14 2008
9 Author's interview March 31 2008
10 Author's interview April 24 2008
11 Author's interview April 22 2008
12 Author's interview March 31 2008
13 Author's interview April 22 2008
14 Author's interview March 14 2008
15 Author's interview April 7 2008
16 Author's interview April 2 2008
17 Author's interview May 15 2008
18 Author's interview April 24 2008
19 Author's interview April 9 2008
20 Author's interview March 31 2008
21 Author's interview March 31 2008
22 Author's interview April 7 2008

15. LEGACY (pp259-266)
1 Author's interview June 18 2008

16. FUTURE (pp267-278)
1 Author's interview March 13 2008
2 Author's interview October 29 1992
3 Author's interview April 24 2008
4 Author's interview March 13 2008
5 Author's interview April 24 2008
6 Author's interview April 23 2008
7 Author's interview April 18 2008
8 Philipp Blom *To Have And To Hold: An Intimate History Of Collectors And Collecting* (Allen Lane 2002)
9 Author's interview April 23 2008
10 Author's interview May 1 2008
11 Author's interview March 31 2008
12 Author's interview May 1 2008
13 Author's interview April 7 2008
14 Author's interview May 15 2008

17. LESTER (pp279-281)
1 *Guitar World* June 1991
2 Author's interview April 2 2008
3 Author's interview April 25 2008

INDEX

ACKNOWLEDGEMENTS

AUTHOR'S THANKS (in addition to those named in Original Interviews below) to: Nicholas Aleshin; Galadrielle Allman; Tony Arambarri (NAMM); Jimmy Archey (First Act); Julie Bowie; Dave Brewis (Rock Stars Guitars); Larry Briggs (Texas Amigos); Dave Burrluck *(Guitarist)*; John Callaghan *(Guitar & Bass)*; George Case; Paul Cooper; Diane Dalton (August Capital); Syd Davey; Paul Day; Gary Dick (Gary's Classic Guitars); Greg Dorsett (Rock Stars Guitars); Seymour Duncan; Alex Echo; Bob Elliott; Bill Fajen; Betsy Fowler; Alan Greenwood *(Vintage Guitar Magazine)*; Dave Gregory; Sue Hargreaves; Vincent Hartong; Greg Howard; Joan Hudson; Dave Hunter; Rachael Iverson (J&R Adventures); Chris Jackson; Brian Jacobs (Rittor); Emi Keffer; Martin Kelly; Howard Kramer (Rock & Roll Hall Of Fame); Marcus Leadley *(Guitar & Bass)*; Dave Lewis *(Tight But Loose)*; Petri Lunden; Stuart Maskell; Joel McIver; Warren Mendonsa; John Morrish; Cecil Offley; Graeme Pattingale; Erin Podbereski (Jensen); Ronny Proler; Julian Ridgway (Redfern's); Alan Rogan; Meredith E. Rutledge (Rock & Roll Hall Of Fame); Amy Sciarretto (Roadrunner); Tom Seabrook; Harry Shapiro; David Simons; Jeremy Singer (Gibson London); Jeff Suter (Eagle Rock); Mick Taylor *(Guitarist)*; John Thomas; Chris Walter (Photofeatures); Chris Welch; Guy White (Snap Galleries); Brad Whitford; Adam Yeldham.

SPECIAL THANKS to Walter Carter for much help and enthusiastic encouragement throughout.

ORIGINAL INTERVIEWS conducted by Tony Bacon and used during research for this book are as follows: Scot Arch (Apr 08); Andy Babiuk (Apr 08); Max Baranet (May 08); John Bates (Apr 93); Jeff Beck (Jan 84, Feb 93, Apr 05); Binky Brinkworth (Apr 08); Allen Bloomfield (May 08); Bruce Bolen (Jan 93); Joe Bonamassa (Jun 08); Clive Brown (Apr 08); David Dann (May 08); Vic DaPra (Apr 08); Jim Deurloo (Oct 92); Dan Erlewine (Apr 08); Melvyn Franks (Apr 08); Joe Ganzler (Apr 08); Billy Gibbons (Apr 08); Roger Giffin (Oct 92); Clay Harrell (May 08); Dan Hawkins (Apr 08); Tony Hicks (Apr 08); Christopher Hjort (May 08); Mike Jopp (Jun 08); Kerry Keane (Mar 08); Kunio Kishida (May 08); Mark Knopfler (Apr 02); Timm Kummer (Apr 08); Kim Lafleur (Apr 08); Randy Larson (Jun 08); Albert Lee (Apr 08); Jason Lollar (Jun 08); Chris Lovell (May 08); Seth Lover (Oct 92); Ted McCarty (Oct 92); Tom Murphy (Dec 01); Les Paul (Mar 89, Mar 93, Apr 08); Andy Rappaport (Mar 08); Stan Rendell (Dec 92); J.T. Riboloff (Mar 93); Chris Robertson (Apr 08); Tim Shaw (Feb 93, Mar 93, May 08); Mike Slubowski (Mar 08); Steve Soest (Nov 92); Peter Svensson (May 08); Ben Wells (Apr 08); David Wilson (May 08); Edwin Wilson (Apr 08); Phil Winfield (Apr 08); Tom Wittrock (Mar 08); Michael Wright (Mar 08). The sources of previously published quotations are endnoted where they occur in the text.

ACKNOWLEDGEMENTS

BOOKS

Tony Bacon *Electric Guitars: The Illustrated Encyclopedia* (Thunder Bay 2000); *50 Years Of The Gibson Les Paul* (Backbeat 2002)

Tony Bacon (ed) *Echo & Twang: Classic Guitar Music Of the 50s* (Backbeat 2001)

Tony Bacon & Paul Day *The Gibson Les Paul Book: A Complete History Of Les Paul Guitars* (Balafon/Miller Freeman 1993)

Julius Bellson *The Gibson Story* (Gibson 1973)

Walter Carter *Gibson Guitars: 100 Years Of An American Icon* (General Publishing Group 1994); *The Gibson Electric Guitar Book: Seventy Years Of Classic Guitars* (Backbeat 2007)

George Case *Jimmy Page: Magus, Musician, Man* (Hal Leonard 2007)

Eric Clapton *The Autobiography* (Century 2007)

Alan Clayson *The Yardbirds: The Band That Launched Eric Clapton, Jeff Beck, Jimmy Page* (Backbeat 2002)

A.R. Duchossoir *Gibson Electrics – The Classic Years: An Illustrated History Of The Electric Guitars Produced By Gibson Up To The Mid 1960s* (Hal Leonard 1994)

Mo Foster *17 Watts?: The Birth Of British Rock Guitar* (MPG 1997)

George Gruhn & Walter Carter *Gruhn's Guide To Vintage Guitars: An Identification Guide For American Fretted Instruments* (Miller Freeman 1999)

Christopher Hjort *Strange Brew: Eric Clapton & The British Blues Boom 1965–1970* (Jawbone 2007)

Christopher Hjort & Doug Hinman *Jeff's Book: A Chronology Of Jeff Beck's Career 1965–1980* (Rock'N'Roll Research 2000)

Yasuhiko Iwanade *The Beauty Of The Burst: Gibson Sunburst Les Pauls From 58 To 60* (English edition Hal Leonard 1998)

Robb Lawrence *The Early Years Of The Les Paul Legacy 1915–1963* (Hal Leonard 2008)

[No Author] *Gibson Shipping Totals 1946–1979* (J.T.G. 1992)

Terry Rawlings & Keith Badman *Good Times Bad Times: The Definitive Diary Of The Rolling Stones 1960–1969* (Complete Music 1997)

Jay Scott & Vic DaPra *'Burst: 1958–60 Sunburst Les Paul* (Seventh String 1994)

Andy Summers *One Train Later: A Memoir* (Portrait 2006)

PICTURE CREDITS

The pictures in this book came from the following sources, and we are grateful for everyone's help. Location or page number is followed by an identifier and then the name of the source. **Jacket Front** 1960 Burst: Balafon Image Bank. **4** Page: Jorgen Angel/Redfern's. **6–7** Richards: David Redfern/Redfern's; Clapton club snaps (3): Betsy Fowler; Clapton studio: Snap Galleries Limited; ex-Richards 1959 Burst: Balafon image Bank. **8–9** Clapton squatting: Jan Persson/Redferns; Clapton with shades: Michael Putland/Retna; Clapton with shiny jacket: Michael Putland/Retna. **10–11** Gibbons: Fin Costello/Redfern's; Bloomfield (2): Michael Ochs Archives/Getty Images. **12–13** Taylor: Balafon Image Bank; Green colour: Tony Gale/Pictorial Press; ex-Green 1959 Burst: Balafon Image Bank; Green black-and-white: Chris Walter/Photofeatures. **14–15** Page left: David Stratford/Redfern's; Page centre: Jorgen Angel/Redfern's; Page's 'No.1' Burst: Balafon Image Bank; Page right: Neal Preston/Retna; **16–17** ex-Allman Burst: Collection of Galadrielle Allman; Photo by Design Photography, Inc., Cleveland, Ohio; Courtesy of the Rock And Roll Hall Of Fame And Museum; Wells: Neil Lupin/Redfern's; Allman: Michael Dobo/Michael Ochs Archives/Getty Images; ex-Kossoff Burst: Balafon Image Bank; Kossoff: Jan Persson/Redfern's. **Jacket rear** Beck: David Redfern/Redfern's. We have tried to contact all copyright holder but if you feel there has been a mistaken attribution please contact the publisher.

FEEDBACK

Comments? Complaints? Updates? Email us – lesmillions@jawbonepress.com – or write – Million Dollar Les Paul, Jawbone Press, 2A Union Court, 20-22 Union Road, London SW4 6JP, England.

"I see the young guy out there – young guy, old guy, doesn't make any difference – and he has the same affectionate feeling for that instrument that I have. He loves that guitar like a mistress, a bartender, and a housewife. It's the best psychiatrist out there, that guitar. To this day, if I've got a problem, I'll probably pick up my guitar and solve it."
Les Paul, 1993